The Marriage Book

Nicky and Sila Lee

Harper*Christian* Resources

HODDER

The Marriage Book

Contents

Foreword   vii

Acknowledgments   ix

Introduction   1

Section 1: Strengthening Connection   13

  1 Taking a Long View   15

  2 Planning to Succeed   29

Section 2: The Art of Communication   43

  3 How to Talk More Effectively   45

  4 How to Listen More Effectively   59

Section 3: Love in Action   75

  5 The Five Expressions of Love   77

  6 Words and Actions   89

  7 Time, Presents, and Touch   99

Section 4: Resolving Conflict   111

  8 Appreciating Our Differences   113

  9 Focusing on the Issue   135

10 Centering Our Lives   147

Section 5: The Power of Forgiveness   161

11 How Can Intimacy be Lost?   163

12 How Can Intimacy be Restored?   177

Section 6: Parents and In-Laws   197

13 How to Get Along With Our Parents and In-Laws 199

14 How to Leave Behind Parental Control   219

15 How to Address the Effects of Childhood Pain   233

Section 7: Good Sex   249

16 Sex–What is it All About?   251

17 Six Qualities for Great Lovers   261

18 Protecting Our Marriage   281

19 Keeping Sex Alive   291

Section 8: Epilogue   303

20 The Opportunity of a Lifetime   305

Appendix 1: Ready for Marriage?   313

Appendix 2: Engagement, Sex, and the Honeymoon   321

Appendix 3: Working Out a Budget   333

Appendix 4: Praying Together   341

Endnotes   349

Recommended Further Reading   359

Other Relationship Resources Available
    from Alpha International   361

Foreword

Marriage is under attack in our society. Many feel it is an outdated institution. In the UK, the number of marriages per year has been falling steadily. Those who do get married find it increasingly difficult to stay married. Today, forty-two percent of all marriages in the UK will end in divorce.[1] What is the answer to all of this? Why should we get married? How can we stay married?

In this book, Nicky and Sila answer these questions, showing us the value and potential of any marriage. They suggest how we can not only stay married but also make the most of our married lives together.

Nicky has been my closest friend for more than forty years. We were at school together and we shared a set of rooms at university. He has always been one step ahead and I have tried to follow in his footsteps. He became a Christian on February 14, 1974. Forty-eight hours later he led me to Christ. Nicky and Sila married in 1976. Eighteen months later, Pippa and I followed suit. Our first three children are approximately the same age. They went on to have a fourth.

After university our paths separated as Nicky went off to teach in Japan and I practiced as an attorney. Then Nicky went to theological college and one year later I followed. Nicky and Sila returned to London to join the staff of Holy Trinity Brompton Church (HTB). One year later, we followed. Nicky and Sila ran Alpha for five years, then passed the baton to us in 1990.

They have taught us many things. In particular, we have learned so much from the example of their marriage and family life. We have observed in their home something to which we can aspire.

Nicky and Sila have run The Pre-Marriage Course at HTB since 1985 and The Marriage Course since 1996, and many couples have found their marriages enriched through attending them. For some, the course has literally saved their marriage from separation or divorce. Others have turned the water of an ordinary marriage into the wine of a strong one, a transformation made possible by the presence of Jesus Christ. For still others, the courses have provided a forum to think creatively about making a good and healthy marriage even better.

While reading this book, you may feel that the Lees' marriage is "too good to be true," but having observed it for more than forty years, let me assure you that it is entirely true and that it inspires us to aim for the very best.

My hope and prayer is that, through this book, many more people would be able to enjoy the fruit of Nicky and Sila's example and wisdom.

Nicky Gumbel

Acknowledgments

We would like to thank the many people who have helped us with this book. Between them they have spent hundreds of hours reading the manuscripts and suggesting changes and additions. The book could not have been written without them. We are particularly grateful to John and Diana Collins and Sandy and Annette Millar, who have inspired us through their teaching and their lives. We are also very grateful to those who have told us stories from their own marriages, which have rooted the theory in everyday experience.

We would like to express our enormous gratitude to Philippa Pearson-Miles, Mary Ellis, Joanna Desmond, Jo Soda, and Sam Snedden for all the tireless help they have given with the manuscript, and to Charlie Mackesy for the fun he has brought to our family as well as to the book. To Jo Glen, our editor, we want to say a special thank you. Without her compelling enthusiasm, humor, imagination, and new ideas each time we got stuck, this book might never have been finished. We would also like to thank Nicky and Pippa Gumbel, not only for their friendship and encouragement over so many years, but also for persuading us to start this project.

Finally, we would like to thank our own parents for their constant love and for the model of two long and happy marriages.

Nicky and Sila Lee

Love is patient,
love is kind.
It does not envy,
it does not boast,
it is not proud.
It does not dishonour others,
it is not self-seeking,
it is not easily angered,
it keeps no record of wrongs.
Love does not delight in evil
but rejoices with the truth.
It always protects,
always trusts,
always hopes,
always perseveres.
Love never fails.

1 Corinthians 13:4–8a

Introduction

Nicky's story

I first set eyes on Sila at Swansea Docks. I was en route to South West Ireland for the summer holidays, having just left school. I was eighteen; she was seventeen. It was love at first sight. We spent two weeks in next-door holiday cottages in one of the most beautiful and unspoiled corners of the British Isles–West Cork. Most of that time I hardly dared believe she might feel anything for me at all. Two days before she left I built up my courage and told her my feelings and found, to my astonishment, that she felt the same.

Sila was still at school and studying for her A levels. (Advanced Levels or A-Levels are subject-based qualifications that British students aged 16 or older must get if they plan to enter university.) I had nine months before beginning university courses and realized she probably wouldn't pass any of them if I stayed in the same country, so I went backpacking in Africa on my own. Africa was unlike anything I had experienced before. I felt in awe of the landscape, people, and culture–but secretly I was longing to be back in England with Sila. I was lonely for much of the time and lived for the letters she wrote to the capital cities of the countries I traveled through, from Addis Ababa to Cape Town. It worked well until I reached South Africa. There had been a gap of more than six weeks when I arrived in Cape Town and I was pinning all my hopes on a letter being there, only to find nothing (except one from my mother). I was devastated.

I began to wonder if Sila had lost interest because of the time I had been away. I felt no desire to go back to England if that was the case. After several weeks of checking at the post office every day, I hitchhiked back to Johannesburg as a last resort and was elated to find a letter I had just missed four weeks previously. I took the first flight home.

I immediately went to see Sila at her boarding school, which seemed like a cross between a prison, to keep the girls in, and a fortress, to keep boys out. After three wonderful hours together, we realized too late that she was locked out. She was caught climbing in through a window at midnight and was "grounded" for her last two weeks of school life.

I went to begin university classes and Sila left school and moved to London. At this time I was starting to hear people talk about the Christian faith in a way that was new to me. Increasingly it made sense and caused me to think seriously about the meaning of my life. Yet at the same time I kept it very much at arm's length as my relationship with Sila was far and away the most important part of my life. I was afraid that, if I became a Christian and Sila did not, we might drift apart.

After five months of cautious investigation I realized that I had reached a defining moment. I had to decide one way or the other. I broached the subject with Sila, who responded with her usual enthusiasm. As she heard for herself the claims of Christianity, Sila, like me, felt she had discovered the truth, and we both embraced it.

Rather than pushing us apart, our new-found faith seemed to add a new and exciting dimension to our relationship. In fact, it opened the door to a perspective on life that I had not known existed before. It seemed as though all the different parts of my life were like the pieces of a jigsaw puzzle: my past, my relationship with Sila, my studying English, my university studies, everything. Suddenly all the pieces fell into place.

In the autumn of 1974, after two years of dating, we both felt, independently, that if we were to know for sure whether we should spend the rest of our lives together, we needed first to spend some time apart.

So, early one Monday morning at the beginning of October, I walked with Sila to the train station. We agreed that we wouldn't see each other or talk until Christmas.

It was a beautiful autumn morning with a carpet of mist in the faintly orange dawn light. Sila was waving goodbye to me out of the train window and I wondered if I would ever see her again. I walked back through the still deserted streets of Cambridge feeling as low as I had ever felt in my life. I decided not to go to London at all during that time as it was too painful to be there without seeing Sila.

However, a week later I was playing football with some friends at my old school. As we set off for the return journey, the friend whose car I was in said, "I hope you don't mind going back via London as I have to pick something up from home." I was horrified but I didn't say anything to him. I just hoped that it wouldn't take him very long. Anyway, Sila lived in another part of London.

The friend dropped us at High Street Kensington and said, "I'll pick you up here in forty minutes," and then drove off. It was pouring down rain and we stood on the pavement trying to decide what we were going to do. At that moment I looked up, and there, about fifty yards away, walking down the pavement towards me, was Sila.

I abandoned my two friends without a word of explanation and ran towards her. Then she saw me. She started running towards me. We flung our arms around each other and I remember swinging her round and round. I shouted back to my friends not to wait for me.

We went to a café and talked for hours. I discovered that Sila had been traveling by bus along High Street Kensington, got stuck in heavy traffic and so had decided to get off the bus and walk the last half-mile to where she was going. That was when she saw me.

Meeting like that was a chance in a million and we took it as a sign from God. We both felt that if God could cause us to meet in such an extraordinary way when we were doing our best to avoid each other, he was more than able to show us over the next three months whether we should spend the rest of our lives together. We agreed again not to see each other until Christmas. This time it felt different. There were still tears but we believed God would guide us.

Being apart was hard, but by the end of the term there was no question in my mind that I wanted to spend the rest of my life with Sila. We resumed dating at the beginning of 1975. I still had another year and a half of university classes. With Sila coming up most weekends, it was a time filled with some of the happiest memories of my life.

We were married on July 17, 1976 in Scotland, Sila's home, two weeks after I had graduated from my university studies.

Sila's story

I grew up in the Highlands of Scotland and my childhood was happy and uneventful. I loved the outdoors, was a tomboy, and thought I lived in the best place in the world. There was only one drawback: a lack of people. So when my best friend at school, Penny, asked me to spend two weeks of the summer vacation with her in South West Ireland along with family and friends, I jumped at the opportunity. I was just seventeen and I had no inkling that those two weeks would change my life.

We had to travel by ferry from Swansea to Cork. Swansea Docks is the most unpromising place I know, and yet that was where I met him. Nicky drove up behind us in line, climbed out of an old green Mini Cooper and smiled—it was love at first sight (or rather an overpowering attraction at first sight, to be accurate). He wore a large black felt hat (it *was* the seventies), jeans, and a white shirt and he was very tanned. He was eighteen and I thought, "He's gorgeous!"

We spent two idyllic weeks with a large group of friends. We sailed and swam, fished for mackerel, rowed out to islands for midnight barbecues, and sat under the stars talking into the early hours. All the time I was falling madly and deeply in love. I didn't breathe a word about my feelings to Penny and had no idea whether the feelings were mutual.

Forty-eight hours before returning home to Scotland I discovered that they were, and Nicky kissed me for the first time. Even then, although I was only seventeen (and he wasn't the only boy I'd kissed!), I remember lying awake that night thinking that I wanted to spend the rest of my life with him. I'd been with him every day for two weeks and I felt as if I couldn't live another day without him.

He then went to Africa for six months, which was agonizing as we were only just getting to know each other. All my friends at school told me not to pin my hopes on the relationship: Africa was far away, six months was a long time, and he was sure to meet someone else during his travels. But our relationship strengthened as we wrote long and increasingly intimate letters, discovering more about each other with thousands of miles between us than we might have done if we'd been together.

The moment I heard his voice on the telephone saying he was back, my heart seemed to stop. The strength of my feelings was almost overwhelming. We parted after that evening of reunion both reassured that our love had only grown during our months apart.

In the autumn of 1973, Nicky left for his university classes and I went to London. I was learning to type in the daytime and taking classes in painting at night, building a portfolio to apply for art college. But the lure of university life and my longing to be with Nicky meant that I spent more time at his university than I did on either of my own courses. Our relationship became close and intense—in some ways too intense for our own good.

Learning about God as I grew up, I never doubted his existence, but this belief had no effect on my lifestyle, except that Nicky and I would occasionally go to the college chapel on a Sunday for the early communion service. I had a vague sense that one day, when I was grown up enough, I would earn my way into heaven if I said a few more prayers, went to a few more services, and did a few more good things in my life. For the moment I didn't need anything. I had Nicky.

By the New Year, I had been accepted by Chelsea Art College for the following September. Life seemed to hold new possibilities around every corner. So when Nicky came to London to see me one evening in February 1974 and started talking to me about Christianity, I was as enthusiastic about that as I was about most other things he suggested. But I had no real understanding of what he was talking about and no idea of the implications.

When I went to see Nicky that weekend he took me straight to hear a Christian preacher called David MacInnes. I was amazed by what I heard. What had been happening for Nicky over a period of about five months took place for me in the space of twenty-four hours.

I was fascinated by what David said. Never before had I heard anybody talk about Jesus Christ like this. Nobody had ever told me I could have a personal relationship with God. For me, relationships were everything. That Friday we talked long into the night with Nicky's best friend, Nicky Gumbel, who at that stage was extremely suspicious about what was happening to us.

On Saturday, we went to hear David MacInnes again. He talked about the cross. It was a revelation to me. I kept saying to myself, "Why did nobody ever tell me before *why* Jesus died on the cross?"[1] It was as if everything I had ever known fitted together, not just intellectually, but also emotionally and spiritually. Everything made sense when the cross was explained. It was as if my life up to that point had been like a black-and-white still photograph and suddenly it started to move, first in a sort of blurred slow motion, and then faster and faster until it was in sharp focus and beautiful color. Life became very real in a way I'd never known it before. It was a radical change of perspective and it was the start of a new freedom in our relationship that I hadn't imagined possible.

Living life with a new faith was exciting. Nicky and I were even more deeply involved with each other. But eight months later we both sensed God leading us to distinguish between our faith and our love for one another. This was one of the most testing times of my life—even more difficult than when Nicky went to Africa. Learning to trust that God had the best plan for us was very hard.

It was a remarkable experience to see God intervening in our lives, as it seemed to us, in a way that could only have been him. On High Street Kensington when we ran into each other's arms and I shouted, "Nicky!" at the top of my voice, I was thinking, *God, I will never doubt you again.* I knew with great conviction that I could trust him with everything, even the most precious part of my life—my relationship with Nicky. I believe that God showed me that day, however much I loved Nicky, it was my love for God and his love for me that were most important.

During those three months apart we each grew in our relationship with God. When we resumed seeing each other it was with a different foundation to our lives, a foundation of personal faith that has strengthened us in our relationship with each other ever since.

Nicky proposed to me in February 1976 and we got married in July. I was twenty-one and he was twenty-two.

We write from the vantage point of more than forty years of marriage. During these years we have lived in Japan, the North East England, and central London. We have experienced together the birth of our four children and approximately 1,528 sleepless nights. We have known the strain and joy of having four children under the age of eight, as well as the turbulence and complexity of parenting teenagers. We have been through illness and financial hardship together. Three of our four children are now married and we have nine grandchildren.

Our experience has not been dissimilar to that of many other couples. We must have driven more than 600,000 miles together, talked for more than 30,000 hours and slept more than 16,000 nights in the same bed. We have worked together and played together. We have laughed and cried. We have been frustrated, irritated, mystified, and entranced by each other. And we still feel passionately about each other and passionately about marriage.

We are not suggesting for a moment that our marriage is more special than any other. Indeed, there is no text-book marriage, no blueprint or faultless prototype. Each couple is unique and has their own story to tell. But do those who reach the heights get there by luck? And is it true that those who feel let down by their marriage have simply married the wrong person? Our own experience has shown us that we need certain tools to build a strong, happy marriage. We have had to find out about communication and ways of making each other feel loved. We have had to learn to resolve conflict and to practice forgiveness. We have discovered that the joy of sexual intimacy cannot be taken for granted.

For the past thirty-five years we have been increasingly involved in seeking to help other marriages. We have seen hundreds of couples and have faced with them a range of diverse and difficult issues. From all of them, and from our own marriage, we have learned that the marriage relationship is not always easy, but it is highly rewarding. These experiences, combined with our own research and plenty of advice from others in the field, enabled us to develop a five-week Pre-Marriage Course for couples who are either engaged or exploring marriage and a seven-week Marriage Course for couples at any stage of their marriage. Thousands of couples have been through these courses and we still offer each of them three times a year. After we produced the courses on film, in response to numerous requests, they started to be taught by thousands of couples in many different countries and languages around the world.

The Marriage Course, on which this book is based, is designed to help any couple invest in their marriage and to make it stronger and better. We have written the book out of our desire to pass on what has caused us to be more in love now than when we were first married. Our Christian faith has had an enormous impact on the way we seek to love each other, and we try to explain in various places the difference it has made to our marriage. However, you do not need to be a Christian to benefit from this book. Most of the advice given could be described as practical guidelines for making a relationship not only work but also flourish.

We have included many stories from our own marriage and from others. Some examples may seem trivial, but it is the little things that can make or break a marriage. The other couples whose stories we tell have been kind enough to share their experiences in the hope that they might inspire others to persevere and discover for themselves what a dynamic partnership marriage can be. (In the majority of cases, we have changed the names to maintain confidentiality.)

The marriage wheel (illustrated below) encapsulates the areas we believe every couple needs to address in order to have "Love" at the heart of this journey they have embarked on together. Each section of the book (and each week of The Marriage Course) represents one section of the wheel. Our experience has shown us that every part is needed if the marriage wheel is not to bump and jar, especially when the road gets rough.

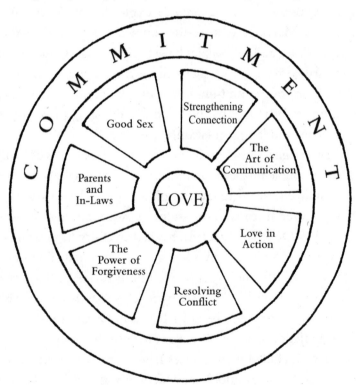

The rim of the wheel, which represents commitment, holds the relationship together. Some argue that the ideal of a lifelong marriage should be abandoned today in favor of an arrangement that makes "coupling and uncoupling" as easy as possible. Is there still a case for the traditional view of marriage? We would answer with a resounding yes.

Our view is that marriage remains of vital importance, not only to us as individuals, but also as the foundation of any society. Marriage is the ideal God-given basis for family life, particularly because the best way for children to learn what committed, loving relationships are all about is through their experience of the commitment between their mother and father. Nothing is more important in a child's education. Children, like adults, always learn far more from what they see than from what they are told. One father said to us recently, "I have realized that the best way to love my children is to love my wife."

But marriage is not just for the benefit of children. There is a desire deep within us all for someone with whom we can be totally open and honest emotionally, spiritually, and physically. Such intimacy is only possible where there is commitment. We will only dare to expose our innermost selves if we know for sure that we are not going to be let down.

Marriage is designed by God to be a relationship in which a man and a woman give themselves to each other in radical and total abandonment. In the wedding service, the minister, priest, or pastor may bless the couple, pray for them, and declare that in the eyes of God and the people they are married, but it is the promises that the man and woman make to each other that establish the marriage, and every phrase of the vows underlines this lifelong commitment:

Groom: I, N, take you, N,
to be my wife,
to have and to hold
from this day forward;
for better, for worse,
for richer, for poorer,
in sickness and in health,
to love and to cherish,
till death do us part,
according to God's holy law,
and this is my solemn vow.

Bride: I, N, take you, N,
to be my husband,
to have and to hold
from this day forward;
for better, for worse,
for richer, for poorer,
in sickness and in health,
to love and to cherish,
till death do us part,
according to God's holy law,
and this is my solemn vow.[2]

The marriage relationship is designed by God to be an adventure of love that lasts a lifetime. The Bible contains much practical advice about how to make such an intimate relationship work. And Jesus Christ says that anyone who hears his words and puts them into practice is like a wise man who digs down deep and builds his house on a secure foundation. When the storms come and the wind beats against it, as they will in any marriage, the house stands firm.

Section 1

Strengthening Connection

Chapter 1

Taking a Long View

There is a woman in bed beside me. Right this moment I could reach out my hand and touch her, as easily as I touch myself, and as I think about this, it is more staggering than any mountain or moon. It is even more staggering, I think, than if this woman happened instead to be an angel (which, come to think of it, she might well be). There are only two factors which prevent this situation from being so overpoweringly awesome that my heart would explode just trying to take it in: one is that I have woken up just like this, with this same woman beside me, hundreds of times before; and the other is that millions of other men and women are waking up beside each other, just like this, each and every day all around the world, and have been for thousands of years.[1]

Mike Mason

Marriage is a unique opportunity. We have the chance to share every aspect of our life with another human being. We have promised to stick together through the highs and lows, and, out of the security of our mutual promise, we dare to reveal everything about ourselves.

We relate to each other in our common humanity, feeling each other's pain and covering each other's weaknesses.

We rejoice in each other's strengths and delight in each other's successes. We are given a counselor, a companion, a best friend—in short, a partner through life. And if we are patient enough, kind enough, and unselfish enough, we will discover that each of us is inexhaustibly rich.

Marriage has brought untold joy to millions, and throughout history has been celebrated around the world in ceremony, poetry, prose, and song.

What is marriage?

That is why a man leaves his father and mother and is united to his wife, and they become one flesh.

(Genesis 2:24)

Marriage is about two people being joined together to become one, and is therefore the closest, most intimate relationship of which human beings are capable. Some might object and say that the parent–child relationship is closest, given that the child's life begins within the mother. However, a healthy parent–child relationship is to be one of increasing separation and growing *independence*, with each child leaving the parental nest to make a home of their own. The marriage relationship is altogether the other way around. Two people, at one time strangers to each other, meet and subsequently get married. They enter into a relationship marked, at its best, by an increasing *interdependence*.

John Bayley writes about his fifty years of marriage to his late wife in *Iris: A Memoir of Iris Murdoch*. Towards the end she suffered from Alzheimer's disease, through which he nursed her himself:

> Looking back, I separate us with difficulty. We seem always to have been together . . . But where Iris is concerned my own memory, like a snug-fitting garment, seems to have zipped itself up to the present second. As I work in bed early in the morning, typing on my old portable with Iris quietly asleep beside me, her presence as she now is seems as it always was, and as it always should be. I know she must once have been different, but I have no true memory of a different person.[2]

This process of growing together is not automatic. Most couples come into marriage with big expectations. As they leave their wedding through a shower of confetti and meander off into the sunset, they cannot imagine ever not wanting to be together. The long-term reality is different and, potentially, far better.

Both husband and wife must be ready to build their marriage. Each stage of the process brings its own challenges and opportunities. In the early days we may be shocked by the things that we discover about each other that had not been apparent during the heady days of courtship and engagement.

For ourselves, even though we had known each other for four years prior to getting married, we both had to make adjustments in the light of what married life revealed: irritating habits, unexpected behaviors, values that differed from our own.

The first lesson of marriage is to accept your husband or wife as they are, rather than trying to make them into the person you had hoped they would be. This mutual acceptance must continue, as the passing years will inevitably bring change. As Shakespeare mused:

Love is not love
Which alters when it alteration finds,
Or bends with the remover to remove. . . . Love's not time's fool,
though rosy lips and cheeks
Within his bending sickle's compass come;
Love alters not with his brief hours and weeks.[3]

Despite our best efforts, we cannot stay the same. Not only will our appearance change, but also our thinking will mature, our character will develop, and our circumstances will alter. Perhaps the greatest change comes with the arrival of children, although equally challenging are the distressing and traumatic circumstances of infertility. Difficulties in conceiving can put great stress on a marriage and will call for much patience, loving support, and a refusal to blame.

The birth of a baby brings supreme joy but is often accompanied by physical exhaustion. Later on, the teenage years can be immense fun and can provide opportunities for growing friendship with our children, but are usually an emotionally exhausting roller coaster ride. When eventually our children move out, we may find ourselves grieving their absence (the expression used by one mother whose children were gradually leaving home in their early twenties).

Through these years of bringing up children, when there is so much to think about at home and at work, it is all too easy to neglect our marriage. Undoubtedly children need to be nurtured, but so too do marriages. When a couple have continued to invest in their relationship and have supported each other through the varying pressures of family life, the later years can be the most rewarding.

A friend of ours was questioning her parents recently about their marriage. Her father turned to her mother and said, "I think we've had a great marriage, but there have been difficult bits and wonderful bits." Both agreed that the hardest phase had been in their thirties when they had young children, not much money, and tough demands at work. But as the children became increasingly independent (although still very much part of their lives), the pressures eased and they had the time and opportunity to rediscover each other in new ways.

British comedian Frank Muir described in his autobiography what this later stage of his long marriage to Polly meant to him:

When brother Chas and I were teenagers our granny decided to give us signet rings. I hated the idea of wearing jewellery and so she gave me something else.

It was coming up to our forty-seventh wedding anniversary and Polly asked me if there was something I would like to have as a keepsake, and suddenly I knew exactly what I wanted. I said, 'Please may I have a wedding ring?'

Polly was very surprised. She said, 'Tell me why you suddenly want a wedding ring after all these years and you shall have one.'

'Well, I wanted to be sure first,' I said, the sort of slick half-joke inappropriate for a rather emotional moment, but it gave me time to think . . .

I find it quite impossible to visualise what life without Polly would have been like. Finding Polly was like a fifth rib replacement . . .

I asked for a wedding ring so that I could wear it as a symbol of the happiness my marriage to Pol has brought. Now that I work at home it is so good just to know that Pol is somewhere around, even though invisible, perhaps bending down picking white currants in the fruit cage and swearing gently, or upstairs shortening a skirt for a granddaughter.

The happy thing is to know that Pol is near.[4]

Why do some marriages stop working?

Tragically, we hear of many marriages today that fail to experience this type of togetherness. For some, after the initial few years, a creeping separation causes them to become disconnected. This may happen when children are young and exhausting or when they leave home. In the latter case a couple may discover that they have nothing to say to each other and they divorce, assuming that they should never have got ten married in the first place.

We grow up believing in a romantic myth: if Cinderella happens to meet her Prince Charming, they will live happily ever after. Should friction arise and we fall out of love, then, the myth states, we have married the wrong person and we are destined to live unhappily ever after or get divorced. This message is reinforced for adults through love songs, books, and films. Underlying this pervasive and dangerous myth is the belief that real love is something that happens to us, and over which we have little or no control.

This view is sometimes reported in the press as though it is beyond dispute. A *Guardian* article stated that some "lucky souls" keep an intimate marriage relationship going for twenty years or more, but the natural time limit is closer to four years. Once you've lost it, "nothing on earth will bring back that magic spark . . . You either feel it or you don't, and that's the end of the matter." In apparent consolation the article ended, "It can always be re-kindled for somebody new."[5]

But anyone who has been in a stable marriage for more than a few years will say that a relationship has to be worked at. It has taken more than romantic feelings to keep them together. It has taken a daily choice, on some occasions having to talk through sensitive issues, on others having to control an attraction to another man or woman, and, if the romantic feelings left for a while, in time they returned at a deeper and richer level. Couples who get married thinking that the line in their vows "for better or for worse" will not really apply to them are in for a shock or a failed marriage.

Marriages that break down are usually the result of a process of growing apart over many years, as this anonymous poem entitled *The Wall* describes:

Their wedding picture mocked them from the table,
These two whose lives no longer touched each other.
They loved with such a heavy barricade between them
That neither battering ram of words
Nor artilleries of touch could break it down.

Somewhere between the oldest child's first tooth
And youngest daughter's graduation,
They lost each other.
Throughout the years each slowly unravelled
That tangled ball of string called self,
And as they tugged at stubborn knots
Each hid their searching from the other.
Sometimes she cried at night and begged
The whispering darkness to tell her who she was,
While he lay beside her snoring like a
Hibernating bear unaware of her winter.

Once after they had made love he wanted to tell her
How afraid he was of dying,
But, fearing to show his naked soul, he spoke instead
About the beauty of her breasts.

She took a course in modern art trying to find herself
In colours splashed upon a canvas,
And complaining to other women about men
Who were insensitive.

He climbed into a tomb called the office,
Wrapped his mind in a shroud of paper figures
And buried himself in customers.

Slowly the wall between them rose, cemented
By the mortar of indifference.
One day, reaching out to touch each other,
They found a barrier they could not penetrate
And, recoiling from the coldness of the stone,
Each retreated from the stranger on the other side.

For when love dies, it is not in a moment of angry battle,
Nor when fiery bodies lose their heat.
It lies panting, exhausted, expiring
At the bottom of a wall it could not scale.[6]

Many marriages break down, not because of incompatibility, but because the husband and wife have never known what it takes to make their relationship work. In our society, fewer and fewer people grow up seeing a strong relationship modeled by their own parents

We live in a consumerist age in which people are not used to mending things. If something doesn't work, it is easier and cheaper to buy a new one. Powerful advertising encourages us to focus on wanting what we do not have rather than being grateful for what we do have. It increases the expectation that we should have our desires fulfilled quickly—as in the slogan for the credit card that promised to take "the waiting out of wanting."[7] We are encouraged to believe that fulfillment comes through what we can acquire with as little effort as possible rather than through working at something.

Alvin Toffler, a sociologist and bestselling author, wrote that people today have a "throwaway mentality." They not only have throwaway products, but they also make throwaway friends, and it is this mentality that produces throwaway marriages.[8]

Marriage is viewed by many today as a temporary contract between a couple for as long as their love lasts. Our culture stresses the freedom of the individual. If the relationship is not personally fulfilling, then it is better to get out. If there is no more love in a marriage, it is better to finish it.

But we are discovering as a society that the consequences are not so easily discarded. The oneness of the marriage bond means that the two people cannot be neatly and painlessly divided. It is like taking two sheets of paper and gluing them together. They become one, and they cannot be separated without causing damage to both.

If you're struggling in your marriage, we want to encourage you that reconnecting is possible. When couples have tended their relationship, we've seen things change dramatically, and they go on to experience a new connection and intimacy.

In an interview, the actor Michael Caine spoke of the break-up of his first marriage. He was desperately short of money and his wife, Patricia, tried to persuade him to give up the theater, but, "rather than relinquish his dreams, he walked away from his marriage." Later he said that, if he'd known the anguish involved, "I would have stayed at all costs. If I'd been as strong as Pat I think we could have made it."[9] Michael Caine is right. A marriage can be made to work but it takes deliberate and determined action.

Tending a marriage

Our daughter Kirsty and son-in-law Rick are involved in making sparkling wine on the south coast of England, and we have learned a lot from them about the work that goes into tending a vineyard in order to produce good wine. It's hard work. It requires care and attention of the vines on a regular cycle throughout the year, every year. Tending a vineyard provides a helpful analogy for what's required to tend and look after a marriage.

The first analogy is the importance of adjusting. Newly planted vines have to adjust to the new soil (a process that goes on for at least three years). In a similar way, in the early years of a marriage, as a couple we have to learn to adjust to each other, as we move from "I" to "we," from being independent to being interdependent. If we're to stay connected, this adjusting has to happen, not just at the beginning, but all the way through our marriage, because change is inevitable. We will both keep changing—physically, mentally, and emotionally—and our situation will keep changing, and we have to be prepared to adjust our ways of thinking and of living.

A second analogy from tending a vineyard is pruning, and vines require a lot. Pruning is a very positive activity for the vine. It involves prioritizing the most important branches and cutting the other ones off in order to direct the vine's energy into the most fruitful branches—otherwise you get lots of leaves but very little fruit. A key skill in marriage as life gets busier, maybe through having a child or work becoming more demanding, is prioritizing, which involves pruning back certain areas of our lives in order to prioritize another. We will only survive as a couple if we learn to prioritize our marriage relationship over every other demand on our time.

A third analogy is supporting. In order for vines to flourish, they need to be supported. The investment in a good, well-kept trellis system of posts and wires is vital for the production of good fruit. Similarly, a marriage needs a support system if we're to work through challenges and thrive over a lifetime. A marriage can't survive in isolation. This support network may include friends and family, or support may come from an older married couple, whom we watch and from whom we learn. But as well as having support from others, it's essential that we support each other.

Sila

Personally, I found the change from parenting young children to parenting teenagers pretty challenging. Parenting teenagers didn't come as naturally to me as it did to Nicky. And I really needed his help not to over-worry or over-control them, to listen to them and give them space to grow in their independence. Nicky's support and encouragement made a massive difference during those years.

Finally, renewing. At the end of the growing season, when the vine is reduced to a stem and a few bare branches, to an uninformed eye it looks as though there's not a lot going on until the buds appear in the spring. But that's not the case. This is a vital time when the vine is putting its energy into extending its roots deeper into the soil. The vine is resting while its roots are fed with compost in order to renew strength and produce a good crop the following year.

We all need times of renewing in our marriage. Renewing means continually taking care of our relationship, particularly when we reach a new season. It involves being prepared to talk about our own individual needs and desires, sharing with our partner our hopes for our future together. Renewing our marriage may mean slowing down long enough to decide on changes we'd like to make, possibly stopping certain activities in order to have more time together, or starting a new pattern in our day or our week or our year that will strengthen or renew the connection between us.

For any of us to grow closer as a couple we must be proactive within our marriage. All too often we are only reactive. We react negatively to each other's behavior or comments, blaming each other when things go wrong and retaliating when we are hurt. Being proactive means taking practical steps to develop new, positive habits.

This book is intended as a toolkit for building a strong marriage. Each chapter provides a different tool with which you can shape, fix, maintain, or repair your relationship. We believe that by using even one of these tools, you will begin to see improvements.

If you are reading and discussing this book as a couple, we hope that you will find it becomes easier and easier to talk together about your relationship. Some people will discover wonderful things about their partner that have never been disclosed. Others will recognize areas of their marriage that need attention. Some of the practical application may at first seem contrived, but we know from our own experience that by persevering it becomes a normal and natural part of our relationship.

Working at a marriage takes time and intention, but the effort involved will be amply rewarded. The former TV chat show host, Michael Parkinson, has been married to his wife Mary for more than fifty years. He first saw her on a bus in Doncaster. She was wearing a red duffle coat and he thought she had a face he could look at forever. He said in an interview that no marriage is without its crises and they have both felt pleased they hadn't walked out when things were tough. "I just can't imagine divorce," he said, "I really can't. I can't contemplate life without Mary." He said he has done everything he wanted to do and been paid very well for doing it, but he concluded, "When you come to the end of your life, having your family intact–that's the really important thing."[10]

Chapter 2

Planning to Succeed

Marriage is a choice you make every day . . . You don't do it because it's easy. You do it because you believe in it. You believe in the other person. It's important . . . to be with somebody who wants you to win as much as you want them to win.[1]

Michelle Obama

We can clearly remember the first time a couple asked us for advice about their relationship. They had been married for sixteen years and had two children. The husband, a successful businessman at the height of his career, called in desperation to say that his wife was about to leave him. They arrived together at our house looking slightly awkward. We opened the door feeling equally awkward and wondering if we had anything to say that could help.

We started by asking where things had gone wrong. They were both highly articulate in describing their version of the events of the preceding months and years. Neither allowed the other to finish a sentence. After ten minutes it became clear that they were more interested in attacking each other than in answering our question. Their marriage looked like a ball of string so tangled that it would be easier to throw it away and buy some more than patiently undo each knot. Thankfully, they were prepared to attempt staying together.

We saw two changes that had to happen if their marriage was to stand a chance. First, they needed to spend more time together. Second, they needed to use that time effectively. And so, very tentatively, we suggested that every day they set aside thirty minutes to talk together. Each would allow the other to speak about their feelings for at least five minutes without interrupting. We also encouraged them to plan an evening once a week to go out as a couple in the way they had before they were married.

Two weeks later, we opened the door to two different people. They had made a start along the road of understanding each other. We were excited to see how a marriage could be transformed when a couple moved from being reactive to being proactive and when they were willing to make time available exclusively for each other.

Time together

To deprive a marriage of time spent together is the equivalent of depriving a person of air or a plant of water. Some plants can survive longer than others, but eventually they wilt and die.

Rob Parsons, founder and chairman of Care for the Family, describes what he calls "the great illusion":

> You can run several agendas in life, but you cannot run them all at a hundred per cent without somebody paying a price . . . We have so many excuses. The main one is that we convince ourselves a slower day is coming. We say to ourselves, "When the house is decorated, when I get my promotion, when I pass those exams–then I'll have more time." Every time we have to say, "Not now, darling . . ." we tell ourselves it's okay because that slower day is getting nearer. It's as well that we realise, here and now, that the slower day is an illusion–it never comes. Whatever

our situation, we all have the potential to fill our time. That's why we need to *make time* for the things that we believe are important–and we need to make it now.[2]

The former Beatle, Paul McCartney, and his late wife Linda, despite the pressures of fame, were very particular about making time to be together. Hunter Davies, their friend and biographer, recalled that Paul had decided that there were two things that were most important to him: being with his family and playing music.

> He was willing to go backwards, to start where he had begun, playing in local halls, college campuses. It struck me as so mature, so clever, so adult, to realise that and act upon it. And so Wings was born, putting his two passions in life together. He would take Linda and the children on tour with him all around the country, sleeping in caravans if need be.
>
> Naturally the critics were horrible to Linda, criticising her musical skills or lack of them, and were snide about Paul, saying how stupid to drag her round. Wings weren't all that brilliant at first, but they got better, learned and improved together. Just as they did in their marriage.[3]

Time together with the people who matter most does not just happen. It requires a deliberate and determined decision. Before they get married, most husbands and wives contrive to spend every available minute together. Gary Chapman, bestselling author of *The 5 Love Languages*, describes it well:

> At its peak, the "in love" experience is euphoric. We are emotionally obsessed with each other. We go to sleep thinking of one another. When we rise that person is the first thought on our minds. We long to be together . . . When we hold hands, it seems

as if our blood flows together . . . Our mistake was in thinking it would last forever.[4]

We have been led to believe that, if we really are in love, such emotions will never fade. Psychologists' research, however, indicates that this state only lasts an average of two years. After that a couple can no longer rely solely upon their feelings. They must *choose* to put each other first.

In marriage, time together can quickly cease to be a priority. As we are living under the same roof, we all too easily think that we no longer need to coordinate our calendars; we can begin to take each other for granted. However, we are convinced that *married* couples need to continue planning special times for each other. The effort that went into meeting when we first fell in love, the anticipation, the excitement, the variety of times and places all added to the pleasure. If once we're married we continue to make time for each other, the romance will be kept alive, we will have the chance to communicate effectively and our understanding of each other will deepen. The regularity and nature of this time together will create the fabric of our relationship over a lifetime.

In our own marriage we have sought to set a pattern of fixed times for one another. What is possible and workable will vary for each couple, but we know that without such a pattern we would have failed to spend enough time together to stay closely connected. When people ask us for one thing that a couple could do to keep their marriage alive and their love growing over the years, our answer would be this:

> Plan a regular time every week of at least two hours to spend alone together, to relax, to do something you both enjoy and to have fun.

We, like many couples, call this our "date night," although our weekly date will not always be in the evening. This time is intended to be different from the other hours spent together during the rest of the week. An evening at home can so easily become just another night when the bills are paid, the broken door handle is mended, or the ironing is done. These dull domestic necessities are an inevitable part of married life, but if we *only* meet around the bank statement or the toolbox, meaningful communication will be stifled and our love will struggle.

Carefully planned time together rekindles romance in a marriage. Exhausting organization is not required: candles on the table, music in the background, ordering takeout (to give the cook a break), and putting phones away are all that is necessary. These times should be fun and memorable. We could go to a movie or out for a meal. In fact, not setting the bar too high on what we do and where we go makes a weekly pattern more easily sustainable. It is time to hold hands, time to laugh, time to enjoy being together and, above all, time to talk. This is the time to share our hopes and fears, excitements and worries, struggles and achievements. Such sharing builds intimacy. It's simple but very powerful.

But keeping this time for each other is not easy. There are obstacles that get in our way: schedules at work over which we have little control, transporting children from one activity to the next, or a self-inflicted pressure that "there is always something else that needs to be done." Many of us are overcome with exhaustion at the end of the day and the easiest option is to sit in front of one or more screens, physically together but mentally apart.

Experience has shown us that keeping our weekly date requires the following three commitments. The first is to *plan it.* This will involve finding a time that works for us both, which will depend on whether we have children, how old they are, whether our work is at home or some distance away. For some years we discovered that a two-hour lunch was the best time for us. Now we can be more flexible between the daytime and the evening. But we still put it in our calendars once a week, and we give it as high a commitment as an invitation we have accepted or an appointment we have made. Because our lives are busy, we usually plan our weekly dates three months ahead, putting each other's name in our diaries once a week like any other appointment.

This idea of planning time together with our husband or wife may seem contrived. However, it is the first thing that can slip quietly out of a loving relationship. We don't set out to neglect one another. Rather, the routines of daily life steal the time we once spent together.

The second commitment is to make this time together a *priority.* This means recognizing the importance of it over and above the many other good things that we could be doing with our spare time, such as seeing family, entertaining at home, going to a party, watching a football game with friends, or commitments at church. Making our time together a top priority is a powerful indication of our love.

When we were first married, we often failed in this. When other people invited us to do something with them, it seemed unfriendly to say we were keeping the evening for ourselves. So now, instead of telling them, "We are having an evening in," we say, "I am so sorry but we are busy," without saying *what* we are doing. If we receive an exciting invitation that clashes with our planned date, we have an agreement not to accept it without consulting the other, and we will usually only make a change if we can find an alternative time that week.

The third commitment is to *protect* it. Interruptions can destroy our time together. Our phones can hold us for ransom. Some of us cannot resist answering it or checking our messages and notifications at frequent intervals; others find it hard not to talk for hours. We made the decision to put our phones on silent and out of sight during our date night in order not to be distracted from focusing on each other.

For others, the television is the prime intruder. Watching TV can easily claim many hours each week, some of which could otherwise be spent in conversation. If the TV is a problem, do something. Banish it from the sitting room, schedule your program and catch up at a more convenient time when it's not going to detract from this quality time you've planned together.

We try to arrange our weekly date at a place where we are not going to bump into people we know. The needs of family and friends are important, but none of them is as important as the need to invest time in our marriage.

The busier we are, the more important and the more inconvenient this time together becomes. On occasions, one or both of us have been distracted by other pressing demands, but the temptation to cancel our time together is far easier to resist when we are convinced of its long-term benefits. Of course, there have been weeks when it has been impossible, but we have discovered that two weeks without the opportunity to relax together and communicate properly is a long time in a marriage. We soon find that we are out of touch with each other and often out of sorts too. When we have had time together, we experience a sense of well-being: the week feels more balanced, we are less worried about the demands of life, and we relate better to each other and to other people.

A day together

Every four to six months we plan a day away together. This is a time to talk over those things that in everyday life we have neither the time nor the energy to discuss. It is a time of looking back to see what is working well and what needs attention, to consider our finances, to look forward to our goals for the future, and to dream up new ideas for our marriage and family life.

Setting aside time every few months helps to prevent a backlog on these bigger issues. These days have become special and fun for us. Because we live in the city we try to get out to the country. We go for a walk and have lunch together, giving ourselves plenty of time to talk. We have sometimes written down plans and goals to refer back to in the months to come.

Vacation

We have discovered the benefits of considering carefully how and where to spend our vacations, taking into account our different preferences. It is all too easy to think we will just "go with the flow," see what comes up, or accept the first invitation to go away with other people. We have been on vacations that we failed to plan and think through properly, and on our return realized that we needed a vacation in order to recover. The main purpose of a vacation is to have fun, to relax, and be re-energized through a break from our usual routine. We have found that vacation with lots of other friends, friends' children, or family are wonderful for *some* of the time, but not all of it.

Mini-honeymoons

Two or three days away as a couple once a year, without our children, have had an amazingly revitalizing effect on our relationship. For couples with young children, it can be difficult to organize, but it is well worth persevering. If you do not have family who could look after them, what about the possibility of taking turns with friends who have children the same age to enable each couple to go away for a few days on their own?

If going away is too expensive, you could have a staycation (but without your children) and do something completely different. Alternatively, swap houses with friends or family who live in another part of the country. We see this time as a mini-honeymoon every year. The benefits more than repay the effort it takes to organize it.

Time apart

While we stress the need to spend time together, we recognize that most couples will spend a certain amount of time apart.

Some friends of ours, who have been happily married for several years, recalled that the husband had to go away for a week only three weeks after their wedding. Everyone felt sympathy for his poor wife. She, however, was delighted. She slept really well for a whole week. The complexities of sharing a bed, with extra limbs kicking around, had totally exhausted her. A week's recovery was exactly what she needed.

Where time apart is not out of necessity, it will need to be with the genuine and freely given agreement of both husband and wife. An overdose of "stag weekends" or "hen parties" will not be helpful to a marriage, and any invitation of this kind needs to be considered carefully and jointly. It is better to disappoint a friend than to harm a marriage.

Some friendships from our single days may deepen when the relationship is enjoyed by both husband and wife. But it will not be possible to maintain every friendship. Those that are in any way a threat to the marriage must be allowed to die, particularly if there is a danger of physical infatuation. In this way we shall be faithful to our marriage vows: "forsaking all others, be faithful to him/her as long as you both shall live." This is part of the new start that marriage involves.

That is not to say that we must do everything together. We are not to try to force our partner to become like us in every way. There may be social occasions, events at church or in the community, work or leisure-related invitations about which we feel differently. This may have much to do with our personality type, our ability in a certain area, or our level of self-confidence. Of course, our priority is to find activities we both enjoy, but there will be some interests couples do not share.

Many couples have trouble with this aspect of marriage. They feel abandoned when their spouse wants time apart. In reality, spouses need time apart, which makes them realise the need to be back together. Spouses in healthy relationships cherish each other's space and are champions of each other's causes.[5]

There are four questions to consider, particularly if we have young children:

- Are both husband and wife being given some opportunities to develop their individual interests?
- Are our separate interests causing mutual resentment or are we genuinely pleased to give each other this time?
- Are we both seeking first to release the other rather than to grasp time for ourselves?
- Are we willing to give up our separate interests if family circumstances require it?

If the attitude of both partners is right, pursuing interests separately can prevent a relationship from becoming one-dimensional or claustrophobic, and brings refreshment, stimulation, new thoughts and stories into the marriage. Some interests, however, will need to be curtailed or dropped if they cause a distance to come between us or put a strain on our marriage.

Sila

One of Nicky's passions is sailing. When we first met in South West Ireland, I soon realized this and I was always the first to volunteer to be his crew for him during the two weeks of racing in August. Some years later we discovered that dinghy sailing and small babies are totally incompatible. After much tension, occasional resentment, and some agonizing, we decided that taking our family vacation with four children under the age of eight during the two weeks of racing was going to cause more conflict than it was worth.

As a result, for many years we overlapped our vacation with three or four days of racing to give Nicky the chance to compete in some of the races and then to have the rest of the time free to spend as a family.

Staying connected

The process of blending two lives into one can only happen as we develop a regular pattern of disclosing to one another our separate worlds. This may at times take great effort, but our different contributions over a lifetime establish a reservoir of shared experiences and a level of mutual understanding that draw us closer.

Normally we start each day by talking about our plans as well as any potential areas of stress or anxiety, and we then pray for each other before we part. (We describe in more detail how we do this in Appendix 4.) These few minutes have had to be fitted into the changing pattern of family life.

There are huge long-term benefits if we stay in contact about the daily minutiae of our lives. If we are having to spend one or more nights apart, we still try to keep in touch with each other at least once a day. This enables us to be a part of each other's "world" and has an impact on our understanding of one another. It also helps us to reacclimatize ourselves to each other when we are back together.

In the evening, the day can easily grind gradually and separately to a halt: one of us falls asleep on the sofa and the other crawls into bed alone. For the sake of our relationship, and despite our tiredness, we generally try to connect with each other at the end of the day. One wife, after twenty-five years of marriage, described the late evening in these words: "This is the cream of our marriage: this nightly turning out and sharing of the day's pocketful of memories."

Section 1 – Strengthening connection

Conclusion

At the heart of a strong marriage is a strong friendship. Even good friendships drift apart unless they are positively fed and held together. A pattern of regular time spent together daily, weekly, and annually is the first investment needed to keep our friendship growing, and this will provide a firm foundation for a strong marriage.

Our weekly date has been for us a wonderful investment and has become the single most important means of staying closely connected with each other at an emotional level and keeping the romance alive. Time planned, prioritized, and protected counters the illusion that "the slower day" is coming. We often remember Rob Parsons' words: ". . . we need to *make time* for the things that we believe are important and we need to make it now."[6]

First golden rule of marriage

Make time for each other and have fun together regularly.

Section 2

The Art of Communication

Chapter 3

How to Talk More Effectively

The only real essential is to carry on the conversation you started.[1]

Libby Purves

Liz and Steve met through their careers in the police force and were married shortly afterwards in 1997. They went on to have three daughters, with Liz running the family home in order to support Steve in his role as an undercover police officer, leading an armed surveillance team working to infiltrate gangs in South London.

Despite their relationship looking ideal from the outside, the strain and trauma of Steve's job soon began to take its toll on their marriage. Steve recalls, "I wouldn't talk about my work at all. I thought the best thing for my family was to protect them from all the stuff I'd see—the murder scenes I'd go to. When I got home and Liz asked how my day was, I'd say it was fine. I began to stick everything into little compartments."

This was when everything started to unravel. Instead of sharing her feelings about Steve's intense workload and the effect it was having on their family and marriage, Liz would bottle them up. She reflected, "I wouldn't put any expectations on him whatsoever. I wouldn't complain about his long hours. I would just deal with it all. I was the true martyr."

Although she was wanting to avoid putting any additional pressure on Steve by taking on everything to do with the family, she later realized that her actions inadvertently communicated that he wasn't needed. With Steve not feeling needed at home, he began to stay even later at work, and the downward spiral of their miscommunication increased. Their lack of understanding towards each other was constantly simmering beneath the surface. Liz said, "We began to talk only about basic things to get through life. We were living quite separately, only occasionally getting together for family events."

It was at this point that the various pressures of his work, his lifestyle, and his marriage began to mount for Steve. Following the sudden death of his twin sister in 2007, Steve suffered a heart attack and was taken to the hospital.

He relayed, "The one good thing that I was ever any good at was being a policeman, and I couldn't do it anymore—it crushed me. I couldn't be a father; I couldn't be a husband. That's when we decided, right there in the hospital, to firm up our separation." Steve moved in with his parents, with Liz staying in the family home.

As time went on, Steve describes how he hit rock bottom and was planning to end his life. At a critical moment, he was visited by their local vicar who listened at length to Steve's problems. Before leaving, he offered Steve one piece of advice: "Try reading the Psalms." Steve weighed up his choices and decided that the Psalms might be the better one to try first. The impact on him as he read was profound. He said, "I found a God I could shout at and be angry at with all the different things that had happened, and I found a God who loved me despite the mistakes

I'd made. Soon after, Liz came over and knocked on the door and said, 'I still love the man I married and I'm here until you find yourself again.' And, from that moment, we started falling in love again."

Steve describes the changes they have made since they moved back in together: "I think it's been a process of us learning how to communicate deeply, not just on a surface level. This means that we know where our weaknesses are and where we have a tendency to fall down. Allocating dedicated time each day to being present with each other has really changed things. It was gradual, but putting space on the calendar and making sure that we kept on doing so really made the difference."

Liz added, "We learned through that time that we really needed to work on our marriage and that we needed to make it our number one priority. It's so easy, especially when you've got young children, to just get on with your own stuff. We realized that we needed to work hard on each other, concentrate on and listen to each other, respect each other and seek to understand where the other was coming from.

"Quite often, even now, we just stop for a moment and say, 'We don't feel we've connected for a few days. We need to connect.' We can recognize now when we're starting to drift away from each other and we need to regroup and come back together."

What was true about Liz and Steve's difficulties in communication is true in many marriages. To communicate is not just to exchange information but means, literally, to "make common" our thoughts and feelings. In this way we make ourselves known to each other.

Even though Winston and Clementine Churchill spent much of their fifty-six years of marriage apart owing to the demands of politics and two World Wars, they constantly communicated by letter, notes, telegrams, and memoranda, of which more than 1,700 still exist.[2] They maintained the habit of making common with each other all that they were thinking and feeling. This constant communication must help to account for their lifelong love for each other.

In the best marriages there are no secrets between husband and wife. In a television drama about Queen Victoria there was a conversation between the queen and her prime minister, Lord Melbourne. The queen was seeking advice as to whether she should talk to her new husband, Prince Albert, about affairs of state with which he, as a German, might disagree. Lord Melbourne's reply was very wise: "In marriage, disagreements are not nearly as dangerous as secrets. Secrets breed mistrust."

Of course, we may need to learn *how* to communicate with one another. An article in *The Mail on Sunday*, describing the break-up of a celebrity marriage, quoted the husband as saying, "When we went to marriage guidance counselling, I was shocked to find we had never really talked. I heard my wife telling a complete stranger about feelings I never knew existed. And I heard myself doing the same. We could only communicate through a stranger."

Professor John Gottman, who runs the Family Research Laboratory at the University of Washington and has been analysing marriage relationships for more than forty years, has observed:

> What typically happens is that one person reaches out to the other to get the person's interest and it falls flat. The basic problem is emotional connectedness . . . people are asking their partner to "show me you love me." Many people live in an emotional desert. That's why they are so needy.[3]

Talking

The importance of conversation
Robert Louis Stevenson described marriage thus:

> Marriage is one long conversation, chequered by disputes. Two persons more and more adapt their notions to suit the other and in process of time, without sound of trumpet, they conduct each other into new worlds of thought.[4]

Some years ago, when our children were young, we left them with their grandparents for three days so that we could spend some time on our own. We went to stay in a small hotel in the Highlands of Scotland and had been looking forward to having an extended opportunity to talk. We arrived at the hotel in the evening, unpacked, and went down to the dining room.

It was full of other couples, most of whom looked as though they had been married for twenty-five years or more. However, apart from the sound of knives and forks on plates, there was total silence. We were given a table in the middle of the room and sat as close to one another as possible, talking in whispers so as not to be overheard by everyone else.

We are sure that, if those same couples had been out with friends or even if they had been at a party with complete strangers, they would not have sat in silence throughout the evening. They would have made an effort to initiate conversation. The tragedy for many husbands and wives is that they fail to recognize that their *greatest effort* should be made with each other.

Of course, unless we plan time for each other, we usually meet at our worst moments: first thing in the morning when we are barely awake or last thing at night when we are exhausted. Social media and the TV take the place of talking. What conversation there is consists of little more than functional requests—"Would you pick up some milk on the way home?"—or a simple exchange of facts—"The woman across the road has had her baby."

Making an effort

If, when we first went out with our partner, we had never bothered to talk to them, we would probably not be married now. Relationships grow when we make an effort. One woman, who was on the point of being drawn into an affair, told us why she was so attracted to another man: "He seemed to be interested in me—asking me questions and so on."

Many couples spend their days in different ways. We were talking to a businessman from Australia. He has a frenetic job and spends most of his time on his cell phone. The phone rings as he gets into his car in the morning and does not stop ringing all day until he turns it off in the driveway of his home when he returns.

His wife, who used to have a similarly demanding work schedule, is now at home full-time looking after three children under the age of five. As she hears the door open she is desperate to talk to an adult and longs for stimulating conversation. All *he* wants is to unwind on his own. Both know they have to make a supreme effort to be sensitive to each other's needs.

Another couple we know has devised a strategy to deal with this situation. As soon as they leave work, they consider the time to belong to the other. So, during the journey home, they start thinking about how their partner has spent their day, thus preparing themselves for seeing each other again and for their evening together. Such mutual effort leads easily into conversation and can scarcely fail to draw a couple closer together and deepen their friendship.

Other situations require a similar degree of effort: a doctor in a cancer ward married to someone in sales—each will have to try hard to understand the other's pressures and to respect the other's job. The husband or wife of a schoolteacher may need to be extremely patient in semester changes as a considerable part of each evening is spent preparing lessons and marking books, with less time for conversation and relaxation together.

Increasing our topics of conversation

A couple we know decided they would avoid talking about their work or their children on their date night. In order to have other topics of conversation, the wife says she always has a quick glance at the past week's news.

Another way to find more things to discuss is to increase our pool of joint interests. Shared experiences lead naturally to stimulating conversation. A friend of ours told us of the interests her parents have come to share over the last forty years:

> When Mum met Dad, she had never held a pair of binoculars to her eyes and her knowledge of birds did not extend past a sparrow. It is quite touching to see her incredible ornithological knowledge at the age of sixty-five. She got interested because she loved Dad and this was his passion. They have walked thousands of miles together in pursuit of birds over their forty-plus years of marriage.
>
> Dad is not remotely arty and an evening at a concert or the theatre would not have been his choice as a young man. This is Mum's kind of thing. Over the years, he has chosen to go with her and tried his best to be interested. On occasions, he comes home having genuinely loved a piece of music or a play, but he sometimes falls asleep, often can't remember either the title or

anything that happened upon his return, and has mainly spent the evening working out the mechanics of the scenery.

It will sometimes require a conscious decision to show an interest in what our partner already enjoys. This may mean doing again what we did together when we first met, or we may need to find a new activity that attracts both of us. The list of possibilities is endless and could include taking up a new sport, remodeling the house, gardening, going for walks, listening to music, going to street markets or exploring a different part of the city, watching sports, going to concerts or festivals, the theater or a movie.

We can then discuss our different reactions to what we've seen or heard or done, drawing out of the other their thoughts and feelings: what they liked or didn't like, what they want to do next time and so on.

Making use of mealtimes

The original meaning of the word *companionship* is *taking bread together*. The comedian and travel writer, Michael Palin, commented after his journey around the world:

> In almost every country I visited . . . the sharing of food was an important social activity, which is as it should be. A shared meal is the best forum for the airing of grievances and celebration of pleasures that has yet been devised.[5]

In biblical times, meals were an opportunity for developing friendships. Perhaps this lies behind Jesus' words when he describes his desire for a relationship with us: "I stand at the door and knock. If anyone hears my voice and opens the door, I will come in and eat with that person, and they with me'" (Revelation 3:20).

Eating together has always been valued as a means of drawing a family together, and only since the second half of the twentieth century in the West has this been neglected. The danger of convenience foods and microwaves is that they allow people to eat quickly and separately. In some countries now, this has gone so far that houses are being designed with no place for communal eating, but with a place for a screen in every room. This is a great loss. One couple commented to us, "We find mealtimes one of the most important occasions for conversation. No matter how convenient the food, laying the table and sitting down to eat together without interruptions or distractions is always beneficial."

Talking about our feelings

Many years ago, we received a sad letter from a woman who had been married less than a year. She wrote, "To all the world we look like a happy newly married couple. He puts on a veneer when we are with others. But a few weeks after we were married, I felt so disappointed. I thought we would be able to talk about everything, but he never tells me about his feelings."

Men in cultures like our own typically have a harder time than women when it comes to showing emotion. Certainly in the past, and to some extent today, men have been expected to keep their feelings to themselves while women are encouraged to talk about theirs with friends and family. A friend of ours said about the breakdown of her marriage, "Our marriage collapsed because we failed to share our real feelings with one another. I began to confide in my sisters and close friends rather than in my husband. This began—subtly at first—to drive a wedge between us."

Some people think of themselves as "not the emotional type." But emotions are a fundamental part of being human and we must learn to talk about our feelings if we are to communicate effectively in our marriage and stay connected. A woman who participated in The Marriage Course, when asked what she had most enjoyed about the course, wrote, "My husband *had* to communicate with me his thoughts and feelings. There are many lovely things he thinks but never puts into words." To ask our husband or wife at appropriate moments, "What are you feeling?" can help them to talk more freely. If we learn to express our feelings when we are feeling fine, then there is a much greater chance we will be able to do the same when we are under pressure.

In the course of any marriage, we are all likely to go through difficult times: maybe financial hardship, serious sickness, a road accident, problems with a teenage child, a miscarriage, or a bereavement. The handling of a crisis can make or break a marriage. The death of a child in particular puts an enormous strain on a relationship, and the divorce rate among such couples is significantly higher than average. In times of bereavement or sadness we easily slip into denying our feelings, withdrawing from each other, or disappearing into our work. But an essential part of coping with these experiences as a couple is to voice our feelings, however painful that might be, to allow each other to respond differently, and to work through the grief together.

In a magazine article entitled "Do Men Understand Intimacy?" a wife called Alison is quoted as saying, "James relies on me to do all the feeling in our relationship . . . He is English and very remote—he was sent away to boarding school when he was eight years old. When that happens to a little boy, he soon learns that having emotions will just make life a lot harder."

After Alison suffered a miscarriage, the couple began to grow apart. Alison continued, "I found it helpful to talk about the tragedy; but James suppressed his feelings. He dealt with it by becoming highly critical of me and angry over the smallest things. Then one night in bed, I realized that he had been feeling depressed for weeks too. 'Why didn't you tell me you were feeling this way?' I asked him."[6]

Deep communication requires us to be open about our inner selves and to make ourselves vulnerable to each other. If we fail to communicate painful and complex emotions and try to cope on our own, we drift apart.

One husband, who had spent some time separated from his wife, wrote to us: "If I had to identify one reason for our separation it would be ineffective communication. I remember so well the ease with which it is possible to settle downwards into a norm in which the air is filled with words but nothing is really said. All current wisdom on this subject stresses the importance of quality time being carved out of hectic schedules. But this, in my experience, only marks out the space. Effective communication must mean revealing all parts of our lives, in my case the parts that I am well practiced at keeping hidden. For me, at least, it requires more than time; it requires courage."

For those of us who feel unable to *recognize*, let alone *talk about*, our feelings, change is possible. A good way to start is to write down three or four things (of minor or major significance) that have happened to us over the course of a normal day. Against each of these events we should record what we felt about them. For example:

> Caught the train–felt bored/alert/tired; made a telephone call–felt angry/hopeful/anxious; went to the bank–felt ashamed/calm/annoyed; met my husband or wife–felt happy/tense/excited.

It will require courage to begin to articulate these emotions if we are not used to doing so. We are likely to feel exposed and vulnerable, so we will need to know that our husband or wife is not going to reject us, get angry, or blame us for what we reveal.

Choosing the right moment

While it is important not to keep secrets from each other and to be able to express our feelings, it is not always right to say immediately what we think. We need to consider carefully the effect of our words. The book of Proverbs in the Bible asserts: "The right word at the right time is like a custom-made piece of jewelry" (Proverbs 25:11, MSG).[7] Restraining ourselves until a more suitable moment is part of the costliness of love. This may require waiting until neither of us is over-tired or preoccupied and we have time to talk the matter through.

Expressing affection

While we are wise to delay raising sensitive issues, there are no right or wrong moments to talk about our *positive* feelings towards each other. And to do so frequently has a powerful effect upon a marriage, as Frank Muir relates:

As far as Pol and I are concerned, being in love certainly developed into something more lasting–love. And love is altogether a much deeper, give-and-take, *affectionate* relationship than being 'in love'.

Polly and I confirm our feelings towards each other every night along with prayers for the rest of the family and Sal's Dalmatian Dotty, and our cat Cinto (named after the tallest mountain in Corsica, such a sensible name for an Abyssinian cat), so should a journalist from a women's page telephone me today and ask me how often I have told my wife that I love her, I will reply (after a quick arpeggio on the calculator to check) roughly 16,822 times. And I spoke the truth every time.[8]

Chapter 4

How to Listen More Effectively

Two may talk together under the same roof for many years, yet never really meet.[1]

Mary Hartwell Catherwood

Our partner is talking to us about their day. We go on looking at the television or reading the news, making the occasional grunt. Our phone rings. It is one of our friends. We put down the newspaper and listen to every word they say. Our partner hears us responding animatedly, showing avid interest, deep sympathy or robust enjoyment during the conversation. There are long silences as we take in exactly what our friend is saying. We motion to our partner to turn the television down and we sit on a chair with our back turned, giving the conversation our full attention.

Most of us are perfectly capable of listening, but we often neglect to do so with the person we see most and whose voice we hear most. It is easy to think that the most important part of communication is *talking*: being articulate, being a good storyteller, having knowledge to divulge and opinions to proclaim.

The Bible strongly challenges this view, placing much greater emphasis on the need to listen. We are told in the book of Proverbs, "To answer before listening—that is folly and shame" (Proverbs 18:13). But how many of us do just that? The apostle James in the New Testament urges us similarly, "My dear brothers and sisters, take note of this: everyone should be quick to listen, slow to speak and slow to become angry" (James 1:19). Perhaps that is why God created us with two ears and one mouth—that we might learn to listen twice as much as we speak.

As human beings, one of our greatest longings is to be listened to and understood. It meets the fundamental need we all have—not to be alone. Some people pay to visit a counselor or a therapist simply to be heard—to have someone who will listen to them for an hour or so. The Samaritans once launched an advertising campaign with a poster of a huge ear and a caption under it saying, "Open 24 hours a day." The organization exists to give support through listening to anyone at any time. In marriage, the danger is that we don't bother to listen, either out of laziness or because we think we already know what is going to be said. We easily fall into bad habits such as interrupting, switching off, or finishing each other's sentences. In the words of one counselor:

The gift of being a good listener, a gift which requires constant practice, is perhaps the most healing gift anyone can possess; for it allows the other to *be*, enfolds them in a safe place, does not judge or advise them, and communicates support at a level deeper than words.[2]

Listening is a powerful way of showing that we value each other, but it is also costly. It takes effort to listen to our husband or wife as they pour out their feelings or express their opinions.

Many of us are not the listeners we might be. Yet to improve our listening is to improve our marriage. The following list of five bad habits has been helpful for us to recognize the various ways we might have a tendency to fall short.[3]

Five bad listening habits

Giving advice

Instead of aiming to empathise with our partner, the advice giver *offers a rational explanation* for the problem and gives a solution, completely ignoring the feelings of their partner: "It's because you're under too much pressure. You just need to . . ." Carried to an extreme and unchecked, this can destroy a marriage. Gary Chapman recounts:

I met Patrick when he was forty-three and had been married for seventeen years. I remember him because his first words were so dramatic. He sat in the leather chair in my office and after briefly introducing himself, he leaned forward and said with great emotion, "Dr Chapman, I have been a fool, a real fool."

"What has led you to that conclusion?" I asked.

"I've been married for seventeen years," he said, "and my wife has left me. Now I realize what a fool I've been."

I repeated my original question, "In what way have you been a fool?"

"My wife would come home from work and tell me about the problems in her office. I would listen to her and then tell her what I thought she should do. I always gave her advice. I told her she had to confront the problem. 'Problems don't go away. You have to talk with the people involved or your supervisor. You have to deal with problems.'

"The next day she would come home from work and tell me about the same problems. I would ask her if she had done what I had suggested the day before. She would shake her head and say no. So I'd repeat my advice. I told her that was the way to deal with the situation. She would come home the next day and tell me about the same problems. Again I would ask her if she had done what I had suggested. She would shake her head and say no.

"After three or four nights of that, I would get angry. I would tell her not to expect any sympathy from me if she wasn't willing to take the advice I was giving her . . .

"I would withdraw and go about my business. What a fool I was," he said, "what a fool! Now I realize she didn't want advice when she told me about her struggles at work. She wanted sympathy. She wanted me to listen, to give her attention, to let her know that I could understand the hurt, the stress, the pressure. She wanted to know that I loved her and that I was with her. She didn't want advice; she just wanted to know that I understood. But I never tried to understand. I was too busy giving advice. What a fool! And now she is gone."[4]

Interrupting

Instead of listening when someone else is speaking, we can easily be working out what we are going to say next. Best-selling author Stephen Covey writes:

> Most people do not listen with the intent to understand; they listen with the intent to reply. They're either speaking or preparing to speak. They're . . . reading their autobiography into other people's lives.[5]

A number of years ago on a family vacation, our children had been taken water-skiing and were talking excitedly about their achievements. A man standing nearby joined in the conversation. No sooner was he aware of the subject matter than he started to regale them with tales of his own prowess at water-skiing, his children's water-skiing, the speed of his boat, the price of his wetsuit and so on. Our children, even though they were quite young at the time, have not forgotten him. He spoiled a very happy afternoon through his inability to listen and his tendency to interrupt with his own autobiography.

An individual listens on average for seventeen seconds before interrupting. This has sometimes become such a habit that husbands and wives are not even aware that they are doing it to each other. It will be a particular danger to the one who is more articulate than their partner. Some tend to work out what they think as they speak, while their partner's way is to sort out their thoughts first and then speak. In these cases, it can take great restraint not to finish our husband or wife's sentences or respond to what we think they are going to say. We need to learn to wait and listen, as the interrupter can discourage his or her partner from expressing themselves at all beyond the minimum reporting of facts required for daily living.

Reassuring

The reassurer is the person who jumps in prematurely before a sentence is finished with comments such as, "It probably isn't as bad as you're making out," or, "I'm sure it will work out all right," or, "You'll feel so much better tomorrow." Reassurers prohibit any real expression of feelings, whether of anxiety, disappointment, or hurt, often because they themselves need the reassurance that there is no major problem and that their own life can go on uninterrupted.

Disengaging

Sometimes we disengage from what our partner is saying because there is a separate conversation going on in our heads, which distracts us. Perhaps something they have said triggers a memory of our own and, as we recall this memory, we can become distracted and stop listening to what's being said.

Our physical environment may equally cause us to disengage, particularly if we're in front of a computer screen, we're on social media, or the TV is on in the same room. With the streaming of information today, we are very used to filtering what we think is interesting from what we think is not. So we may find ourselves disengaging through a lack of interest in what may be very important to our partner.

Going off on a tangent

Some people, instead of commenting on the issue raised, take the conversation off at a tangent, usually on to an event that interests them. They say, "That reminds me of when . . ." and away they go.

We can all become good listeners, but we need to be willing to recognize where we fail and then to learn new skills. The following guidelines may appear artificial at first, but they are essential for good listening and have certainly been helpful to us over the years.

Learning to listen

Giving our full attention

We watched a film recently about a teenage daughter who rebels against her parents' values. In an early scene, the daughter wants to talk to her father about some issues that are worrying her. He is desperate to finish a piece of writing and he continues to work at his computer while she tries to summon up the courage to voice her concerns. His eyes never leave the computer screen and after a few minutes she decides not to say anything.

The father's failure to listen has disastrous consequences in his daughter's life.

By contrast, a woman wrote of her father:

> I had been so proud of him, with his high posts in the Indian government. I could still see him, impeccably dressed, adjusting his turban at the mirror before leaving for his office. The friendly eyes under bushy brows, the gentle smile, the chiselled features and aquiline nose. One of my cherished memories was seeing him at work in the study . . . Often, as a little girl, I would have a question to ask him and I would peek at him from around the door of his office, hesitant to interrupt. Then his eye would catch mine.
>
> Putting down his pen, he would lean back in his chair and call out, 'Keecha?' Slowly, I would walk into the study, my head down. He would smile and pat the chair next to his. 'Come, my darling, sit here.' Then, placing his arm around me, he would draw me to him. 'Now, my little Keecha,' he would ask gently, 'What can I do for you?' It was always the same with Father. He didn't mind if I bothered him. Whenever I had a question or problem, no matter how busy he was, he would put aside his work to devote his full attention just to me.[6]

One father showed that he was listening. The other failed to do so. In marriage, as with parenting, giving our full attention communicates love.

Studies in communication reveal that less than ten percent of what we want to communicate involves the words we use. The tone of voice with which we say them accounts for approximately forty percent and our body language for the remaining fifty percent. This is as significant for listening as it is for talking.

Physical proximity aids communication: shouting our conversations from one room to another is not very effective. If our partner needs to tell us something that has upset them, sitting close to them, putting an arm around them and, most of all, looking at them will show that we are concerned. Eye contact conveys the message, "I am interested in what you are saying and I am giving you my undivided attention."

Coping with distraction

Sila

I find it difficult to give my full attention to Nicky if there are practical jobs that need doing. Nicky can happily sit among the chaos or be clearing up and holding an in-depth conversation at the same time. All I can think about is getting the debris from breakfast cleared, the house tidied, or the dirty clothes put into the washing machine. I know that I am not concentrating on what Nicky is saying and therefore it is better for me to ask, "Can you give me ten minutes to tidy up?" Sometimes, however, there is no time for that and it takes a great effort for me to stop what I am doing, look at him, and listen properly.

It can also be very hard to listen to someone if we sense our phone is demanding our attention or if there is a lot of background noise.

Nicky

If there is a television on in the room, I find it practically impossible to concentrate on what someone is saying to me. Equally, I am easily distracted by another conversation within earshot or a newspaper with an interesting headline that catches my eye.

But a still greater hindrance to listening even than these things is that, unconsciously, we often spend time in conversation listening to *ourselves*. It is as though there is a television switched on inside us that constantly distracts our attention. The other person's words trigger thoughts and memories of our own.

If our partner says, "I was talking to Chris today; he's just lost his mother," we immediately start thinking about what it felt like when one of our own parents died. Or if they say, "As I was driving home, the blossom looked amazing," our mind becomes preoccupied with how much needs to be done in our garden. Thus our own thoughts and memories obstruct our listening, and our next remark may have little to do with our partner's conversation and more to do with our own internal narrative.

It can be hard not to hold a separate conversation in our own head, especially if we are busy and our mind is full. Our aim should be to put our own views and agenda aside and to try to grasp what our partner is saying. Stephen Covey underlines the impact this has:

> If I were to summarize in one sentence the single most important principle I have learned in the field of interpersonal relations, it would be this: *seek first to understand, then to be understood.*[7]

Significantly, the Chinese character for hearing includes symbols for the eyes, the heart, and the mind, as well as for the ear.

Showing an interest

If we decide to be interested in what another person is saying, we listen carefully; otherwise we can easily switch off. A woman told us about her visits to see her mother. She wanted to use the opportunity to talk about deeper—and what she considered to be—more meaningful issues. Her mother, however, enjoyed discussing more mundane matters such as the price of potatoes, the neighbour's dog, or a recent television program. The daughter quickly stopped listening, thinking what a boring life her mother led.

Then one day she suddenly saw that this *was* her mother's life. This brought her up short. She recalls, "I said to myself, 'My mother is always interested in everything I do,' and I suddenly realized I had not been very generous towards her. So I made a conscious effort to be interested and to listen, and this has made a huge difference to our relationship."

Inevitably, people have different interests. Making an effort to listen to what others find interesting is a compelling way of showing our love. Author and speaker, Dale Carnegie, writes of the skill of being a good conversationalist:

> To be interesting, be interested. Ask questions that other persons will enjoy answering.[8]

Listening intelligently

To relive and describe in detail some hurt or long-standing problem can be costly. It is easier to skirt around the subject or allude to it through humor. It is sometimes necessary to listen to what is *behind* the other's words to detect a hidden agenda. A good listener will have the courage to draw the other out by probing with gentle questions at the right moment.

We must give each other enough time to talk, because often we are only half-aware of why we feel as we do. Articulating our pain enables us to begin to see things in perspective. Do not be afraid of silences. For some people, silence allows them to organize their thoughts, and waiting quietly shows our concern.

Listening uncritically

Communication flourishes with acceptance of each other and is crushed by criticism. We need to be able to listen without becoming defensive and without butting in. If we can fathom what our husband or wife is feeling, we will be at least halfway to resolving a difficult situation. One wife said, "I've learned to recognize non-verbal clues from my husband. And now I try to listen, not only to his words, but to how he is saying it; listening to the feelings, rather than becoming defensive."

We will sometimes talk to our partner when we feel raw emotionally. Our words may seem confused and contradictory. We may change our mind about what we feel in the course of expressing ourselves. The listener fails totally (and cruelly) if they start to pick holes in their partner's case or in their logic.

Acknowledging our partner's feelings

To repeat back in our own words what our partner has been telling us can be very powerful, particularly when deep feelings are being expressed. This enables our husband or wife to know that we are on the same wavelength and that we have properly understood them.

For example, our partner says, "The children have been driving me mad–they haven't stopped crying and arguing all day." Rather than immediately suggesting a solution or quibbling over whether it really was "all day," they will feel heard when we simply acknowledge their feelings with something like, "That must have been really hard for you."

Or if our partner says, "I can't see how we are going to make ends meet. I can't earn any more. I'm really worried about it," we can show we have listened to their feelings by saying, "I'm really sorry you've been so worried about our finances. Let's talk about it."

Or one of us says, "It really upset me when you suddenly told me about the possibility of a new job. If we have to move to a different house, I hate the thought of losing contact with our friends." Again, the other needs to show they have heard and understood what their partner is feeling, perhaps by replying, "I didn't realize that you'd be worried about losing contact with our friends." Using their exact words will indicate to them that we have been listening.

Acknowledging feelings in this way may seem unnatural and contrived at first, but it is a powerful tool in learning to listen and in building emotional intimacy.

Nicky

I vividly remember a time when a group leader dropped out of one of the courses we were offering. Although my calendar was already crowded with evening commitments, I saw no alternative but to agree to lead the group myself for four evenings. When I told Sila, I expected sympathy from her for the extra commitment of time and work. Instead Sila was cross and unreasonable, or so it seemed to me.

A few weeks later she started to tell me how upset she was that I had given away some of our free evenings without discussing it with her. Feeling full of self pity, I immediately defended my decision. I realized later that the real need was to listen to Sila and understand her feelings. She was hurt. She felt that the people participating in the course were more important to me than our family.

In situations like this, the aim of listening is to understand and accept our partner's feelings, not to judge whether they are right or wrong.

The impact of listening

Learning to listen like this, rather than trying to fix each other, and only giving advice when asked, can transform our whole marriage. Many couples participating in The Marriage Course have commented on the difference it has made:

- "We listen much better and we don't feel we have to blame one another."
- "I learned to listen to what my partner's needs really are."
- "It has helped us to listen to each other with compassionate ears."
- "Listening has improved for both of us. We allow each other to finish their say."
- "I have learned to listen with new ears; the small things *are* important."

Section 2 –
The art of communication

Conclusion

Diane Vaughan, a sociologist and professor, spent ten years working at Oxford University researching reasons for the failure of marriages. As part of her conclusion she wrote:

> It starts with the partner who first feels discontented. At first, he or she will try to hide the discontent, pretend it doesn't exist, or that it will go away. Instead it grows stronger and after some time the initiator will attempt to convey the discontent to the other partner usually with vague hints or complaints that are *almost always ignored or unnoticed.*[9]

In other words, her ten years of research revealed that, in almost every marriage that breaks down, there is a failure of communication.

There is no substitute in marriage for effective talking and effective listening. Two individuals with separate thoughts and separate feelings come together as one. Communication is the bridge that connects one to the other, for we cannot read each other's minds nor see into each other's hearts. If we fail to communicate, we draw up the bridge and retreat to our lonely castle.

As we choose to communicate, we let down the drawbridge and invite each other in. We allow each other access to the secret places. We connect at an emotional level.

Second golden rule of marriage
Keep talking and keep listening to each other.

Section 3

Love in Action

Chapter 5

The Five Expressions of Love[1]

It is possible to give without loving, but it is impossible to love without giving.

Anonymous

A group of children were asked their opinion as to why people fall in love. One nine-year-old replied, "No one is sure why it happens, but I heard it has something to do with how you smell. That's why perfume and deodorant are so popular."

An eight-year-old boy had a different theory: "I think you're supposed to get shot with an arrow or something, but the rest of it isn't supposed to be so painful."

Gary, aged seven, was convinced it had something to do with more than your appearance: "It isn't always just how you look. Look at me, I'm handsome like anything and I haven't got anybody to marry me yet."

Some adults are equally in the dark about the real nature of love. They have been brought up to believe that love is principally an emotion over which we have little control, a belief that is reinforced by the lyrics of many popular songs. As teenagers, our children discovered (to their great amusement) some of our records from the sixties with phrases such as:

> Before this dance is through,
> I think I'll love you too.[2]

and

> I didn't know just what to do
> So I whispered, "I love you."[3]

Infatuation, which can be triggered as easily by physical appearance as by any real knowledge of the other person and which is likely to go as quickly and mysteriously as it came, is often portrayed as the sum total of love. The popular understanding of love has largely been reduced to *feelings*.

But there is another kind of love which is deliberate and which is cultivated over a period of time. In Louis de Bernières' novel, *Captain Corelli's Mandolin*, Dr. Iannis describes to his daughter the type of love that lasts:

> Love is not breathlessness, it is not excitement, it is not the promulgation of promises of eternal passion, it is not the desire to mate every second minute of the day, it is not lying awake at night imagining that he is kissing every cranny of your body. No, don't blush, I am telling you some truths. That is just being "in love," which any fool can do. Love itself is what is left over when being in love has burned away . . . Your mother and I had it, we had roots that grew towards each other underground, and when all the pretty blossom had fallen from our branches we found that we were one tree and not two.[4]

Some people get married on the basis of infatuation. Eventually and inevitably, however, when their infatuation wears off, if there is no understanding of how to create a love that develops with time, their roots will fail to entwine and their marriage will wither.

Christian love, as the New Testament describes it, is not so much an abstract noun as an active verb. Love involves doing. It means reaching out to meet the needs of another, often at a cost to oneself. In marriage, it may mean doing the washing-up out of love for our partner when we would rather be watching television. It may mean sitting down to talk with our husband or wife when we would rather be getting on with some work.

It may mean hugging our partner when we know that they have had a hard day. Only *this* sort of love is able to sustain a marriage relationship over many years, causing it to mature and to deepen.

In practice, there are five ways through which we can actively show love to our husband or wife:

1. Loving words
2. Kind actions
3. Quality time
4. Thoughtful presents
5. Physical affection

These ways of putting love into action are called *The 5 Love Languages* in Gary Chapman's excellent book, in which he uses the metaphor of language to examine the different ways in which we communicate and understand love.

He explained what led him to write the book:

> The five love languages grew out of my counselling with couples. They would sit in my office and one of them would say, "I just feel like he doesn't love me or she doesn't love me," and the other would say, "I don't understand that. I do this and this and this. Why would you not feel loved?"
>
> I heard similar stories over and over again and I knew there had to be a pattern. I asked myself the question, "What were they complaining about when they said, 'I feel my spouse doesn't love me?' What did they want?"
>
> Their answers fell into five categories and I later called them the five love languages. I now explain to couples, "If you want him or her to feel love, you've got to express love in his or her love language," and I would help couples discover their own and each other's primary love languages.[5]

All five are important ways of showing love, but which is primary? We may shower our partner with *presents*, but they may first and foremost need to hear kind words in order to feel truly valued. A husband or wife might work hard in their home, thinking that in so doing they are showing love, but their partner might need regular *physical affection* in order to *feel* loved and appreciated.

The greatest need we all share is to know we are loved, that we matter to another, that we are special to them. We must therefore ask ourselves, "What is it that makes my husband or wife feel most loved?" We can find this out through conversation and through deliberate and careful observation. A friend of ours who has been married for many years claims that in order to have a happy marriage, a husband and wife must "study each other." In doing so we discover important, and sometimes unexpected, information.

While there may be plenty of romantic ways on a honeymoon to demonstrate love with the minimum of words, daily life would be near impossible without being able to speak the same language. Daily *love* will be impossible if we never find out and learn our partner's primary love language (and quite possibly their second and third too).

Our tendency can be to try to show love in the way we like to receive it and to be surprised when our partner doesn't appreciate our efforts.

Nicky

I have come to realize that time and touch convey love most powerfully for Sila while words and actions are most important for me. So I find it relatively easy to show Sila love through my words and my actions, but they have proved ineffective if I am not using the love languages that are most important to her.

One particular Saturday, just after we had received several boxes of books from Sila's late father and had nowhere to put them, we decided to spend the day going to IKEA, buying a bookshelf system, and putting it up. I felt rather resentful about the whole exercize as I was fairly sure Sila was unlikely to open the books, let alone read them. However, I recognized they held emotional value for her.

When we got home, we divided the job between us. Sila was in one room sorting through the books and I was in another trying to put the shelves together, which took me considerably longer than I had anticipated. But, while I worked, I was thinking that I was doing this for Sila so it was worth the effort.

Finally, at about 10 p.m., I finished and was feeling rather pleased with my handiwork, when Sila came in and failed to say anything encouraging at all about the shelves, which left me feeling very hurt as affirming words are so important for me.

Sila

We hadn't talked about it, but I was hoping we'd be finished in time to at least have dinner together. So, I was feeling very grumpy with Nicky, not because I didn't appreciate his hard work, but because we hadn't spent any of the afternoon or evening with each other, and spending time together is so important for me to feel loved and to feel good.

Having found out what makes our partner feel loved, we must then decide to act on our discovery. It may seem unnatural at first and, as with learning a foreign language, it will require time, determination, and a great deal of practice. Some have grown up in homes where there has been little or no physical affection and they will not naturally and spontaneously give this to their partner. But this expression of love can be learned. And it will be essential to do so if this is the way our husband or wife feels loved. Others have not heard loving, affirming words being spoken during their upbringing. In this case, if this is particularly important to their partner, they will need to practice this way of showing love. As they do so they will become increasingly fluent.

"If only I'd known you liked this before, Mildred"

We write in detail about these five expressions of love because we know from our own experience that, in its simplicity, it is a profound and far-reaching principle, which any couple can utilize for the strengthening and well-being of their relationship. Numerous couples we know are still very much "in love" many years after the initial infatuation has worn off because they have a thousand times each year shown love to their partner in the particular way that he or she understands it best.

Some couples never discover what makes their partner feel loved. They may study each other but with the wrong intention–they are looking to criticize rather than to find out each other's needs. In a short story, *The Eyes of Love*, we read about an American couple, Kenneth and Shannon, who are in their car driving home after a family party.

Before he can suppress it, anger rises like a kind of heat in the bones of his face. "Okay, what is it?" he says . . .

She doesn't answer right away. "I'm tired," she tells him without quite turning to look at him.

"No, really," he says. "I want to hear it. Come on, let it out."

Now she does turn. "I told you this morning. I just don't like hearing the same stories all the time."

"They aren't all the same,' he says, feeling unreasonably angry.

"Oh, of course they are . . . Your mother deserves a medal."

"I like them. Mom likes them. Everybody likes them. Your father and your sisters like them."

"Over and over," she mutters, looking away again. "I just want to go to sleep."

"You know what your problem is?" he says, "You're a *critic*. That's what your problem is. Everything is something for you to evaluate and *decide* on. Even me. Especially me."

"You," she says.

"Yes," he says. "Me. Because this isn't about my father at all. It's about us."

According to Kenneth, she has looked upon the evening and his father's storytelling in the same way as she looks upon him: as a critic. The conversation continues:

He's quiet a moment, but the anger is still working in him. "You know the trouble with you?" he says. "You don't see anything with love. You only see it with your *brain*."

"Whatever you say," she tells him.

"Everything's locked up in your *brain*," he says, taking a long drag of the cigarette and then putting it out in the ashtray.

He starts the car. "You know those people that live behind us?" he says. The moment has become almost philosophical to him.

She stares at him with her wet eyes, and just now he feels quite powerful and happy.

"Do you?" he demands.

"Of course I do."

"Well, I was watching them the other day. The way he is with the yard–right? We've been making such fun of him all summer. We've been so *smart* about his obsession with weeds and trimming and the grass."

"I guess it's really important that we talk about these people now," she says.

"I'm telling you something you need to hear," Kenneth says.

"I don't want to hear it now," she says. "I've been listening to talk all day. I'm tired of talk."

And Kenneth is shouting at her. "I'll just say this and then I'll shut up for the rest of the year if that's what you want!"

She says nothing.

"I'm telling you about these people. The man was walking around with a little plastic baggie on one hand, picking up the dog's droppings. Okay? And his wife was trimming one of her shrubs. She was trimming one of the shrubs and I thought for a second I could feel what she was thinking. There wasn't anything in her face, but I was so smart, like we are, you know, Shannon. I was so smart about it that I knew what she was thinking. I was so *perceptive* about these people we don't even know. These people we're too snobbish to speak to."

"You're the one who makes fun of them," Shannon says.

"Let me finish," he says. "I saw the guy's wife look at him from the other side of the yard, and it was like I could hear the words in her mind: 'He's picking up the dog droppings again. I can't stand it another minute.' You know? But that *wasn't* what she was thinking. Because she walked over in a little while and helped him–actually pointed out a couple of places he'd missed. And then the two of them walked into their house arm in arm with their dog droppings. You see what I'm saying, Shannon? That woman was looking at him with love. She didn't see what I saw–there wasn't any criticism in it."

Finally, Kenneth and Shannon stop arguing.

> The fight's over. They've made up. She reaches across and gives his forearm a little affectionate squeeze. He takes her hand and squeezes back. Then he has both hands on the wheel again. Their apartment house is in sight now, down the street to the left. He turns to look at her, his wife, here in the shadowed and watery light, and then he quickly looks back at the road. It comes to him like a kind of fright that in the little idle moment of his gaze some part of him was marking the unpleasant down-turn of her mouth, the chiselled, too sharp curve of her jaw–the whole dishevelled, vaguely tattered look of her–as though he were a stranger, someone unable to imagine what anyone, another man, other men, someone like himself, could see in her to love.[6]

As the story ends, we realize that, unlike the husband and the wife who live behind their house, Kenneth and Shannon have become each other's critics. We reap what we sow. "You don't see anything with love," Kenneth said. But then nor does he look at her with love. In a world full of critics, we are called as husband and wife to study each other, not with critical eyes, but with the eyes of love, searching for what our partner needs to make them feel loved and special.

Gary Chapman underlines the importance: "When you feel loved in the relationship, it's easier to process all the rest of life because the need for love, the emotional need for love, is the deepest emotional need we have as humans."[7]

Over the next two chapters we will describe each of the five expressions of love. As we do so, ask yourself the following three questions:

- Do I regularly express love in this way?
- How important is this expression of love for my husband or wife to feel loved?
- How important is this expression of love for me?

It is easy to expect our husband or wife to know instinctively about our needs and then to get hurt when they fail to meet them. We all tend to express love in the way that we like to receive it. Despite our good intentions, this will not work if our partner has different needs from our own.

We can let our marriage fall apart. Or we can take the opportunity to have the best possible marriage. If we are to have a real sense of intimacy and a true enjoyment of each other, we must study one another with the eyes of love, and then use our words, our actions, our time, our money, and our body to communicate our love effectively.

Chapter 6

Words and Actions

Gracious words are a honeycomb, sweet to the soul and healing to the bones.

Proverbs 16:24

Where love is lacking, sow love and you will soon gather love.

St. John of the Cross

Loving words

The playground rhyme, "Sticks and stones may break my bones but words can never hurt me," is only true in a physical sense. The Bible often reminds us of the power of our words: "The tongue has the power of life and death" (Proverbs 18:21).

Studies have shown that words can affect a person's behavior and achievements to an extraordinary degree. If children are told that they are useless at math, they are likely to do very badly in that subject. Conversely, if they are told their creative writing is brilliant, they are likely to become aspiring novelists overnight. People will live up to the expectations they are given.

This has enormous implications for the way we speak to each other in marriage. We need to maintain love, gentleness, and respect in our tone and avoid getting into the habit of putting each other down. We need to build up our partner both at home and in public; it is highly destructive for them to be made the butt of our jokes.

The way to make each other feel loved through our speech is by affirming each other. This will include how we give compliments, how we say thank you, how we encourage, how we show kindness and how we make requests. The failure to do these things skillfully and graciously leaves our marriage partner open to temptation from outside. The following extract from a poem, written more than a hundred years ago by Ella Wheeler Wilcox, is a wife's explanation (though not her excuse) for having an affair:

Each day,
Our lives that had been one life at the start,
Further and further seemed to drift apart.
Dead was the old romance of man and maid.
Your talk was all of politics and trade.
Your work, your club, the mad pursuit of gold

Absorbed your thoughts. Your duty kiss felt cold
Upon my lips. Life lost its zest, its thrill
Until
One fateful day when earth seemed very dull
It suddenly grew bright and beautiful.
I spoke a little, and he listened much;
There was attention in his eyes, and such
A note of comradeship in his low tone
I felt no more alone.
There was a kindly interest in his air;
He spoke about the way I dressed my hair
And praised the gown I wore.
It seemed a thousand, thousand years and more,
Since I had been so noticed. Had mine ear
Been used to compliments year after year,
If I had heard you speak
As this man spoke, I had not been so weak.[1]

There are many different ways of using words to convey love to one another.

Paying compliments

People who have not been used to hearing compliments during their upbringing may not easily accept them, let alone give them. But we can learn. Compliments draw attention to what we admire and appreciate in our husband or wife. Many of us keep such thoughts locked up in our mind, thinking they are too trivial to verbalize or unneeded because our partner already knows that we love them. Yet the marriage service speaks of cherishing one another. Paying compliments is a great way to cherish each other, and we can all learn to do it. Try something as simple and direct as:

"You look really great in that shirt."
"You handled that meeting brilliantly."
"I love the way you always think of the right thing to say."

Offering thanks

Gratitude confers value and worth upon someone. When we live together day by day, we all too easily overlook the many things our partner does for us. Some are small and regular; others show great care and may require a lot of effort if we're not used to saying, "Thank you."

"Thank you for taking out the trash," or "Thank you for taking my trousers to the cleaners," sound mundane, but it is important to give recognition for small acts of kindness. "I'm so grateful you remembered my mother's birthday" gives appreciation for what could easily be taken for granted. "Thank you for planning all the food for the weekend; it's been such a busy week for me" shows gratitude for the other's support.

Being encouraging

Another way we can use words positively is by encouraging, that is, inspiring *courage* in each other. All of us have areas of our lives where we feel insecure: we lack courage. It is within our power to give the encouragement that will help our partner to reach their potential. Conversely, if we criticize, our words have the power gradually to rob our partner of their self-worth and self-confidence. When we encourage, we are saying to each other, "I believe in you."

Sila

There have been many areas in my life since we've been married where Nicky's encouragement has spurred me on to do things that I might otherwise not have done. Both looking after our children full-time at home and then gradually transitioning back into employment had their challenges, and his words often made all the difference, giving me confidence I could do it and helping to build my self-esteem.

Being thoughtful

Thoughtful words build someone up, whereas untimely, thoughtless words cause much hurt in a relationship.

Sila

In our own marriage, I have had to learn to be careful with my words. I like to discuss things immediately after an event and, when we were first married, I had little concept that I might need to choose a better time to voice my opinion to Nicky, particularly when he had made himself vulnerable.

It took me some time to realize that after he's given a talk, he needs some encouraging words from me right away. I've learned that Sunday lunch is not the right moment to give my analysis of his sermon and that it's better to wait until at least the next day, when he is more able to be objective.

Even then I have to choose my words carefully. I am not advocating false flattery, but for me it requires a conscious effort to make sure that my words are encouraging, kind, and affirming, and that they will build Nicky up. I have come to realize over the years how important these words are for Nicky. For him, affirming words are the key way in which he feels my love, and this gives him a foundation of confidence that affects all other aspects of his life.

Making requests

There is a world of difference in a marriage between making demands and making requests. When we make requests of our husband or wife, we are affirming their worth and their abilities. If we make demands, we become intolerant and tyrannical in our own home, often without realizing it. That kind of person is not easy or pleasant to live with. We can become demanding when we start to take our partner (and their gifts and abilities) for granted.

Sila

Nicky is very practical and capable of turning his hand to anything that needs repaired in our home. Yet there are times when I can be complacent about that. I've heard myself say, "You haven't fixed that flat yet, have you? I need my bike by tomorrow." A better way of saying it would be, "Nicky, would you be able to fix the flat on my bike before tomorrow?" A request like that creates the possibility for him to express his love for me by responding to it. Demands exclude that possibility.

If verbal affirmation is deeply important to your husband or wife and they have not received any for some time, they will probably be feeling low. To hear positive words from you again will be like reaching an oasis in the desert. As we learn to build our partner up with words, we will reach a new level of love and intimacy in our marriage. The words we use have the power to renew love daily. Criticism and self-pity are powerful separators. Words of affirmation are powerful uniters.

Kind actions

"Love is patient, love is kind" (1 Corinthians 13:4). The apostle Paul describes kindness as love's second characteristic. We show kindness to our husband or wife when we serve each other in practical ways. Within a marriage, this can take many different forms: making a cup of coffee, taking out the trash, cleaning the windshield of the car, cooking a favorite cake, ironing a shirt. Of course, routine activities may be taken for granted, but, when they are done willingly, they constantly express love. However, it is the non-routine acts of service that communicate love most powerfully to those for whom this is one of the ways they feel loved.

Nicky

I can recall many occasions when Sila has done things for me which I was not expecting. She has packed for me when I have had to go away overnight and have been under pressure. She has brought tea and toast to my desk when I have been struggling to prepare a talk. Often the crisis has been self-inflicted through taking on too many commitments and I have felt much loved by Sila's thoughtfulness.

After many years of marriage, I continue to be amazed and delighted by all that Sila does for me, routine and non-routine. I sometimes catch myself wondering why she does it. And the only answer I can come up with every time is that she loves me!

In *Captain Corelli's Mandolin*, Dr. Iannis succeeds in curing an old man called Stamatis of deafness by removing a dried pea that has been in his ear since childhood. Stamatis returns to the doctor to ask him to reinsert the pea as he cannot stand his wife's constant nagging. Dr. Iannis refuses, but suggests an alternative. He recommends a cure for his wife's nagging:

"My advice is to be nice to her."

Stamatis was shocked. It was a course of action so inconceivable that he had never even conceived of conceiving it. "Iatre . . ." he protested, but could find no other words.

"Just bring in the wood before she asks for it, and bring her a flower every time you come back from the field. If it's cold put a shawl around her shoulders and if it's hot bring her a glass of water. It's simple . . ."

"Then you won't put back the . . . the, er . . . disputatious and pugnacious extraordinary embodiment?" [*referring to the dried pea*]

"Certainly not. It would be against the Hippocratic oath. I can't allow that. It was Hippocrates, incidentally, who said that 'extreme remedies are most appropriate for extreme disease.'"

Stamatis appeared downcast. "Hippocrates says so? So I've got to be nice to her?"

The doctor nodded paternally, and Stamatis replaced his hat . . . He watched the old man from his window. Stamatis went out into the road and began to walk away. He paused and looked down at a small purple flower in the embankment. He leaned down to pick it, but immediately straightened up. He peered about himself to ensure that no one was watching. He pulled at his belt in the manner of girding up his loins, glared at the flower, and turned on his heel. He began to stroll away, but then stopped. Like a little boy involved in a petty theft he darted back, snapped the stem of the flower, concealed it within his coat, and sauntered away with an exaggeratedly insouciant and casual air.

The doctor leaned out of the window and called after him, "Bravo Stamatis," just for the simple but malicious pleasure of witnessing his embarrassment and shame.[2]

A strong marriage consists of both husband and wife finding opportunities to serve each other and to express their appreciation for what the other does. When life is hectic for us both, we instinctively think, "Why isn't he or she helping me?" But when instead our partner asks, "What can I do to help you?" or spontaneously does the job that we most dislike, this is unmistakably "love in action."

A friend describes the effect upon her of such acts of sacrificial love:

My husband often has to leave for work very early in the morning, before the children and I are even awake. Quite often, when we come downstairs, the dishwasher has been emptied, the table is laid for breakfast and he has left some little surprise for each of the children—nothing too dramatic—a jelly baby in an eggcup or a custard cream. When this happens, I can almost feel my heart physically warm as I enter the kitchen, and all three of us seem to start the day with a skip in our step (occasionally the mood lasts all through breakfast). The next challenge I face is to feel cheerful when it doesn't happen. How quickly we take each other for granted!

Chapter 7

Time, Presents, and Touch

You know very well that love is, above all, the gift of oneself.[1]

Jean Anouilh

Quality time

Some friends of ours were traveling back to London from Australia. Their flight had been delayed en route, and consequently they had spent four hours together in the Hong Kong airport reading newspapers and magazines and entertaining their young daughter. They had then spent a further twelve hours sitting side by side on the airplane.

On their way home from the airport, the husband said to his wife, "I've missed having our quality time recently. We must schedule it in."

His wife was astonished. "What do you mean?" she asked. "We've just been together for the past sixteen hours!"

But her husband needed more. He needed a time and a place in which he and his wife could give their total attention to each other without all the distractions and without worrying when the plane would leave or what time they would get home.

Every couple needs to spend time together regularly, as we discussed in Chapter 2, but for some people, this quality time is their primary *love language*. For such people, the longed-for togetherness is more than physical proximity; there is a need, indeed a hunger, for total, focused attention.

Nicky

For Sila, the surroundings and the activity take second place to my spending time with her, talking and listening, discussing ideas and sharing our hopes and fears. Such regular times together enable her to face the pressures in her life because she is confident of the love in our marriage. I have found that the value of our weekly date together is more than doubled if I manage to arrange for us to go somewhere where we are unlikely to see anyone we know.

We wrote in Chapter 2 of our plan each year to go away together for two or three nights. For two years in a row we went to Paris. We spent our time exploring the city, visiting art galleries, and eating in little cafés. Those two or three days were very romantic and great fun. But for Sila, they had a disproportionate effect on her feeling of being loved. For days after our return, nothing was able to diminish her sense of joy and well-being. I have realized increasingly that these breaks are one of the best investments I could make in our marriage.

The Bible tells us to "live a life of love" following the example of Jesus, who "gave himself up for us" (Ephesians 5:2). Most of us will not be called to give up our lives for each other, but we can demonstrate our love for our husband or wife by regularly giving up our time for them.

This may mean sitting down together after work for half an hour to hear how their day has gone. It may mean getting up earlier to spend time together in the morning. It may involve going out of our way to have lunch together. It may mean making arrangements for our children so that we can have a night away from home on our own. Love in action requires effort and sacrifice, but the rewards far outweigh the cost.

Thoughtful presents

Giving presents is a fundamental expression of love that transcends all cultural barriers. They are visual symbols that have a powerful emotional value. For some of us, these symbols are so important that without them we will question whether we are loved at all. A person who is good at *giving* presents probably loves *receiving* them. If this is true of our partner, we will need to practice this art.

This is the easiest of the five expressions of love to learn. However, we may need to change our attitude to money. If we are naturally a *spender*, it will not be difficult for us. But if we are naturally a *saver*, we may well struggle with the idea of spending money as an expression of love. We are not talking here about the difference between being generous and being mean.

Sila

Nicky is one of the most generous people I know, but he is a natural saver. Because he does not easily spend money on non-essentials for himself, I know he finds it difficult to buy such things for me. However, he has discovered that presents are another form of investment. For me, presents are not the most important expression of love, but when Nicky quite spontaneously (without it being my birthday or our anniversary) comes home with a flowering plant or something to eat that he knows

I like, it makes me aware again that he loves me and has been thinking about me.

A few guidelines about present-buying are worth considering:

Presents can be inexpensive—but have a high value. For example, one flower picked from the garden and given with a note can express love as powerfully as a bunch from a shop.

Don't wait for special occasions. Spontaneous and unexpected presents can bring a huge amount of joy and a great sense of being special and loved to our partner. A present can cheer someone up during difficult times, such as when one of us is sick, under pressure, or having a hard time at work. Conversely, if our partner has done something that particularly helped us, a present can show that this has not been taken for granted.

Find out what your partner particularly likes to receive. It is worth noticing which presents our partner has especially liked receiving over the years, either from us or from others. If we are out together, we could make a mental note of something they point out in a shop window.

Sila

Over the years, we have collected blue-and-white china of all different sorts and patterns. Nicky once gave me a pair of large breakfast cups in blue and white, which have become very special. I associate them with a long, leisurely breakfast on a Saturday morning. Each time we use them, I am reminded of Nicky's care and thoughtfulness in choosing them for me.

There are endless possibilities. The key to being a good present-giver is this: the present must be something that the other person will enjoy, not what we ourselves would like to have. This was certainly an issue in Kenneth and Mei's marriage:

Mei: Kenneth does have a tendency to buy me things and then say, "Oh, it's for us to share."

Kenneth: So she got a bench-press for one of her Christmas presents.

Mei: Yes, and a tennis machine for another. So I said to him, "No more gifts."

Kenneth: Sometimes, you get it wrong.

It is easy to dismiss this expression of love as materialistic or shallow. But we are all different. One husband for whom presents mean little only recognized several years into marriage how important they are for his wife to feel appreciated and loved. Initially he paid little, if any, attention to how they were wrapped or presented. Now he realizes the thought and care he puts into the presentation is as important to his wife as the present itself.

If our husband or wife demanded a diamond ring or a sports car every week, we would probably be right to question their motives. Nor should we buy our partner off with presents as a substitute for spending time together or discussing difficulties. The time and thought that go into choosing a present make it truly a gift. And given appropriately, the value of a present can far exceed its cost.

Physical affection

Being shown love through touch is a basic need for every person. Babies need to be shown physical affection to develop healthily; without it they will fail to thrive.

Mother Teresa of Calcutta clearly understood the importance of touch. Whenever she was with people, whether they were babies, children, or old people dying of incurable diseases, she would hold them, stroke them, caress them. She knew that touch can often communicate love more effectively than words.

Physical affection is a powerful communicator in marital love, and not just as a prelude to making love. As Gary Chapman puts it, "To touch my body is to touch me. To withdraw from my body is to distance yourself from me emotionally."[2] For those who feel loved through touch, hugs can sort out all the problems of the week, while a lack of them causes isolation, emptiness, and a deep sense of rejection. If we have grown up in a family where physical affection was lacking, the practice of showing love in this way will almost certainly need to be learned. And it is important to understand that if one of us has been denied physical affection while the other has not, it may cause some initial awkwardness. But persevere!

In marriage, the touch of love can take many forms: holding hands, an arm around the shoulder or waist, a kiss, a hug, a brush of the body as you pass, a back massage, as well as the variety and richness of arousing each other as a prelude to making love.

Sila

I love holding hands with Nicky when we are walking together. Although I know there are certain situations when he would not do that naturally, he has learned that some embarrassment on his part is worth it to have a wife who feels loved.

He also knows from years of experience that if I'm anxious or worried, the best thing he can do is to take me in his arms, hug me, hold me, and kiss me tenderly, at which point my worries feel much less overwhelming!

Both sexual and non-sexual touch have their place, but we should recognize that men and women generally function quite differently in this area. For many women, much of their desire for physical touch stems from their need for emotional connection through being shown affection. By contrast, many men are quickly aroused by physical touch and see it as part of sexual foreplay.

These different ways of responding can become a vicious circle. If a wife does not feel emotionally connected, she will often shut out her husband sexually. And if she is not sexually responsive, the last thing he feels like is connecting at an emotional level. All too often the result is a stalemate. This is often where the sexual relationship starts to wane. We need to recognize what is happening, talk about it, and then agree how to help each other break this negative pattern.

For some people, there is a fine line between their desire for sex and their longing for physical affection. The two cannot be easily separated.

Matt and Penny, a couple completing The Marriage Course, were experiencing great tension after the birth of their second child. Penny did not feel like making love, while Matt became frustrated and tried to persuade her. She stopped touching him at all in case he took it as an encouragement to have sex. The more he wanted sex, the less she did, and the less she did, the more he did. And so they spiralled down in misery. Matt was confused, not understanding why his wife didn't want him. As touch is his primary way of feeling loved, he felt undervalued and unloved.

Meanwhile Penny felt hurt and angry and interpreted his persistence as insensitivity, thinking he was ignoring her emotional turmoil. The result was that they were locked into a cycle of hurting and blaming each other and had no physical contact at all.

Eventually, they sought help. As a result of hearing Penny describe to a third party how she felt, Matt apologized to her for putting his needs above hers, and she forgave him. He then backed off sexually for about two months. This was an important sign to Penny that he meant his apology, and it allowed time for the hurt to heal. As a result, she began to open up to him again. With the lines of communication cleared, they could draw close and start to touch each other again without fear of misunderstanding. Soon Penny was able to accept Matt's advances and even make a few of her own.

If physical affection is our husband's or wife's primary love language, at a time of crisis, holding and hugging them will communicate how much we care. Those gentle, tender touches will be remembered long after the crisis has passed.

Section 3–Love in action

Conclusion

There are few things more important in marriage than discovering what makes our husband or wife feel loved and then making the effort to love them in this way, remembering that their needs may well alter over time and under different circumstances. Rather than trying to change our partner, we must accept their needs and learn to communicate love accordingly.

It is worth noting that, in the Gospels, Jesus showed love in all five ways: through words, actions, time, presents, and touch. He spoke *words* of affirmation to his disciples, saying, "I have called you friends . . . You did not choose me, but I chose you" (John 15:15–16). He served them with practical *deeds*, washing their feet when no one else was prepared to do this menial and unpleasant job (John 13:5). He spent *time* with them, taking them to quiet places away from the crowds (Mark 6:31). He gave them *gifts*, supremely the gift of the Holy Spirit (Luke 11:13). And he showed his love to many through *touch*, taking the children in his arms (Mark 10:16), putting his hands on the leper (Luke 5:13), and allowing the prostitute to dry his feet with her hair (Luke 7:38).

At the Last Supper, Jesus said to his disciples, "Love each other as I have loved you" (John 15:12). We must fulfill this command first and foremost with our husband or wife, showing love in the way that will assure them that they matter and are special to us.

Do you know which is your partner's first *love language*? How about your own? The starting point is to talk together about what each of us does or fails to do that makes the other feel most loved or most neglected.

Don't put it off! It may lead to a surprising discovery about your partner.

Third golden rule of marriage
Study the ways your partner feels loved.

Section 4

Resolving Conflict

Chapter 8

.

Appreciating Our Differences

Pol and I are on paper reasonably incompatible, so important an ingredient in a good partnership.[1]

Frank Muir

Nicky

I remember vividly as a seven-year-old practicing the three-legged race for our school sports day. For several weeks before the event I went around with my left leg tied with a red handkerchief to my friend's right leg. To start with it was agony. Our strides were different lengths; we kept forgetting which leg we had agreed to start with; we fell over on the road; the handkerchief chafed our ankles and we had several heated arguments. However, by sports day we could run almost as fast tied together as we could on our own. And we won the race!

Marriage is a bit like doing a three-legged race, and it would be surprizing if at times we would not prefer to be running on our own. According to Paul Tournier, author of *Marriage Difficulties*, "Disagreements are entirely normal. As a matter of fact, they are a good thing. Those who make a success of their marriage are those who tackle their problems together and who overcome them."[2]

A survey of the principal causes for arguments between British couples revealed that cleaning was number one (including what "clean" looks like!), followed by how often they should have sex, how much time is spent on phones or tablets, and what to spend money on.[3] *The Times* newspaper, reporting on the survey two days before Valentine's Day, said, "The most common form of argument is a blazing row followed by a total lack of communication."[4] In one marriage counselor's view, "The way a couple handles its arguments is the single most important key indicator of whether their relationship will succeed or not."[5]

Marriage involves two people with different backgrounds, personalities, desires, views, and priorities being joined together in the most intimate relationship possible for the rest of their lives. Added to this is the inherent selfishness of human nature: the desire to have it *my* way, to maintain *my* rights, to endorse *my* opinions, to pursue *my* interests.

One woman who had been married for six months commented that she had been more surprized in her marriage by the things she had learned about herself than about her husband: "It was like having a mirror held up in front of my face and I saw how selfish I really was." For all the joys of marital intimacy, our freedom to do just what we want is seriously curtailed.

Sila

I vividly recall one argument between us. Our first child was four months old, we were living in Japan and a bachelor friend who lived two hundred miles away invited us to stay for the weekend.

He was a great entertainer with boundless energy, and whenever we went to stay for the weekend he would arrange a breakfast, lunch, and dinner party every day and organize as many other social activities as he could fit in between meals!

On the Wednesday before we were due to go, I expressed my anxiety about the weekend because I felt exhausted from looking after a four-month-old and anticipated that a weekend socializing with our daughter on show might finish me off. Nicky was adamant. Having accepted the invitation and knowing that a number of parties would have been arranged around us, he insisted we had to go.

We both felt our particular point of view very strongly. When I had failed to convince Nicky with my words and he did not seem to appreciate how tired I was, I completely lost it.

Unfortunately for Nicky, it happened to be the Japanese season for apples, and we had just bought a large box of them. They were arranged in a pyramid in a basket near where I was standing and, starting at the top, I proceeded to hurl these apples at him one by one across the room. He managed to escape injury by ducking down behind the sofa until the basket was empty.

I'm glad to say these are the only objects I have ever thrown at Nicky. However, I know my tendency is still to hurl words at him when I get angry.

Disagreement and conflict either build or destroy a marriage. When a husband and wife are determined to get their own way and to do all they can to change the other to their way of thinking, the result is usually a type of trench warfare. We dig in to defend our own position, protecting ourselves by keeping the other at bay and occasionally launching an offensive. One of us may seem to win the odd skirmish, but really we have both lost, as there are a hundred yards of no man's land between us, full of barbed wire and barbed comments, unexploded bombs and unresolved issues. Conflict has destroyed our intimacy.

Disagreements can, however, lead to growth when both partners are prepared to tackle them together. The resolution may, of course, require us to change profoundly. Rowing a boat together means both of us adapting our strokes in order to row in time with each other. The church reformer, Martin Luther, observed that there were two ways of becoming less selfish and more like Jesus Christ. The first was to enter a monastery; the second to embark upon marriage!

What follows is the first step towards resolving conflict effectively.

Recognizing our differences

Uniqueness makes for conflict, but it also makes for excitement and color. If we shared the same views on everything, marriage would be dull. It is about teamwork. And in the most effective teams, people contribute their different gifts, temperaments, and insights for the benefit of everybody A football team is ineffective if all eleven players are defenders. A business will not operate successfully if every member is a visionary and nobody is interested in working out the details.

In the last section we looked at one common difference: the particular way we each feel loved. There will be many other differences in our approaches to life, particularly as opposites are often attracted to each other. Unconsciously we are drawn towards someone who has the qualities we lack.

Typically, at the start of our relationship we accommodate ourselves to each other. Many couples are not even aware of their fundamental differences. Infatuation causes us to be highly tolerant and to adapt our behavior to fit in with each other. Then, when the "honeymoon phase" has worn off, those very differences that attracted us can become the irritants that cause conflict.

At this stage, mutual accommodation is replaced by attempts to eliminate the differences. We try to force our partner to think and behave as we do. If we like planning ahead, we expect them to like planning ahead. If we put our clothes away each night, we expect them to do the same. If we squeeze the toothpaste from the bottom of the tube, we expect them to follow suit. We make demands, we manipulate, we become irritated, and we voice our dissatisfaction. All of this inevitably extinguishes intimacy. Sadly, many couples then conclude that they are not compatible. But this is not so. Differences can be complementary and made to work to our advantage. We need to move on from attempted elimination to deliberate appreciation of our diversity.

Monty Don, a horticulturist, jewelry designer, and author, writes about the different ways he and his wife, Sarah, approach gardening:

> If you make a garden with someone else, it is partly a celebration of your sameness, just in the way you enjoy the same food or laugh at the same things, but it is equally a celebration of your difference. It is only by allowing the other to take you where you would not have gone yourself that the garden

becomes greater than the sum of its parts. In practice, this means that although we never impose our horticultural wills on each other, we often profoundly disagree over what we should do and plant. I am by nature impetuous and impatient and like to execute an idea while it is still warm. Sarah would rather think through all possibilities and come to a conclusion that she is sure is right. She would rather do nothing than the wrong thing. I would rather do something than nothing. We appal and admire each other in equal measure. But it is a good mix and–you've guessed this already–an important part of our marriage.[6]

Our different personalities

What follows is a description of some differing personality types. In each category we all have preferences which may be mild or may be extreme. Where extreme, we shall find it easy to see ourselves; where mild, we may only recognize them in contrast to our husband or wife. As you look at each of the following five categories, ask yourself towards which personality type you and your partner tend. Where we differ, we need to consider whether these differences cause conflict or a greater appreciation of each other.

Category one: extrovert or introvert

This first category relates to our energy source. Those with extrovert tendencies derive energy from their interaction with people. They want to spend much of their time with others and come alive at a party. They will often be "external processors"– that is, talking to other people may well be the way they organize and clarify their thoughts. In fact, much of their speaking is likely to be thinking out loud. Extroverts enjoy solitude now and then, but too much of it drains them emotionally; they need to be stimulated by the outside world to recharge their batteries.

Those who tend more towards introversion, by contrast, derive energy from quiet reflection. Their natural focus is on the inner world of thoughts and ideas. They may be warm, friendly, and caring, but too much social interaction drains them and they need time on their own to recover. They usually prefer a few close friends to many acquaintances and often opt for a night at home in preference to a party. They tend to be quieter and, as "internal processors," will usually organize their thoughts before they speak.

The introvert may value the extrovert's ease of relating to many different people, while the extrovert may value the introvert's quiet thoughtfulness.

Category two: logical or intuitive

This category involves the way in which we view the world around us. Those with a preference for logic use their five senses to gather information. They tend towards wanting facts. They look to the past and they learn through experience. They feel an urge for clarity and prefer matters of practical importance to conjecture. They are interested in details and solve problems through a careful analysis of the facts. Other people may describe them as methodical, pragmatic, and focused on the here and now.

Those who tend to be more intuitive prefer ideas to facts. They are more innovative than practical. They look at the big picture rather than the detail. They love to speculate about what could be and are likely to concentrate on the future. They often solve problems through hunches and will easily move from one activity to the next. They are often seen by others as unconventional and imaginative.

The first type could be seen as a "stickler for detail" while the second might be described as having their "head in the clouds." But any project requires both personalities. The more intuitive person is drawn to vision, ideas, and goals; the more logical focuses on practicalities, details, and a plan of action.

Category three: task-oriented or people-oriented

This category determines the way in which we make decisions based on the information we receive. Those who are more task oriented are clear about their goals. They are motivated by efficiency, justice, and truth. In business, productivity and profit have the highest priority. Given a clear objective, the task-oriented person moves quickly and in an orderly way to the destination.

For those who are more people oriented, the heart rules the head and relationships are prioritized over goals. Such people probably feel deeply themselves and empathize easily with the feelings of others. Their decisions are heavily based on how their choices will affect others. They tend to excuse rather than blame, and will often see grey where the task-oriented person sees black and white.

Those who are more people oriented may admire the more task-oriented person's single-minded pursuit of a vision, while the latter may value the former's ability to create an atmosphere of tolerance, encouragement, and care of others. An effective team requires both personalities.

Category four: structured or flexible

This category is concerned with whether we like plans to be drawn up in advance or whether we tend to be spontaneous. Those who prefer a structured life decide easily on their course of action and then follow it through. Those who prefer to remain flexible like to keep their options open for as long as possible in case they receive new information, a better offer, or a cheaper deal.

Those who enjoy structure are good at setting priorities. They tend to be well organized. They gain satisfaction from beating a deadline, but are not so good at handling the unexpected.

Those who prefer to remain flexible tend to go with the flow. They like freedom and spontaneity and hesitate to finalize plans. They may appear laid-back and unconcerned with the exact timing of events as they are confident that things will probably turn out for the best. They sometimes miss an opportunity through delaying a decision. However, they are good at adjusting to the unforeseen and will sometimes find success where others see failure.

Category five: initiator or supporter

This category reflects whether naturally we prefer to take the initiative and to lead, or whether we would rather take a supporting role. Initiators enjoy coming up with new ideas, make decisions easily, and are not afraid of change. They like to take charge and are confident leaders. Those who like to support prefer others to take the initiative. They listen carefully and hesitate to express their opinions. They prefer to avoid confrontation and are prepared to adapt their own preferences to maintain harmony.

In order to obtain the right balance of leadership and support, there are two dangers to avoid. Initiators can fail to consult their husband or wife. Supporters, on the other hand, may defer all responsibility for joint decisions to their partner. Neither tendency is healthy in a marriage, as both partners should be included in all decisions that affect them as a couple.

In practice, in a healthy marriage, each partner will take the lead in some areas of their marriage and support their partner in others, depending on their respective interests, gifts, and experience. It is worth remembering that taking the lead in a particular area does not mean dominating, controlling, or imposing our own agenda. Nor does giving support mean following passively or remaining unheard. In order to work effectively as a team, both the initiator and the supporter are actively involved in each area.

Making the most of our differences

To put ourselves into these categories is not to deny our uniqueness. Each different personality type contains enormous variety. Our typical responses do not mean we cannot develop characteristics from the opposite end of the spectrum. These traits do not suggest that the task-oriented person is not interested in relationships or that the people-oriented person has no goals, nor does it conclude that the introvert cannot enjoy a party or the extrovert a solitary walk in the countryside. The preferences are, however, fundamental for our different approaches to life.

The first step is to recognize our differences. The second is to accept that there is no right or wrong way. Our instinctive way of thinking is not better or worse than our partner's. It is just different. Each preference makes a valuable contribution, yet is limited on its own. If we regard our own way of behaving as "normal" and the behavior of others as "defective," we are unlikely to build an intimate marriage.

The third step is to believe that our different approaches can be complementary. A marriage is strengthened immeasurably when we concentrate on what we admire in each other's personality rather than what irritates us.

In her autobiography, *Becoming*, Michelle Obama writes about the differences between her and her husband, Barack:

Each day brought small discoveries: I was a Cubs fan, while he liked the White Sox . . . He was a lefty with immaculate handwriting; I had a heavy right-hand scrawl.[7]

When something sets me off, the feeling can be intensely physical, a kind of fireball running up my spine . . . meanwhile, tends to remain cool and rational, his words coming in an eloquent (and therefore irritating) cascade.[8]

She goes on to describe how they've learned to build a strong partnership despite their differences:

Over time, we have figured out how to express and overcome our irritation . . . As different as we were, we fit together in an interesting way.[9]

In the table at the end of the chapter, we have listed some of the areas where a husband and a wife can have very different approaches. With each area, decide how far along the line each of you comes. Then see where you differ and ask yourselves whether this causes conflict. At the end of the table there is space to write other areas where there are significant differences between you.

Discussing differences over money

With each issue on the table it is easy to assume that *your* way is the *better* way, and to criticize your husband or wife for thinking differently. Nowhere is this clearer than with the issue of money. The natural saver usually blames the natural spender and assumes that all the virtue lies on their side.

Nicky

Sila and I embarked upon marriage with very different attitudes towards money. This reflected our personalities, although our parents certainly helped to shape our views.

Put simply, there are three choices we can make with our money: save it, spend it, or give it away. We have had no problem agreeing on how much and when we should give. With the other two options we are poles apart. Sila is better at spending, while I prefer saving. (As a child I remember saving the old silver sixpences. Eventually I discovered that the coins were no longer legal tender and my full moneybox was worthless!)

When we were first married, I was employed while Sila was still a student. Each month we would assign a portion of the money I earned for household expenses and I would put it into Sila's account and hope that she would avoid going overdrawn. I hoped in vain! I would regularly have to pay off the overdraft from our savings, which made me feel resentful about how much Sila was spending, while she felt guilty about the whole subject and didn't want to talk about it. At that stage we both thought that I was better than Sila with money because I didn't spend it as easily as she did.

It was only after several years of conflict, a lot of tension, and one particularly big argument about our finances that it suddenly came home to me that I'm not better with money than Sila. In some respects she is much better with money than I am. Rather we realized that we're better at different things. Sila is better at using money: she is better than me at working out what is needed each week, as well as buying occasional treats and surprises for the family and presents for others. I, on the other hand, am better at managing money. I don't mind working out how much we have (or haven't) got. I manage our savings and make sure the bills can be paid.

Since that realization that our different tendencies are complementary, I have stopped feeling resentful and money has ceased to be a source of tension. By talking through how much we should allocate for our different needs and creating a budget, we've been able to identify the areas where each of us could help the other. Sila has certainly helped me not to be over-cautious and to use money more freely for the benefit of others and ourselves.

As an example of how cautious I can be, for their weekly pocket money, we would give our children one penny for each year of their age: six pennies when they were six, eight pennies when they were eight and so on. I saw no problem in this until Sila pointed out that ten pennies was not really going to teach our ten-year-old daughter much about handling money sensibly. I am so glad that Sila, with the strong support of the children, persuaded me that we needed to increase the amount substantially, which we did one memorable day by 1,000 per cent!

Now, instead of me keeping money back each month to pay off an overdraft, Sila takes charge of our household budget and uses it for what she feels we need.

Sila

Nicky has definitely helped me to keep track of my spending and to stay within our budget. The discipline of budgeting does not come naturally to me. The fact that I am not good with figures certainly has something to do with it. I would not describe myself as extravagant and I do not particularly enjoy shopping. However, I buy most of the necessities as well as anything extra for entertaining or presents. On the whole, I do most of the spending while Nicky does most of the saving. This happened without us planning it.

Each month I would feel guilty about being overdrawn

(although I was convinced I couldn't manage on less) and Nicky felt frustrated that I couldn't do anything about it. We didn't face our differences over handling money until quite a few years into our marriage.

Eventually we had an honest discussion about our feelings and what to do about the situation. Our roles have remained much the same since then, but with Nicky's help I've started to plan ahead and, more importantly, to tell him when I think I might have overspent. In the past, because I was fearful of managing money, I was reluctant to discuss it. I realize now that it's better to bring things out into the open and talk to him about it, rather than bury my head in the sand and hope that the problem will somehow resolve itself.

As finances are one of the greatest sources of tension in most marriages, every couple will need to discuss how they use their money. This sounds absurdly obvious, but it is extraordinary how few of us actually do it.

John Kirkby, who founded the debt advice service Christians Against Poverty (CAP), says:

> We're all different. We're all a sum total of our upbringing, of our experience, of our life. When you come together as a couple, it's very possible that you could have diametrically opposed views about how you deal with, think about, and manage your money. And the truth is, that's really okay. The thing in to understand that, somehow, you have to learn to live with some of the differences, but also have a togetherness around where it affects you in your marriage. So, you need to have an overall budget as a couple. You need to decide: Where are your priorities with your money? What do you have to spend and what do you want to spend? What would you like to have and what do you need to have?

> It is difficult; it can be painful; but the rewards are enormous as you come together and find the compromises. And from that building block of a budget spins a wonderful, confident, decision-making process upon which you are in control of your money.[10]

Marriage must be based on the understanding that everything you have, including your wages or salary, belongs to both of you. That means both husband and wife should be aware of their true financial position. If one partner is kept in the dark about their joint level of income or the value of their savings or the extent of their debts, it can cause serious problems—not only with regard to spending but through feelings of deception and betrayal.

Often, couples have different spending priorities, so planning ahead and agreeing to allocate a certain amount to each area is important. Keeping the money in different accounts can help: a joint account for housekeeping, bills, and necessities, and separate accounts to buy presents for each other and other non-necessities. In this way each partner has some room for making their own decisions, although it will usually be worth setting a limit on how much each of you can spend on any one item or activity without consulting the other.

Sometimes couples adopt the same responsibilities for their finances as their parents, but this may not make the best use of their respective gifts. A couple told us how they used to argue regularly about how their money was spent. The wife didn't know how much money they had, yet the husband regularly blamed her for overspending. Eventually they worked out a detailed budget, deciding together how they should spend their money and making sure their expenditure matched their income. Whereas previously he had kept track of their accounts (in a somewhat haphazard manner), as this was what both of their fathers had done in their parents' marriages, they agreed that she was better suited for this role. Since that time, she has managed their money and they have not had a single quarrel about money.

You need to work out together how you are going to use your money. Discussion about finances and making a budget can draw a couple closer together, but, left undiscussed, misunderstanding and resentment will push you apart. To help you make informed decisions, we have included an appendix on how to work out a budget. The very process of doing it together will cause you as a couple to discuss any fears and frustrations regarding money. And it will help you to recognize your respective strengths and weaknesses.

If you find yourselves struggling and under pressure financially, you are not alone. Many couples struggle with financial worries. John Kirkby advises:

> The most important question to ask is: Is it for a season or is it a long term, significant, life-long problem? If it's for a season, is there something you can do to get yourself out of the financial difficulties, or can you weather the storm? Do you have family or friends who can help you?
>
> If it's not a seasonal thing, do you need to make some radical, significant decisions? I would always suggest that, if you find yourself in a situation like this, whilst it's important that you as a couple work through it together, you must not do it alone. Find someone who specialises in financial difficultion. Go and speak to someone whom you trust, who can give you the proper advice. Don't just make a decision based on your own thinking.
>
> And one of the most beautiful things about being able to manage money well as a couple is that the things you learn about each other—the ability to compromise, the ability to work through some difficult things, those skills and the communication

that you will have to develop as you talk about money—will spill out into many other areas of your life.[11]

Maintaining a sense of humor

Differences between us make for either conflict or color. Appreciating our differences means continuing to enjoy each other's uniqueness. For most couples when they first start going out together, laughter will be a part, and often an important part, of their relationship. They are amused by those aspects of each other's personality and behavior that are different from their own, and as their relationship develops they will often start to laugh at these individual traits of character. Such "teasing" further enhances their enjoyment and appreciation of each other.

This is the opposite of cruel teasing, which seeks to expose and humiliate. It is a gentle, affectionate teasing which expresses a deepening intimacy in a marriage: our mutual laughter marks out the exclusive territory of our relationship—a place of private jokes, shared funny memories, and a lifetime of reciprocal humor. All of this stops us taking ourselves too seriously and prevents our relationship from becoming intense and heavy.

In her research surveying fifty happily married couples and seeking to discover the common factors that make marriages last, Judith Wallerstein identifies humor as a key ingredient:

> Over and over again, the couples in these happy marriages said that their laughter was one of the most important bonds between them. Many used the word "funny" to describe a spouse. But by humour and "funny" these couples meant something deeper than the latest jokes making the rounds. They were referring to an intimate way of relating to each other, a low-key, spontaneous bantering that kept them connected.[12]

Continuing to enjoy our differences and to tease each other kindly and gently will keep laughter and humor alive in our marriage. It is the opposite of taking each other for granted and will put many of the little annoyances of life in perspective. Michelle Obama wrote about the importance of humor in her relationship with Barack: "In our house we don't take ourselves too seriously, and laughter is the best form of unity, I think, in a marriage."[13]

Being prepared to change

While we cannot change our own or each other's basic personalities, we can change our habits and behavior. Indeed, marriage requires us to do so in order that our strides match. It is no good saying, "That's just the way I am." In working through our differences, there is a simple but important principle for a happy marriage:

We *can* change ourselves; we *cannot* change each other.

This willingness to change needs to continue throughout our marriage. Richard Selzer (1928–2016), surgeon and author, witnessed a husband doing just that:

I stand by the bed where a young woman lies, her face post-operative, her mouth twisted in palsy, clownish. A tiny twig of the facial nerve, the one to the muscles of her mouth, has been severed. She will be thus from now on. The surgeon has followed with religious fervour the curve of her flesh, I promise you that. Nevertheless, to remove the tumour in her cheek, I have cut a little nerve.

Her young husband is in the room. He stands on the opposite

side of the bed and together they seem to dwell in the evening lamplight, isolated from me, private. "Who are they?" I ask myself. "He and this wry mouth that I have made, who gaze at and touch each other so greedily."

The young woman speaks. "Will my mouth always be like this?" she asks. "Yes, it will," I say. "It is because the nerve was cut." She nods and is silent, but the young man smiles. "I like it," he says. "It's kind of cute." And all at once I know who he is and I lower my gaze. One is not bold in an encounter with a god. And unmindful I see he bends to kiss her crooked mouth, and I, so close, can see how he twists his own lips to accommodate hers, to show the kiss still works. And I remember that the gods appeared in ancient times as mortals and I hold my breath, and let the wonder in.[14]

Mark with your initial where on the line your different preferences lie.

For example: (N = Nicky, S = Sila)

Money	Spend	___S_____N_____	Save
Punctuality	Time to spare	S_____N	Cut it close
ISSUE:			
Clothes	Casual	_____	Formal
Disagreements	Thrash it out	_____	Keep the peace
Vacations	Seek adventure	_____	Seek rest
Money	Spend	_____	Save
People	Time with others	_____	Time alone
Phone	Frequent use	_____	Minimal use
Planning	Make plans & stick to them	go with the fl ow	Be spontaneous &
Punctuality	Time to spare	_____	Cut it close
Relaxation	Go out	_____	Be at home
Sleeping	Get up early	_____	Go to bed late
Sport	Enthusiast	_____	Uninterested
Tidiness	Keep everything tidy & under control		Be relaxed & live in a mess
TV	Keep it on	_____	Throw it out
OTHER ISSUES:		_____	
		_____	

When either husband or wife is willing to embrace the inconvenience of change, the marriage has a chance to move forward. When both choose to embrace it together, a marriage that is static and stuck finds a new and enticing horizon.

Nancy, whose marriage to Ric was rescued from the brink of disaster, described the most important insight she gained from the experience:

> A relationship won't work if you try to make someone fit into your way of thinking. Making a marriage work is not about tolerating your partner's differences; it's about treasuring them.[15]

Chapter 9

Focusing on the Issue

Speak when you are angry and you will make the best speech you will ever regret.

Anonymous

In *Love in the Time of Cholera*, Gabriel García Márquez portrays a marriage that disintegrates over a bar of soap. The husband feels that his wife has failed him supremely in forgetting to replace the soap and comments, somewhat accusingly, "I've been bathing for almost a week without any soap." She vigorously denies the error, so for the next seven months they sleep in separate rooms and eat in silence. "Even when they were old and placid," writes Márquez, "they were very careful about bringing it up, for the barely healed wounds could begin to bleed again as if they had been inflicted only yesterday."[1]

When conflict arises, it is all too easy to retreat into sulks and silence, building a wall that grows higher by the hour, day, week, month, or even year. Alternatively, we start to attack on all fronts—by sea, land, and air—attempting to weaken our partner's position and persuade them to surrender. This can lead to verbal or even physical abuse as we try to force our partner around to our point of view. Whatever our tendency, the following advice helps us to face our point of conflict by focusing on the issue rather than attacking each other. The aim is to prevent specific areas of disagreement affecting our whole relationship.

Negotiating our differences

There will be times in every marriage when our different approaches require discussion.

Nicky

One of the differences between Sila and me is the time we allow
when catching a train or a plane. Sila, left to herself, would be
likely to arrive in time to catch the previous flight or train. I, on the
other hand, prefer to cut it close and arrive as close as possible
to the actual departure time. Otherwise, I feel that I am wasting
valuable time that could be used productively on something else
at home.

Sila

For me, the time spent waiting at a station or an airport is not
being wasted at all–I love the opportunity to people-watch and
to talk to Nicky, or to take the opportunity I would never find at
home to sit and read a magazine.

" But - it leaves
at Midday
tomorrow Sila "

Nicky

For many years we did not discuss the reasons for our different
preferences but were aware that journeys were always preceded
by some of the most stressful moments in our marriage.
We clearly needed to make some changes.

> We sometimes manage to reduce the tension prior to jour-
> neys by having a discussion well in advance about what time we
> ought to leave, allowing a reasonable amount of leeway to avoid
> a rush. I usually have to fight my instinct that I am wasting time by
> arriving early, and Sila sometimes has to control her urge to tell
> me repeatedly to hurry up when we have plenty of time to spare.

When our behavior is incompatible, what do we do? There are four main options: attack, surrender, bargain, or negotiate. Some people attack, trying to force their partner around to their way of thinking. That won't work. The most common reactions to attempts at coercion are either to become defensive and dig our heels in or to cooperate outwardly but seethe inwardly.

Others surrender: they let their partner have it all their own way and never express a view. That is not healthy either, as it allows one person to dominate in the relationship.

Still others bargain, working on the basis of meeting halfway: "I'll do that for you if you'll do this for me?" The difficulty with this is that our behavior becomes conditional on our partner's response. When we regard marriage as "give and take" in equal proportions, we easily focus on what we are giving and what our partner is taking. We each have our own perception of where halfway lies. If we feel our partner is not doing their part, we stop doing ours.

The fourth and best way is negotiation about our differences. This requires both of us to be prepared to move towards each other. Unlike attack, which is "me-centered," or surrender, which is unhealthily "you-centered," or bargaining, which also becomes "me-centered," negotiation is "us-centered." We are both asking, "What is the best solution for us together?" Sometimes that will involve a husband saying, "I need to change." Sometimes a wife will say, "I need to do things differently." Usually, both need to make adjustments.

Negotiation is a skill that can be practiced and learned by choosing to adhere to some basic principles.

Finding the best time

A survey by the British magazine *Relate* revealed that "half of all arguments between couples take place in the evenings and a quarter of those surveyed admitted to arguing in the most stressful moments leading up to a special occasion."[2] Some close friends told us of a simple but highly effective rule they have practiced in their marriage. They call it the *ten o'clock rule*. The rule states that, if after 10 p.m. a disagreement has erupted between them and strong feelings are being expressed, either one of them is able to call the ten o'clock rule into play, which means that any further discussion has to be postponed until a more suitable time.

We soon adopted a similar rule. We recognized that the majority of our heated arguments happened late in the evening, when tiredness distorts our perspective and we find it harder to listen and see each other's point of view. Adhering to the ten o'clock rule requires us to press an imaginary "pause" button. This demands self-discipline, but we have found it has prevented many disagreements developing into hurtful and futile arguments.

There is (usually) no perfect time to air grievances or differences of opinion, but it is well worth working out together the moments to avoid. These are likely to include the often hectic moments before leaving for work, when one of us has just got back from work or when we are getting ready to go out. Time constraints usually cause a greater sense of urgency to persuade each other of our point of view and a commensurate unwillingness to listen to theirs.

We have tried to avoid using our weekly date as an opportunity to bring up contentious issues. We heard of two couples where one partner in each marriage dreaded the idea of a "date night" as they found themselves waiting in trepidation to discover what they'd done wrong *that* week! The benefit of this weekly time together will be lost if it is not enjoyable to both of us.

Being ready to listen

Rather than seeing a disagreement as our partner's problem, we need to see it as our joint problem for which we need to work out a solution together. Reaching an agreement may require some hard talking, but, rather than fighting against each other, really we are on the same side as we attack a difficulty that we both have. It is often helpful to make a list of all the possible solutions and then to weigh up together the pros and cons of each one.

Listening is vital. In the heat of a disagreement we instinctively want to make sure our partner has really grasped our point of view, but we don't feel quite so passionately about understanding theirs. Taking turns to talk will help us to negotiate effectively.

As we listen to each other's perspective, we will often see a way forward that is neither my way nor your way but a new way; it becomes an "us" solution.

Being prepared to express your views

While conflict causes some people to become loud and argumen-
tative, others become quiet and withdrawn. The latter may keep
the peace, but this response does not build intimacy in a marriage.
While extroverts often need to learn to control the expression of
their feelings and to take time to listen, introverts need to be
prepared to express their views and to learn to be open about
their feelings.

A woman called Jane gained the confidence to do so in her
marriage to Rick as a result of her new-found Christian faith:

> For the first few years of our marriage I was very passive and compli-
> ant; I would rarely put forward my own opinions. Through my relation-
> ship with God I've gained a new self-confidence, which allows me to
> express myself more freely. Also, I don't fear that Rick might leave if
> the relationship gets difficult, as I sometimes used to. I know that we
> can work through our differences, and that gives me the freedom to
> disagree with him. *I am more assertive but less judgmental.* The way
> we handle conflict has changed . . . I no longer let things fester, our
> relationship is more honest and differences can be aired.[3]

Avoiding accusations

A few weeks before our wedding, the clergyman who married
us gave us some valuable advice. More than forty years later we
can still remember it:

> In marriage, there are two phrases you should avoid at all costs:
> *"you always"* and *"you never."*

The wisdom that lay behind that simple rule escaped us at the
time, but we came to see how in the heat of battle those two
phrases can easily be used to label and denigrate each other:

"You never lift a finger to help."
"You always come home late."
"You never think of anybody except yourself."
"You're always talking on the phone."

If we catch ourselves saying "never" or "always" at times of conflict, we have probably stopped focusing on the issue and started attacking each other's character. The use of *you* with "never" or "always" is generally an explosive combination.

Sentences that use "I" and "me" and which express our own feelings are more productive than accusing our partner. The previous sentences could be rephrased thus:

"I am exhausted and would really appreciate your help in the house."
"I feel lonely and I miss you when you come home late in the evening."
"I feel upset because you don't seem to be as interested in me when we are together."

"I feel hurt when you spend so much of the evening on the phone rather than talking to me."

Using "I" statements like this demonstrates a greater gentleness, a vital component of love, and makes it easier for our partner to respond positively. Rather than feeling attacked and going on the defensive, they are more likely to see the issue from our perspective. Otherwise disagreements can easily become like a sword fight, except that unkind words leave deeper wounds which take longer to heal than physical pain. The journalist, radio broadcaster, and author Libby Purves makes the point powerfully, quoting a young wife she knows called Maureen:

"My husband once told me I was a selfish, stupid, fat, frigid bitch. Admittedly I had just called him worse things, but when he said that about being frigid, I couldn't forget it. Whenever we make love now, I keep thinking that's what he thinks about me. I sort of stopped trusting him." She is also dieting obsessively, slim though she is, because of the "fat" bit of the insult. Saying "I didn't mean it" is all very well, but in that case, broods the victim, what made you say it? The old line that angry people "always say things they don't mean" is counterbalanced by the equally old line that *only* when you are angry do you dare say what you really mean. Most of us have a fairly total recall of things said to us in anger.[4]

Dragging up past incidents or making cruel personal comments will not help to resolve a disagreement. Even if our partner's words have hurt us, we must resist the temptation to retaliate. Restraint is part of the cost of true love. No single contentious issue, however strongly we may feel about it, is more important than our marriage relationship. The Bible emphasizes the potential of our words to hurt or to heal:

> Be gracious in your speech. The goal is to bring out the best in others in a conversation, not put them down, not cut them out.
>
> (Colossians 4:6, MSG)

> Make it as clear as you can to all you meet that you're on their side, working with them and not against them.
>
> (Philippians 4:5, MSG)[5]

Nowhere is this more relevant than within marriage.

Being prepared to back down

There are few things we find harder than to admit that we are wrong. We desperately want to justify ourselves, to show we are right and so be vindicated. Rob Parsons describes the process:

> We each have what I call an "inner advocate," a hidden lawyer within, who springs to our defence whenever we enter a conflict situation. This eloquent speaker is determined to present to our mind the best possible case in our favour . . . We are portrayed as sensible, logical and gracious–the other party as raving and unreasonable . . . By the time this inner lawyer takes his seat, we are totally vindicated, the jury have brought in a verdict: "Innocent!" And all would be well, save for the fact that at that very moment, not very far away, the other person's lawyer is making his closing speech and, incredibly, getting the same verdict.[6]

Winning an argument can be counterproductive. For those who are good with words, who can make others feel small or stupid, the ability to win will prove to be a disability in the long run.

We so often feel that admitting we are wrong puts us in a weak position. But when we decide that we don't always have to win and try instead to see the issue from our partner's point of view, they will no longer feel the need to defend their corner. As the book of Proverbs says, "Starting a quarrel is like breaching a dam; so drop the matter before a dispute breaks out" (Proverbs 17:14). Backing down and, if necessary, saying we're sorry may cost us some pride, but we will gain a happier marriage. If we find it difficult to lose an argument, we should try doing so a few times to see the benefits to our relationship.

Facing the issue together

Martin's parents separated when he was a child. His father lived abroad and his mother became an alcoholic. Martin was sent to boarding school from the age of seven. His parents often forgot his birthday and at Christmas he was lucky to get a present. Occasionally there was some token, but it was certainly never wrapped. With the adaptability that is so admirable in children, Martin accepted his circumstances and threw himself into school life.

As an adult, he found it difficult to form lasting relationships. But eventually he fell madly in love and got married, dreaming that his marriage and family life would somehow redeem and heal the miseries and failures of the past.

His wife Lucy came from a close-knit family and idolized her parents. She particularly loved the way they had always celebrated birthdays and Christmas with so much plotting and fun: the surprizes, presents, silliness, and secrecy.

Her birthday came a few months into marriage. Martin asked her what she wanted. She made some suggestions, hoping he would also think of some surprizes. He bought two items from the list and left them unwrapped on top of the fridge sticking out of the shopping bags. He felt that he was making a real fuss of her—no one had ever bought him two expensive presents for his birthday. Three days before her birthday she saw the two items on the fridge, unwrapped. She felt confused and unloved, but she kept her thoughts to herself. What could she say?

On her birthday, they woke up—there was no card, no breakfast in bed, no flowers. Then, just before they left for work, Martin took the two items off the fridge (still in their shopping bags) and gave them to her, smiling. She burst into tears and rushed out of the house.

Their relationship never really recovered from the events of that morning. It was never discussed. Lucy presumed that either Martin did not love her or he was by nature mean and thoughtless, possibly both. Martin noticed that Lucy had turned cold and assumed that she had simply lost interest in him. The pattern of rejection was well established in his life. For Martin and Lucy, years of misery with similar silent misunderstandings followed, until they finally divorced.

What a tragedy that on that fateful day (Lucy's birthday) they did not see the need to focus on the issue. They could have listened to each other's childhood experiences of birthdays. They could have expressed their views, feelings, expectations, and disappointments. They would have seen that there was only one, relatively simple, issue causing conflict in their marriage that day. They could have resolved it so easily. Instead, it was the first dark blot on their relationship, which then spread, like ink on blotting paper, until it had darkened and destroyed their marriage.

If there is unresolved conflict in your marriage, discuss the following questions:

- What is the main issue causing the conflict?
- When would be the best time to discuss it?
- Have we listened to each other's perspective?
- What possible solutions can we think of?
- Which solution should we try first?

Chapter 10

Centering Our Lives

Matrimony: an absurd invention that could only exist by the infinite grace of God.[1]

Gabriel García Márquez

Dear God, I bet it is very hard for you to love all of everybody in the world. There are only four people in our family and I can never do it.[2]

Dan

Conflict is inevitable with those closest to us, and it is not always easy to find the love we need.

David and Anne met when they were both fifteen years old and started going out at the age of eighteen. After seventeen years of marriage and with two teenage children, Anne was on the point of giving up. David, who had come from a difficult home background, had turned to drink to help with the pressures of his job. In his own words, "I had nothing else to fall back on. There were weaknesses in me I was not able to cope with. They seemed more manageable after a drink or two."

Their marriage spiraled downward. David's unpredictable moods and quick temper frequently led to criticism being hurled back and forth. Anne defended her corner, but his ridicule left her totally undermined in her role as wife and mother. Their respect for each other had gone. Both felt isolated.

Then David was invited to attend Alpha—a ten-week course exploring the Christian faith.[3] He had recently started a new job but knew that he would fail the medical and lose his job if he did not curb his drinking. During the third session his desperation made him tell some of the course leaders. They offered to pray with him, and that evening David put his future into God's hands, asking for his help.

He was not prepared for the difference it would make, and was surprized that by lunchtime the following day he had felt no urge to have a drink. Normally, he would have been craving one by 11:30 a.m. and would have needed several at lunchtime to get him through the day. Miraculously, his addiction disappeared, leaving no physical side effects.

David started to pray for Anne and for his marriage to be healed. Although Anne was suspicious of David's involvement with the church and poked fun at him about it, she and the children noticed the difference. David didn't fire back when she was critical of him and she felt that he had begun to care about her again. Anne attended the next Alpha course, mainly to investigate what had happened to David. As she continued to witness the profound change in him, her understanding of Christianity increased and her trust in him was rebuilt. Anne recalls, "There was total, unspoken forgiveness between us."

Instead of attacking each other, they began to discuss the issues that were raised week by week on Alpha. They would phone each other during the day to tell each other about a new idea that had occurred to one of them.

Love was returning to their marriage, increasingly affecting their home and their children. "David courted me all over again," said Anne, "and the second honeymoon was even better than the first."

For David, "Our love was more soundly based. I didn't slip back and the newness and freshness didn't wear off in the same way."

There are still times when David and Anne are infuriated by each other, but there is no longer the old destructive pattern of trying to get back, to score a hit. They now have someone to fall back on. David sums up the difference: "We are more controlled in trying not to answer back when we think we are being attacked unfairly. I am not always on the defensive. I have started to dare to believe that I am an equal—without the alcohol. Before becoming a Christian, I was like an unguided missile. Now I have this stabilizing influence inside—like a gyroscope."

In Anne's words, "When one of us is out of sorts, we turn to the Bible and pray to put God back at the center. He fills us with love to keep our marriage going."

Most marriages have their times in the desert. In our own marriage we have discovered that the presence of God is like a spring of water that never stops, regardless of our situation or circumstances. When both husband and wife put their lives into God's hands and ask him to be at the center of their marriage, their relationship is refreshed from within and is continuously fed by an external source of love that keeps flowing in dry times.

For some, the presence of God in a marriage allows trust to be re-established; for others, loving concern will replace selfishness; for others, destructive patterns of behavior will be transformed.

God is the ultimate healer of conflict. We know many couples like David and Anne who would not be together but for God being at the heart of their marriage. Whether we have huge obstacles to face or just the smaller issues of everyday life, having God at the center makes an enormous difference. We suggest four reasons why this is so.

Marriage is a gift from God

When Adam first saw Eve, he said, "This is now bone of my bones and flesh of my flesh" (Genesis 2:23). These beautiful words speak of identification, intimacy, celebration, and a sense of completion.

Often without realizing it, after even a few months of marriage, we can find ourselves focusing on each other's faults and being critical of them. Instead, if we concentrate on how good it is to have one another's companionship and try to see each other's strengths, thanking God for them, our love will be reinforced.

Our thoughts should never dwell on the question, "Why did I marry my husband or my wife rather than . . . whoever?" Instead, thanking God for our husband or wife on a regular basis will increase our appreciation of each other. Criticism and ingratitude only highlight the other's weaknesses. When we perceive our partner as a gift from God, we remain grateful for each other.

The Bible requires mutual respect

Jesus' teaching on marriage was given in an age when a wife was considered to be inferior and a husband expected to impose his will on her. Under Roman law, the husband had total rights over his household—his wife, children, and slaves. His wife had no protection from the abuse that his generally superior physical strength allowed him to inflict.

In this context, the teaching of the New Testament was nothing short of revolutionary: "Husbands, love your wives, just as Christ loved the church and gave himself up for her," and,

"husbands ought to love their wives as their own bodies"
(Ephesians 5:25, 28).

St. Paul's instructions reflected the extraordinary respect and
concern that Jesus himself showed towards women. On one
occasion, against the opinion of the crowd, Jesus offered acceptance and forgiveness to a woman arrested for committing adultery (John 8:2–11). On another occasion, we read of him breaking with social tradition by talking with an unknown woman in
public (John 4:4–26). At a dinner party, and to the disdain of his
host, he allowed a prostitute to anoint his feet with her tears and
wipe them with her hair (Luke 7:36–50).

Jesus gave equal value to men and women. This affected the
marriage relationship profoundly as Christian belief and teaching
spread through the known world and beyond. To follow the
example of Jesus means to respect each other and to value each
other's opinions. It rules out the possibility of either husband or
wife expecting to impose their will in decisions that affect them
both, causing couples to build an equal partnership and work
together as a team.

God is the source of love

Many people marry with unrealistic expectations of their
husband or wife: they hope that in each other they will find the
answer to all their needs, that their insecurity will be solved
through the other's unconditional and unfailing love, that their
life will be given ultimate purpose and significance through their
relationship. But experience shows us that another person can
never fully meet these needs. Only God can do that.

A couple who marry presuming their partner can meet their
deepest needs will end up disappointed. Unrealistic expectations

can then lead to a downward spiral of demands followed by blame, as in the diagram on page 153.

The Bible encourages us to look to God with great expectation and to call upon him for the love, patience, hope, forgiveness, courage (or anything else) that we lack. We are to draw on his limitless resources and to find in his unending love the security and significance that we crave. The Christian pattern is to experience love through a close personal relationship with God and then to give love to each other.

We heard recently of a couple called Billy and Debbie who live in Northern Ireland. They had been married for eight years. Their marriage was a nightmare. Two years into their marriage, Billy's mother had died of cancer and his father from an accident. In Billy's own words, "When Dad died, I decided I was never ever going to get hurt like this again and I made a conscious decision to harden myself and not let myself be close to anybody. I got to the stage where I became a really horrible person . . . I was bad-tempered and not much fun to be around."

When Debbie's mother died, Billy was unable and unwilling to help her in her grief: "I thought, 'Debbie wasn't much help to me when my parents died, so why should I be any help to her?' This meant Debbie couldn't share her feelings with me at all. Instead I started blaming her because the whole family was breaking apart."

They went to Paris in a vain attempt to restore love to their marriage, but found they couldn't talk to each other any longer. Debbie said, "Our relationship was coming to an end. Everything was just going rapidly downhill and I couldn't fix it and neither could Billy."

Billy acknowledged, "I knew I loved Debbie but it was a

downward spiral. We were spiraling down, out of control. There was only one outcome—separation."

At that point they met a Christian couple who invited them to attend Alpha in their home. To their surprise, Billy and Debbie found it fascinating and became more and more interested in what they were hearing. Billy described what happened after the third session, by which time Debbie had already committed her life to Christ:

> I told Debbie, "I want to become a Christian tonight." So that is what I did.
>
> I sat on the bed and said, "Lord, I've lived in this world for thirty-two years without you and I've just heard about you for the first time. I'm so, so sorry for all the things I've done done wrong in my life. I need you in my life."
>
> As the weeks went on, I started to forgive everyone who had ever hurt me and I felt the bitterness being lifted from my heart.

Debbie described the effect on their relationship:

After that, our marriage began to mend, big time. It felt like we had started all over again and all those years before were just nothing. I felt like I hadn't lived. I felt like I was opening my eyes for the very first time.

"As for Billy, he was like a new person—more loving, more caring. I fell in love with him all over again."

"Before doing Alpha, I felt that I'd done without love for so long that I couldn't give love out and I didn't want to receive it from anyone. Afterwards I felt I was going to burst if I took in any more love."

Billy concluded:

What God has done in my life is amazing. I was the most ungentle person you've ever met and he's come into my life and turned it around. Patience wasn't a virtue for me—I didn't have it—but now I seem to have it in spades. I find I rarely get angry. I don't raise my voice. I couldn't possibly have made that much of a change in myself on my own. There is only one person responsible: Jesus.

I always thought Christianity was about what you couldn't do—"You can't do this," or, "You can't do that"—but it's not. It's about what you can do.

Calling upon Jesus Christ for his help gives a marriage a strength from a source outside itself. We are free to love out of the knowledge and experience that we ourselves are loved passionately and unconditionally by God. As the apostle John puts it in his letter, "We love because he [God] first loved us" (1 John 4:19). We are set free to give to each other out of the confidence that God knows all about our own needs and promises to look after us.

God brings harmony into a marriage

Over the course of our own marriage, we have tried to submit important decisions and disagreements to God and to seek his way forward. Time after time, we have seen that prayer brings great harmony to a marriage.

The Bible assures us of the power of two people praying with or for each other. "Confess your sins to each other and pray for each other so that you may be healed" (James 5:16). This is a promise as much for the healing of our relationships as for physical healing.

There have been times when we have disagreed and there has seemed to be no way forward. Praying about the issue is not designed to enlist divine help for our own particular point of view! To pray with integrity involves asking God to give us his wisdom and to show us *his* way forward.

After praying together (even through gritted teeth), we have often been amazed that we have come to appreciate each other's point of view and have seen a third option of which we had previously been totally unaware. In the process of bringing the issue to God, our feelings of anger and resentment have gradually dissipated and we have ended up closer to one another than before.

Nicky

To return to the apple-throwing incident described in Chapter 8, that evening Sila and I decided we should pray together for God's help and wisdom. We were both still convinced that we were right.

By the time we finished, however, I somehow had a new perspective. I realized that I hadn't taken sufficient account of Sila's tiredness, the result of breastfeeding a small baby. I had also become aware that supporting her was more important than my embarrassment over letting down our friend. So I told Sila I would call to say we were unable to come.

Sila

Meanwhile, I felt that, if Nicky understood what I was feeling, he'd be able to support me over the weekend and I'd be able to cope. So we ended up going, and we had a great weekend!

Praying at moments of conflict is hard. We are forced to examine our attitudes and the emotions we are harboring. Prayer, rage, and resentment don't go together. We will, of course, only be able to pray in times of disagreement if we pray together at other times. We describe together in Appendix 4 some practical suggestions for how a couple can get started in praying together.[4]

When a marriage becomes dry, God can water it. When a marriage is stuck, God can remove the obstacle. When a marriage seems to be dying, God can breathe in new life.

Section 4–Resolving conflict

Conclusion

Differences and disagreements do not need to destroy a marriage. Indeed, it can be their very resolution that strengthens and develops our relationship. Marriage is not about suppressing our personality. Rather, it involves discussing our different points of view, seeking to understand each other, and finding ways of combining our wisdom and gifts. When we do this, we discover that the issue that threatened to divide us has drawn us closer together and caused our marriage to move forward.

To live consciously in the presence of God–in the knowledge of him around us, in us, and with us in our marriage–and to call on him for his wisdom and love is not opting out of the hard work of reaching agreement and unity. It is rather affirming our belief that God has brought us together and that there is always a way through.

Fourth golden rule of marriage

Discuss your differences and consider praying together.

Section 5

The Power of Forgiveness

Chapter 11

How Can Intimacy Be Lost?

Do not let the sun go down while you are still angry.

Ephesians 4:26

Two weeks before the wedding, Deborah went to have the final fitting for her dress:

I was going from my office in a taxi at Christmas time, so London was very busy. I was in a traffic jam, feeling very excited, when I saw this couple in front walking away from me with their arms around each other, and I thought, "Hey! They look really great together."

As the taxi drew nearer to them I was shocked to see that it was Miles—my fiancé—with his arm around another woman. What's more, I knew her and knew that Miles had gone out with her before he went out with me. It was like a horror movie.

My taxi was going very slowly, so I watched them for a bit longer and thought, "What shall I do? Shall I jump out of the taxi?" My heart was beating like mad. I couldn't believe my eyes. Then I saw them arrive outside her office. They said goodbye and briefly kissed. It wasn't a passionate kiss, but it was enough of a kiss. At that moment my taxi suddenly picked up speed and I arrived for my fitting. I was so upset that I couldn't even cry.

During the fitting, I kept asking them to hurry up. All I wanted to do was to get on the telephone. As soon as I could I rang Miles and said to him, "Did you have a good lunch?"

He replied, "What do you mean?"

I said, "I saw everything!"

He again asked, "What do you mean?"

Again I said, "I saw everything."

He replied, "Well, I meant to tell you about it this morning. I tried to get you on the phone to say I was going to meet Anne for lunch."

I slammed down the phone and went back to the office, bawling my eyes out. Miles tried to call me but I wouldn't talk to him. When the next day I tried to explain to Miles what it was like for me to see all this happening, he didn't understand how I felt.

Then we got married and, to add insult to injury, this story kept coming up at parties, as a joke. Miles would tell it as his party piece: "Guess what happened as Deborah was on her way to the wedding dress fitting . . ."

Miles tells his side of the story:

I really blew it. I realized that before I got married I needed to apologize to Anne for my failure to end our relationship properly. Anne and I talked and had a great lunch. I was elated that I had gone through with it. I had tried to call Deborah a couple of times in the morning to tell her what I was doing. Unfortunately, I had failed to get hold of her.

Once I had apologized to Anne, it was a great relief for both of us, so I put my arm around her and gave her a kiss before we parted.

When I was back at the office, Deborah phoned me and asked, "How was your lunch?" I told her, "I tried to call you." So, as far as I was concerned, I had done what I could and my intentions were honorable. In fact, I was quite defensive. I never said I was sorry to Deborah, because I never felt the need to.

Then, on The Marriage Course, when we were asked to write down ways we had hurt each other, we each came up with about four or five. Deborah's were all from well in the past and this was clearly number one. So we talked about it.

I really tried to see it from her point of view, to sit in a taxi and to see your future husband walking along the road with his arm around another woman. No matter what the reason, just to have experienced that and never to have had the hurt recognized or acknowledged in some way, I realized, was the issue. Even then, I found it hard. I said grudgingly, "Okay, we will deal with it now."

It was when I said I'm sorry to God that I realized how much it had hurt Deborah. So I said I was really sorry to her and asked her to forgive me. She did, which was wonderful. It is a very powerful process to go through, step by step, dealing with the emotions that come up, and it has brought us much closer to each other.

Deborah concludes:

When I actually started to talk to Miles, I realized that I had suppressed how upset I was because the incident had turned into a good story. As a result, I had continued to feel hurt. Every time the topic came up it hurt a bit more. But, because I felt Miles wouldn't listen to me, I tried not to let it affect me. During The Marriage Course, when he really listened to me for the first time, I felt that my emotions were valid and that Miles understood them. That was important for me. I was then able to forgive him and let it go.

Dealing with ways we have hurt each other is essential for maintaining or restoring the trust between us. Trust is as vital to a marriage as glass is to a window. The function of the glass is to allow the light in but to keep wind and rain out. Being one of the hardest materials, it is capable of withstanding the most violent of storms. And yet it can be shattered with a single blow from a brick or a hammer.

Trust between a couple, however strong it has grown, is equally breakable. It can be shattered with an act of adultery, abuse, or violence. Or it can be destroyed by an accumulation of "white" lies, deception, critical comments, unkindness, or some other form of emotional abuse.

Intimate relationships are built on trust and openness. These two qualities belong together and feed each other. Where trust exists, a couple can be open about their deepest feelings, their hopes and fears, their joys and sorrows, their thoughts and dreams. They allow each other into their inner world to know them as they are. This openness then causes trust to grow stronger, allowing for even greater openness.

When we hurt each other, whether intentionally or unintentionally, we damage the trust and become less open. Our tendency when hurt is to close up, sometimes unconsciously, to keep our partner at a distance and to protect ourselves against further hurt. The greater the hurt, the greater the damage.

Often in a marriage it is not one deliberate act that destroys the intimacy between us but rather the accumulation of smaller hurts that are left undiscussed and unhealed. One husband, whose marriage had failed, wrote a sad and moving account of the situation he and his wife had got into:

After all, our marriage wasn't hellish, it was simply dispiriting. My wife and I didn't hate each other, we simply got on each other's nerves. Over the years we each had accumulated a store of minor unresolved grievances. Our marriage was a mechanism so encrusted with small disappointments and petty grudges that its parts no longer closed.[1]

Hurt occurs every time we act in an unloving way towards each other: when important decisions are made without consultation; when the desire for an intimate conversation is met with coldness; when criticism predominates over encouragement; when our times together are used up by other people or other activities; when no presents are forthcoming on birthdays and anniversaries pass without notice; when selfishness and laziness replace loving deeds; when kindness is met with ingratitude; when an attempt to hug is met with a brush-off or the response, "Can't you see I'm busy?"

Even within the most loving marriages, there are times when a husband and wife will hurt each other. Occasionally this is deliberate, but usually it is unintentional and we are unaware of the pain we have caused. Hurt like this *must be resolved* if trust and openness are to grow. Indeed, the very process of resolving the hurt builds greater understanding and closeness. But where it does not happen, the walls around the heart get higher and the cement gets harder until there is no intimacy left and, sometimes, no marriage at all.

In this section we want to provide tools to enable us to resolve past hurts, to dismantle any walls that have been built and to prevent future hurts having such serious consequences. The process is not complicated, but it is challenging and it always involves a choice. The choice is this: whether we are going to let the hurt fester and poison our relationship, or whether we are going to lance the boil and deal with it.

The more open we are to healing the ways we hurt each other, the easier it becomes. But if we fail to do so, even relatively minor issues can become large mountains that separate us.[2]

Getting angry

After being hurt, sometimes only a split second later, comes the next emotion: anger. While hurt is what we feel in ourselves, anger is what we instinctively feel towards those who have inflicted the hurt upon us.

It is important to recognize that the *feeling* of anger is not wrong in itself. It is the way we deal with it that can cause damage. The behavior of two different animals when physically hurt or threatened illustrates two typical human reactions. A rhino, when provoked, acts aggressively and is likely to charge at you. By contrast, a hedgehog, when in danger, withdraws and throws up a protective shield by curling into a ball and raising its prickles in an attempt to keep its attacker at bay.

Just as animals respond differently to attack, so people react differently when they are hurt and angry. There are two main patterns of behavior, and it would appear that the population is split roughly fifty–fifty. Half of the population are like the rhino: when they are angry, they let you know it. The other half of the population are like the hedgehog: when they feel angry, they hide their feelings. They become quiet or withdrawn. It is not that they do nothing with their anger, but they tend to express it in less obvious ways: they may withhold their affection, suddenly develop selective hearing towards their partner, or run them down in company. This group sometimes regard themselves as more virtuous than the rhinos, but their reactions can be just as damaging to a relationship.

Many couples, like ourselves, are made up of one who is liable to respond like the rhino and one more like the hedgehog.

Nicky

The story of the apple-throwing in Chapter 8 illustrates quite graphically into which category Sila falls! The following story shows what my natural reaction is more likely to be.

One of the differences between Sila and myself is that, when we go out to a party in the evening, we have very different ways of leaving. My way, when we have agreed that it is time to go home, is to say thank you and goodbye to our host and hostess, and then to leave. Sila's way is to start to say goodbye and then get involved in what will usually be her most intense conversation of the whole evening.

I have discovered over forty-three years of marriage that if we are to get home by an agreed time, we need to start leaving just as the first course is being served.

I remember going to the birthday party of a great friend. As the following day was going to be particularly busy, we agreed on the way to the party that we should aim to be home by midnight. To make this possible, I decided to double the time needed to get home and we both started to leave at 11:30 p.m.

I duly said goodbye and, to encourage Sila to tear herself away, I went to get the car that we had parked at the other end of the road where they live. I double-parked outside our friends' house in a narrow and crowded London street and waited for Sila to join me.

After fifteen minutes there was no sign of her. I decided to repark the car, a manoeuvre that had not been easy the first time and proved to be no easier the second. I walked back up the street to our friends' house, rang the bell and went in to find Sila standing at the bottom of the basement stairs deep in conversation with our hostess.

Keeping a fixed smile on my face so as not to spoil the party, I mentioned to her that I had been waiting in the car and that it was now past midnight. Sila replied, "Oh, I didn't even know you had left." At that point I had to cope not only with my frustration about getting home late, but also with the fact that she hadn't even noticed my absence. I went to get the car for the second time, and after about ten minutes she joined me.

On the way home we were talking about the party. Sila was animated about the people she had met and the interesting conversations she had had. I was keeping up a cheerful exterior while seething inside. It is amazing how our mind can operate on two levels. As well as carrying on the conversation, I was weighing up whether to say anything about my frustration and the fact that we were going to get to bed quite a lot later than we had planned. I didn't want to spoil Sila's happy mood; on the other hand, I was finding it hard to be as relaxed as she was.

In the end, I struggled through my tendency to hide my feelings and said as casually as I could, "Did you realize I was sitting waiting in the car for more than fifteen minutes?"

Sila stopped dead in her tracks, looked at me and said in a worried voice, "Oh, no! Were you feeling cross with me?"

When I told her about how frustrated I was feeling, she immediately said, "I am so sorry. Please forgive me."

As soon as it was out in the open, it wasn't difficult to forgive, and my feelings of annoyance evaporated even more quickly than they had built up.

I think I knew the situation would happen again—indeed it has several times since then. But getting my feelings out into the open meant there was no unresolved hurt left buried inside me.

My tendency to bury my anger is potentially no less harmful for our relationship than Sila's tendency to vent hers. In order to have a strong marriage, I have had to learn to talk about my feelings as much as Sila has had to learn to control the way she expresses hers.

Getting revenge

If the hurt and ensuing anger remain, our next instinctive reaction is the desire to get revenge: hurt for hurt, insult for insult, rejection for rejection. We want to retaliate, not least to let our partner know what it feels like to have been hurt in this way. We must get even.

One summer vacation we drove to the southernmost tip of Greece, a part of the Peloponnese called the Mani. It was hot and the population sparse, yet there was evidence from the deserted and ruined villages that more people had once lived there. What puzzled us were the remains of many unusually high towers that had been built as part of the houses. We learned that these towers were the result of feuds between families in the same village. An aggrieved family would build their house higher than the surrounding houses in order to be able to throw rocks or pour hot oil on their opponents. Their neighbors would then build higher still to try to steal the advantage and get revenge. These feuds eventually led to the collapse of the whole village.

There is a similar pattern within marriage when both partners are intent on seeking justice and revenge. This is a pattern that no marriage can survive.

Giving in to fear

A third reaction to hurt is fear: we are afraid of being hurt again and, as a result, we withdraw. This will be particularly true for those who, like the hedgehog, keep others at a distance to protect themselves. We stop being open and close down deep communication. In the words of C.S. Lewis:

> To love is to be vulnerable. Love anything, and your heart will certainly be wrung and possibly be broken. If you want to make sure of keeping it intact, you must give your heart to no one, not even to an animal. Wrap it carefully round with hobbies and little luxuries; avoid all entanglements; lock it up safe in the casket or coffin of your selfishness. But in that casket–safe, dark, motionless, airless–it will change. It will not be broken; it will become unbreakable, impenetrable, irredeemable.[3]

Carrying guilt

Hurt will never be all one way in a marriage. We give as well as receive. There is great destructive power in the guilt we carry around if we fail to own up to our part in hurting our partner. The self-deception involved in denying our responsibility leads quickly to emotional separation.

These four effects of hurt–anger, retaliation, fear, and guilt–can lurk beneath the surface of a marriage. The danger of such unresolved hurt on a domestic level has its counterpart internationally in the dilemma of how to rid old war zones of landmines, which are hidden from sight but which maim and kill. In a marriage, all can look well on the surface, but one or both partners might be forced to tread carefully, not knowing when the next explosion will come. There is a loss of trust and openness, which has usually built up gradually over a number of years as the grievances accumulate. Finally, intimacy is quenched.

When this happens in a marriage, the symptoms can be a lack of communication, criticism, outbursts of anger, resentment, little interest in one another, a lack of desire to make love, and a preference for doing things separately. There may be other emotional effects, such as low self-esteem and depression, and, for some, it becomes easier not to allow themselves to feel anything any more, to avoid the pain.

Some who are on the verge of separation say words to this effect: "I don't feel love any more. In fact, I don't feel anything at all. I feel numb." This is hardly surprising. The unhealed hurt that has accumulated inside them needs to be resolved before there can be any space for the return of positive feelings of love, romance, and attraction. It is not so much that there is no possibility of love being restored; it is rather that it has been squeezed out by hurt and anger.

The author Valerie Windsor tells the story of an English woman on vacation in Paris who decides on the spur of the moment to leave her husband. It becomes clear that any intimacy they once had in their marriage has been lost and in its place there is a simmering irritation with each other just beneath the surface:

> I try to think what it was that made me do it, and I have no idea. I mean what specific thing made me choose that moment rather than any other? It was an odd afternoon. I don't know what was

the matter with me. It was windy: either the wind or the noise of the plastic chair scraping the pavement started a strange sensation in the bones of my head. Tony chose the café: one of those *salons des glaces* where they serve expensive cocktails.

"Will this do?" he said. "Here?" and he flicked at the seat with his handkerchief. "Don't sit down yet," he said. "They haven't been wiped." But I deliberately sat down anyway, without looking, even though I was wearing a white skirt. It annoyed me to hear him fussing about such things. A man should not fuss about such things. A man should not even notice them. I didn't. So was he implying that I should; that because I so patently failed to notice them, he was forced into doing it, against his will? The odd sensation in my head turned into a thin, high buzzing as if a wasp were trapped in the hollows of the skull.

"What will you have?" he asked.

It was June, I think. May or June, I forget which. But cold. Warm enough to sit at a pavement café but cold enough to want something hot to drink.

"Coffee," I said.

He was reading the menu. Behind him was a bank of potted plants with spiky orange flowers.

"Plastic," said Tony turning to look.

"Are they? I don't think they are." I leant over to touch one. I wanted it to be real. I wanted it to be alive and as vicious as it looked. But he was right, of course it was plastic. The buzzing in my head grew worse.

"What's the matter?" he asked.

I lied. "I think there's a wasp."

"Where?"

"I don't know."

Any kind of uncertainty infuriated him. "Well, either there is or there isn't."

"I don't know what the matter is," I said, pressing my fingers against my temples. And then the waiter came.

"*Deux cafés*," said Tony, without even glancing at him. I had to do the smiling for both of us.

The waiter smiled back. "*D'accord*," he said and wiped the table. Tony leaned back in his chair and breathed out. "Well, this is nice," he said. And that was all. That was the sum of what happened between us. There was no atmosphere. The unpleasantness of the previous day when I had got us lost in Neuilly because of incompetent map reading was forgotten. And by mutual understanding we never allowed the surfaces to be disturbed by any mention of the unsatisfactory nightly rituals which, by some failure of imagination, I could never connect with love.

I sat there with my hands folded in my lap, and the buzzing in my head grew thinner and higher, a whining electrical noise in the bone. I stood up.[4]

She stands up and abandons her marriage.

In real life, so many who leave a marriage while still full of unresolved emotions find that they carry them into another relationship. The unhealed hurt can then become the cause of a breakdown in the next one—often more quickly than the first. We see this in those who marry several times and find each successive marriage failing for a similar reason.

No wonder the Bible says, "Do not let the sun go down while you are still angry" (Ephesians 4:26). Anger, whether expressed or suppressed, must be resolved and the underlying hurt healed for the relationship to grow. The wonderful news is that we don't need to let hurt destroy our intimacy. Although the process described in the next chapter may be hard and costly for some, it will set us and our marriage free.

Chapter 12

How Can Intimacy Be Restored?

Forgiveness is not just an occasional act; it is a permanent attitude.[1]

Martin Luther King

Getting to the heart of the problem

When intimacy has been lost, often we do not look deeply enough for the reasons. We are aware only of the symptoms rather than the underlying cause.

Nicky

When we first moved to London in 1985, I discovered that working for a church has more facets to it than I was trained for at theological college. In the middle of a torrential downpour, the drains that served the church toilets blocked and the alley next to our house was six inches deep in water. Together with Derek, the youth pastor, I managed to open the cover of the drains. The sewer was completely full and the contents rapidly started mixing with the rainwater. At that point, the make-up of the flood didn't bear thinking about too carefully.

We tried to remove the blockage with drainage rods but soon realized that it was impossible to do so from above. Someone had to go down thigh-deep into the drain to use the rods at a better angle.

Before I could offer, Derek, who is one of the most selfless men I have ever had the pleasure to know, was down there, rod in hand, crouching up to his waist in the stinking water. He pushed with the rods as hard as he could, and after a few moments there was a wonderful gurgling that soon gave way to a rushing sound, which then turned into a strong sucking noise as the blockage cleared and the water flowed rapidly away. In a short time, the alley was clear. We hosed it (and I hosed Derek) down with fresh water; the smell was gone and the crisis had passed.

It would have been no good if, instead of dealing with the blockage, Derek and I had tried to mop up the surface water. The next time it rained or someone flushed a toilet, the alley would flood again.

Looking at the ways we have hurt each other can be a painful, messy process, one that we instinctively shy away from. But when both partners summon up the courage to face the past, the results will bring lasting change. When there is a backlog of unresolved hurt and anger, we must unblock the drain by doing the following:

- Talking about the hurt.
- Being prepared to say I'm sorry.
- Choosing to forgive each other.

This process acts like a drain, carrying away the hurt so that it does not spoil our relationship. Once we have cleared out days, weeks, months, or even years of unresolved issues, we must both make a choice to resolve every big or small hurt as it happens and never again to allow such an accumulation.

For those who have been married a long time and have never felt able to address and resolve painful issues effectively, this three-fold process will take time and may be very testing, although ultimately liberating. The positive emotions may not return immediately. But as we persist, this process of healing hurt will become an ingrained habit and our marriage will change for the better.

Talking about the hurt

Sila

Dealing with hurt is not thinking, "Our love for each other will somehow magically resolve any ways we hurt each other, so it doesn't matter." I think that's pretty much what I thought when we got married.

I remember vividly the first time I realized I had to say directly to Nicky how hurt I was feeling. It was after a big argument we had had about money and I felt he was accusing me unfairly. It coincided with going away for a special weekend that we had been looking forward to, and at first I tried to bury the hurt. But the result was that I felt full of resentment and self-pity, and went into a mood, which spoiled both the weekend and our relationship.

Eventually, after thirty-six hours, I couldn't contain it any longer and I poured it all out to Nicky–he listened and really understood why I was upset, and he then said he was sorry.

It was at that point I realized for the first time I had to say out loud, "I forgive you." I had never done that before and I found it really hard, but the moment I did, I felt completely different. The self-pity and resentment left me, and we felt reconnected.

What I realized that weekend was that bringing the hurt out into the open and talking to Nicky about it was the way for our relationship to be restored. Rather than saying the hurt didn't matter, I needed to acknowledge that the hurt did matter and it needed to be faced. And after that, the rest of the weekend was great because the hurt I had felt had been healed.

This part of the process is like making the decision to get into the drain. It is no good pretending that all is well. Hurt acts like those big plastic beach balls that you play with in the sea. You can, with some difficulty, push the ball down under the water for a while but then it suddenly comes shooting back up again with a whoosh when you don't expect it.

We must tell our husband or wife when and how they have hurt us. We do not need to do it in a way that is harsh or judgmental. Indeed, the more gently we do so, the easier we make it for our partner to apologize. It is worth rehearsing again the advice in Chapter 9 about using "I" statements. Rather than general criticism or an attack on our partner's character, we are seeking to make our husband or wife aware of how we felt over a particular incident, as when Deborah told Miles how painful it was for her to hear him tell the story about his lunch with Anne (Chapter 11).

So, for example, "I felt hurt and rejected when you pulled away from me in bed the other night," is much more helpful than, "You never show me any physical affection."

"I felt unsupported and unappreciated when you didn't notice the hard work I put into decorating the house for Christmas," is much better than, "You never show any gratitude for what I do."

"I haven't got over the fact that you weren't truthful to me about that letter," is easier to respond to than, "You're a liar and I can't trust you."

"It upset me a lot when you went out to the bar the first night we got back from our honeymoon," is more helpful than, "Your friends are more important to you than I am."

"I felt hurt and humiliated this evening when you said I was 'so slow' in front of our friends," is more gentle than, "You always put me down in front of others."

We may feel that our partner is like a rhino, thick-skinned and short-sighted, charging around causing a lot of damage, in which case it will not be obvious to them that they have hurt us. Or we may feel that they are like the hedgehog, whose prickles have become somewhat longer and sharper. What matters in identifying hurt is not whether our husband or wife intended to wound us. One marriage counselor said, "We don't deal with many people with a premeditated plan of 'How I am going to destroy this marriage'."

We need regular, private opportunities to deal with the ways we have hurt each other, whether in big or small ways, so as not to "let the sun go down" while we are still angry. Hopefully, the need will not arise often, particularly in the early days of our marriage, but it is important to have a framework in place for dealing with hurtful incidents. Sooner or later it will be necessary, even in the most harmonious relationship.

Being prepared to say I'm sorry

The 1970s film *Love Story* was advertized with the byline: "Love means never having to say you are sorry." It could not be more wrong. In a truly loving marriage, we often have to apologize to each other, perhaps even daily.

Most of us do not like to take responsibility for our mistakes. Parents will see this in young children, who often only say I'm sorry through gritted teeth to avoid more unpleasant consequences. It is easier to rationalize what we have done and to blame everybody else. Some people excuse their behavior by blaming their parents for the way they were brought up. Others blame their circumstances, saying, "If we had more money . . ." or, "If I wasn't under so much pressure . . ."

Nicky

I remember some years ago meeting a woman in the hospital who was very ill with lung cancer. She asked me to pray with her, and as part of my prayer I included an element of confession, asking God to forgive us for the wrong things we have done.

She immediately stopped praying, opened her eyes and said to me, "I can't say that I'm sorry for things I have done wrong. You see, I haven't done anything wrong. I try to be kind to everyone. I do occasionally have unkind thoughts about people but I put them out of my mind as quickly as possible. However, I wonder if you could pray for my husband because, you see, he has a terrible temper and treats me like his servant."

I later talked to the nurses on the ward, who told me that she was one of the most difficult patients that they had ever looked after.

It is never easy to listen to ways in which we have been responsible for hurting others. However, we need to try to see things from their point of view.

Taking responsibility involves finding out from our partner how serious a particular incident was for them. It's finding out where the hurt comes on a kind of "Richter scale," where 1 is a light tremor and 10 is catastrophic. We can ask our partner, "Is this a 2, or is it a 9 or a 10, for you?" Some incidents, such as the one in Miles' and Deborah's story, can appear trivial or even humorous to one of us, but we may discover that they have caused deep pain to our partner.

When our partner knows that we understand the extent to which they feel hurt, our apology will carry more weight. If they feel we do not understand how much hurt we have caused them, they will be afraid that we will easily do it again.

To be effective, our apology must also be unconditional. Rather than saying, "If you had been more reasonable, I wouldn't have lost my temper," or, "If you hadn't made us late, I wouldn't have forgotten to mail that letter," we need to swallow our pride and say simply, "I am very sorry I lost my temper," or, "I am so sorry I forgot to mail the letter."

Equally, we need to be sure that our tone of voice and body language do not contradict what we are saying. It is possible to say "Sorry" in a way that means, "Sorry, but . . ." or, "It was your fault really."

Genuine unconditional apologies are powerful in marriage because we no longer need to be on the defensive, determined to get revenge, volleying hurt back and forth in a tit-for-tat battle. We are suddenly on the same side again. This allows the anger to be dissipated and the hurt to be healed.

Choosing to forgive each other

This is the third and, for many, the most challenging part of the process. Forgiveness is essential and has unparalleled power to bring healing to a marriage.

William and Sarah met while attending a university and married shortly afterwards in 1978. They soon had two children and became active members of their local church. But they struggled to be happy. William recalls, "I had to teach at night school to try to supplement our income. That's probably when the cracks started to appear. We bickered a lot and didn't share our feelings with each other."

Gradually, they stopped going to church and their arguments intensified. When they argued, William would explode in an emotional outburst, sometimes storming out and slamming doors. He reflected, "I usually ended up shouting and Sarah would clam up. This annoyed me further and the argument could last for hours, or even days. Often, I would give a long monologue, which ended with me saying something like, 'And that proves you don't love me!' I took Sarah's unresponsiveness as direct evidence that she didn't care what I said and didn't care about me."

Sarah's natural inclination when angry was to shut down, suspending William in a sharp, icy silence. She said, "Our families were totally different. William's whole family were very volatile and they would shout, whereas in mine we were quiet. We didn't share problems, so nothing would really be discussed. I knew something was wrong but I couldn't articulate it. I didn't like any of the conflict."

William began a new career in banking. That eased the financial pressure but it took him away from home for days at a time. When at home, they spent more time with the children than with each other.

William wrote, "I gave up trying to be romantic." They both had extramarital affairs in search of excitement and a romantic escape. But the affairs only disappointed them further.

"I felt shabby," wrote William. "I didn't enjoy it at all. Everybody loses in an affair."

Sarah agreed, "It was very flattering, but I realized I didn't really know this person. There was no real communication and he wasn't the sort that I'd want to be with forever."

When their two children left home, William and Sarah reached a crisis point. In October 2005, Sarah returned from a summer vacation in France, realizing she couldn't go on much longer. She said to William, "I'm not sure if I love you or if I've ever loved you." Those words cut William to the heart. He bought a book on divorce, started reading it, and consulted a divorce lawyer.

But Sarah wasn't quite ready to give up on their marriage. Encouraged by their daughter to start attending a local church together, William and Sarah began to rediscover their Christian faith. A couple they met had scheduled to attend The Marriage Course and invited them to go along too. William reluctantly agreed, thinking, "We're over. It's obvious Sarah doesn't love me. But at least this will prove that I've tried."

Sarah wrote, "We started the course. It was beautiful the way it was set up. We had a meal and we talked. We couldn't argue because we were in public, but with the background music we knew our conversations were private. It was a safe place for us to be able to talk about things."

For William, it was a turning point. He described how his perception of their marriage started to shift:

The course changed everything, and I found out just how flawed my thinking was. My conclusion that Sarah really didn't care about me was totally wrong. The truth was she simply didn't care for my angry outbursts. During one evening we were asked to write down significant times when we'd felt loved. I thought, "I'm going to have a blank sheet of paper." But as I started writing, memories came back of times when we'd supported each other and shared special moments. When we compared notes, I was choking back the tears, because I recognized that Sarah loved me and had loved me all along.

Through the course I learned to listen: to listen and not blame; to listen and not problem solve; to listen and not be dismissive. And, for the first time in years, Sarah felt able to utter the words I had longed to hear. I listened and discovered how very much Sarah loved me, how much she cared about me and how she wanted to be my wife forever. The course saved our marriage, of that I am certain.

Sarah said later:

I realized that I didn't really understand myself very well and couldn't possibly expect William to be a mind reader. I needed to work at understanding myself so that I could explain to William what I needed. Now we know how to talk to each other and how to listen. I still sometimes feel myself withdrawing if I know we need to face an issue, but I know that William will listen and above all that we are a team as we face challenges.

As we've been getting closer to God again, we have seen how that has brought us closer together as well. I now know how much God loves me and that he's forgiven me, which means we can forgive each other–it's all intertwined. We know we'll have our ups and downs and that we'll argue, but at the end of the day we can forgive each other and say I'm sorry. We are far stronger in our relationship now than we have ever been. We're so excited about our future together.

William spoke about the effect on him of Sarah's forgiveness:

We'd hurt each other over the years. When we started to identify those times and ask for forgiveness, it was extremely powerful. I realize now just how much healing has occurred in our relationship, indeed in my own life, because my wife has been able (frequently) to tell me and to show me her forgiveness. She didn't give up even when I resisted it. I used to suffer, virtually every day, deep feelings of self-loathing and shame, and these resulted in angry outbursts and destructive behavior, like getting drunk.

The feelings and their negative results have truly disappeared. At last I am free and I am much more comfortable with who I am. They have been replaced with something far more positive: a burning desire to be the best husband, companion, and lover to my amazing wife.

This goal is so much more fun, worthy, and satisfying. Of course, I don't always get it right, but forgiveness has made all the difference.

Forgiveness is not earned

C.S. Lewis wrote, "Forgiveness goes beyond human fairness; it is pardoning those things that can't readily be pardoned at all."[2] This is why it is always costly to forgive; we have to sacrifice our pride, our self-pity, and our desire for justice. Our culture places tremendous stress on doing all we can to maintain our rights. When we forgive, we are laying down our right to justice and our desire for revenge.

We cannot demand that our partner earns our forgiveness, nor can we be sure that they will not hurt us again in the same way. There are times when we suspect that they will do it again despite their best intentions. Jesus' instruction to forgive each other, if necessary, "seven times in a day" (Luke 17:4) is not just an exaggeration to make a point.

This does not mean that we are required to condone our partner's behavior where there is physical violence, verbal or emotional cruelty, sexual abuse, or unfaithfulness. Such violation of the marriage vows is a terrible betrayal of trust and should not be tolerated. Where such destructive behavior has become a pattern and there is a fear of provoking further abuse, we would recommend seeking professional help.[3]

The flow of forgiveness

The Christian message is that as we come to God, genuinely confessing our failures, he gives us forgiveness as a free gift. Jesus died in our place, taking the consequences for all we have ever done, said, or thought that is wrong. God freely forgives us, even when he knows we will fail again. He is our model for forgiveness. St. Paul writes, "Be kind and compassionate to one another, forgiving each other, just as in Christ God forgave you" (Ephesians 4:32).

As we begin to take in the incredible truth of God's ongoing forgiveness of our failings, he becomes not only the model but also the motivation for us to forgive others. We feel inspired to echo his generosity in our relationships with others.

But even with a model, even with the inspiration, forgiveness can feel an impossible goal. Where are we to find the means to forgive? We can feel blocked. We find no forgiveness in our own heart. We find only the desire for justice to be done. The Bible repeatedly encourages us to leave the consequences to God. " 'It is mine to avenge; I will repay,' says the Lord" (Romans 12:19). We can leave the justice of our case to God. We are told: "Do not repay evil with evil or insult with insult. On the contrary, repay evil with blessing, because to this you were called so that you may inherit a blessing" (1 Peter 3:9).

As we give up our desire to repay, God promises to look after us and to pour his blessing into our lives.

A lake needs water flowing in and water flowing out to stop from becoming stagnant. We desperately need this dynamic flow of forgiveness in all our relationships, and especially in our marriage.

Forgiveness needs to flow into our lives from God. But it is no good if it is bottled up there. With God's help we must let it flow out into the lives of those around us, and especially those closest to us.

Forgiveness is a choice, not a feeling

Forgiveness means choosing not to hold the past against each other. The question is not, "Do we feel like forgiving?" Often, we do not feel like forgiving at all. Rather, the question is, "Will we forgive? Will we let go of the hurt?"

Of course, there are some things that are much harder to forgive because the degree of hurt is much greater. Sometimes people say to us, "I can't forgive him or her." "I can't" is really another way of saying, "I won't," or, "I don't know how to." Very often people are waiting for the right feelings to come or for justice to be done before they forgive.

We do not want to underestimate how hard forgiveness is, and we will often need to ask God to help us. But if we choose to forgive by an act of our will, the *feelings* of forgiveness will follow. For some this will happen quickly and for others by degrees over a longer period.

Forgiveness sets us free

When we forgive, that forgiveness may benefit our partner, but ultimately we are the ones who benefit most by being free. According to the Christian writer, Philip Yancey:

> The word *resentment* expresses what happens if the cycle goes uninterrupted. It means, literally, "to feel again": resentment clings to the past, relives it over and over, picks each fresh scab so that the wound never heals.[4]

Corrie ten Boom was a Dutch prisoner-of-war in the Ravensbrück concentration camp, where she watched her sister Betsie die at the hands of the guards. In her book *He Sets the Captives Free*, she recalls the moment after the war when she came face to face with one of their former guards, who had become a Christian and had come to ask for her forgiveness. Only through silently calling out for God's help could she fight every human instinct towards hatred and revenge and do the impossible. She wrote later:

> At that moment, when I was able to forgive, my hatred disappeared. What a liberation! Forgiveness is the key which unlocks the door of resentment and the handcuffs of hatred. It is a power that breaks the chains of bitterness and the shackles of selfishness. What a liberation it is when you can forgive.[5]

Only through forgiveness can we be liberated from the pain of previous relationships, which otherwise will affect our relationships today.

Irene was a young South African woman had just completed her of university studies and who enjoyed living and working in

London. Soon she met Roger, an older man who swept her off her feet. He persuaded her to leave her job and move in with him. She became pregnant. They married and moved to a small village outside of London. A few months later, their son Timmy was born.

Isolated at home with a new baby, separated from family, friends, and job, Irene soon began to be plagued by horrible thoughts: she suspected her husband was having an affair. Roger explained his increasing absences and frequent need to use a payphone as being linked with top-secret government work. It sounded far-fetched but he was very convincing.

Irene's worst fears were realized one evening when a middle-aged woman from the village turned up on her doorstep. She was holding a love letter that Roger had written to her sixteen-year-old daughter. He and the girl were lovers. The mother was particularly upset because she, too, was having an affair with Roger.

Soon it transpired that not only was the husband sleeping with both mother and daughter, but he also had a mistress in London. He later confessed to Irene that he had begun his first extramarital affair the day after their wedding. Roger was a sexual addict and a compulsive liar. Irene's world crashed down around her.

She and Roger had months of counseling. Gradually, she put into practice principles from the Bible, learning to forgive and even to love him again, things she admits she never thought herself capable of. She felt they had been given a second chance to make things work. But a year later, Roger finally left Irene and Timmy and went to live with his secretary, who was pregnant with Roger's child. Abandoned and alone, Irene found anger and bitterness towards Roger rising constantly in her thoughts. On occasions, she contemplated suicide.

Then one day, while she was praying, Irene realized that her unforgiveness was like a parasite, feeding upon her and growing stronger as it was allowed to thrive. She determined, by a decision of her will, to forgive. Whenever she found herself replaying her mental video of the ways Roger had hurt and humiliated her, she would remind herself of all the things for which she had sought God's forgiveness. Then she would begin to pray for Roger and his new family. At first she did so through gritted teeth, but after a while she began to mean the prayers. Gradually the bitterness and unforgiveness faded. She began to feel a wonderful lightness and peace, and finally freedom—the freedom to start afresh.

Choosing to forgive enables us to move forward without being weighed down by the "chains of bitterness and handcuffs of hatred." At first, we may still feel acute pain, but forgiveness allows the recovery to start. It is like being stung by a bee. When the stinger is taken out, the skin is not instantly restored but it opens the way for healing to take place. When we forgive, we are still able to remember what happened to us, but, as we keep forgiving, the memories have less and less power over us.

Unforgiveness affects not only our relationship with the person or people who caused the hurt, but every relationship we have. Our marriage can be spoiled if we hold on to anger against a third party, and it can be restored when we choose to forgive. We have a Japanese friend who has done much to bring reconciliation between former prisoners-of-war and her own people. When husbands who suffered terribly during the war have been able to express forgiveness to those who ill-treated them, wives have often commented on the change in their marriage. Their husbands sleep well again and are less easily irritated by the small day-to-day issues.

Time on its own does not heal wounds. Only forgiveness can

do that, but it involves a process. We often have to forgive layer by layer, like the process of peeling an onion. We may find that we need to go on choosing to forgive for the same hurts on a daily basis in order to be set free. The less we forgive, the harder it is to do so. But, if we forgive once, it becomes easier to do so the next time. And as we forgive, the emotional bruising gradually heals and our marriage moves on.

Section 5 –
The power of forgiveness

Conclusion

If this process of resolving hurt and anger from the past is new to you, particularly if you have been married for some time, you will need to proceed sensitively and gradually. Our partner makes themselves very vulnerable when they disclose how they have been hurt. We will need to be gentle so that our partner knows that we empathize with their feelings. Where trust has been broken, it will take time for this to be restored. Do not expect the one who has been hurt to be able to forget and recover immediately, but ultimately the healing will come, and then we can maintain a regular process of keeping the drain clear.

As part of his description of love, St. Paul writes that love "keeps no record of wrongs" (1 Corinthians 13:5). Imagine for a moment that each day of your marriage is like the new page of a spiral notebook. Every day we do or say things, or fail to do or say things, that hurt our husband or wife, sometimes slightly and sometimes deeply.

On some days the list will be longer than on others, but every day there will be something on the page. If these things are not faced and forgiven, the page will be turned and the list left intact. We then start to build up a backlog of resentment and bitterness.

Even if we cannot remember the details of each list, the record of the offences remains and will in time become engraved on our relationship and quench our intimacy.

If we learn to forgive daily, it is like tearing off each page at the end of the day and throwing it away. We start each new day of our marriage with a clean sheet and no backlog. Neither of us will be on the attack or the defense. We will then be acting in love, keeping no record of each other's wrongs.

Fifth golden rule of marriage
Practice forgiveness.

Section 6

Parents and In-Laws

Chapter 13

How to Get on Well With Our Parents and In-Laws

When I was a boy of fourteen, my father was so ignorant I could hardly stand to have the old man around. But when I got to be twenty-one, I was astonished at how much the old man had learnt in seven years.[1]

Mark Twain

"Parents are strange," said Amy, "for their age."[2]

Amanda Vail

We should not underestimate the profound impact of wider family relationships on a marriage. Families are complex; some have caused untold heartache and pain that have rolled on down the years and even the generations; others have been a huge source of joy and happiness where the ripple effect on countless lives has brought much blessing and good. If our wider family relationships are to work for the benefit of each generation, we will first need to understand how our relationship with our parents should have developed as we grew up.

The progress from dependence

Our progress from complete dependence on our parents as children through to eventual independence is of vital importance for our marriage. We move through different stages as we change from being a child to being a teenager, then an adult, and finally a married person. We have devized four diagrams that aim to illustrate appropriate parent–child relationships in these four phases. Of course, no experience of family life will be quite as neat around the edges as these diagrams suggest. Some have been brought up by one parent. There are many very loving and highly effective lone-parent families who create a healthy and happy home in which to grow up. There may have been divorce, death, remarriage, step-parents, and step-families. But the same general principles of moving through each stage apply to us all.

As a couple, look at these diagrams together, remembering that you were once the child in the equation. As you do this, you are seeking to understand more about your own and your partner's upbringing, and whether your relationship with your parents changed as it should have at each stage.

We need to talk openly about the strengths and weaknesses of our parents and their marriages. An adult relationship with them requires us to let go of the fantasies of childhood in which we idealized our parents, as well as the common disillusionment during our teenage years when they could do nothing right, and to see them as they really are. We hope that looking at the four different stages will help you do this.

Early years

During the early years, our parents met our physical needs for food, drink, sleep, cleanliness, warmth, and medication. They were also responsible for our emotional needs, as represented by the arrows on the diagram. These included affection, acceptance, security, encouragement, comfort, and so on. Our emotional needs were every bit as vital, even if not as immediately obvious, as our physical needs. The experience of parental love builds a child's self-confidence, an essential quality for making relationships later in life. Relationships always involve the risk of our love being rejected, and the self-confidence we gain from the knowledge of our parents' unconditional love enables us to take this risk and to reach out in love to others.

The circle in the diagram represents the boundaries that our parents needed to set for our security. A young child's activities must be tightly controlled. Dangers must be avoided. Places that are unsafe to play in must be prohibited. As children, we did not have the maturity to make sound judgments about such things.

Teenagers

Do you remember yourself as a teenager? During these years, our parents needed to give us increasing independence, allowing us to make our own decisions in as many areas as possible. These may have included our choice of friends, the use of our spare time, our clothes, our hairstyle (if they dared), and how we decorated our room.

This gradual letting go is an essential part of the transition from total parental control to eventual independence. As young teenagers, however, we still needed boundaries around our activities. The change from a circle to an oval represents the increasing freedom within set limits. We were not mature enough to make all our own decisions and would usually have admitted, if pressed, that we appreciated the security that these boundaries brought. The adolescent years involved much self-questioning as we established our own identity, and we needed our parents' continued emotional support.

By now we might have started to recognize how we could be of help to our parents. This is represented by the dotted arrow.

"Coming of age" / Leaving home

Between eighteen and twenty-one years of age some of us were still living in our parental home. Nevertheless, we were learning

independence, making our own decisions over further education, choice of career, other relationships, use of money, and
so on.

Most of us at this stage continued to look to our parents for
advice, financial support, and comfort (if things went wrong).
But it was now more of an adult relationship. Hopefully we were
less self-focused and were accepting responsibilities towards our
parents, such as making contact (if we lived away from home)
and recognizing *their* need of appreciation, support, affection, or
encouragement.

Getting married

Many situations look more complex than the one in the fourth
diagram, but, whatever our particular circumstances, the issue is
the same. The circle around us as a married couple represents the
need to establish our own home, make our own decisions and
meet each other's needs. Our first loyalty must now be to each
other and we must leave behind any emotional dependence upon
our parents.

This change of loyalty does not mean cutting ourselves off from our families. When the relationship is on a proper footing, parents (and siblings) will be a huge support to a marriage. This has been our own experience, and our parents have been a wonderful source of love, support, fun, and close friendship. We also greatly value the close and special relationship we have with our brothers and sisters and their families. Despite distances of hundreds of miles between us, these relationships play an important part in our own and our children's lives. They have had to be nurtured over the years as it takes effort from both sides to stay in touch and spend time together.

Gatherings with our extended family around Christmas, New Year, and mid-term vacations as well as special birthdays and anniversaries have all been valuable occasions for the different generations to meet. It is worth making the most of such opportunities because the demands and pressures of life can easily crowd out these unique relationships.

In the next chapter we will look at how to establish our independence as a couple. Here we consider how to develop a strong, mutually supportive, and enjoyable relationship with our parents, parents-in-law, and extended family.

Being reasonable about wedding arrangements

The opportunity to start building for the future usually comes with the wedding arrangements. It is rare for any wedding to be organized without emotions running high. There are often strongly held views by everyone. Some parents have been anticipating and planning this day in their minds for many years.

Meanwhile, the bride and groom hear friends say that this of all days is *their* day. In truth, the day belongs predominantly to the couple, but it also involves the parents, partly because they may well be paying (and showing great generosity), and also because many of the guests will be older relations or longstanding family friends whose views matter to them.

It is natural that the parents should be involved in the plans and preparation. It is their final act of giving to their son or daughter before they get married, and this helps them to let go.

Organizing a wedding can mean hard work for many weeks, and engaged couples are often shocked to discover how many decisions there are to make. Conflicting views, an emotional situation, and tiredness are a powerful cocktail for producing tension and arguments. Patient listening and compromise where possible are often required to maintain the peace.

Showing our appreciation

All parents thrive on being shown appreciation by their children. The weeks before a wedding provide a good opportunity for this. Even if we have not come from a happy or harmonious home and have a difficult relationship with our parents, we can usually think of ways in which they have looked after us, perhaps when we were young or when we were unwell. Very few parents have made no sacrifices at all for their children. Some couples write a letter to their parents expressing their thanks. This can enormously increase the parents' joy and pride as they let go of their son or daughter, as well as set the right tone for their future relationship.

Once we are married, we can try to find opportunities to continue to put our thanks in writing, perhaps in a birthday card or in a Mother's or Father's Day card. A friend of ours wrote a long letter to her father on his sixtieth birthday, recounting her happy memories of his love and support during her upbringing. She has allowed us to reproduce a section of the letter here:

> I liked our journeys, especially when I was allowed one of those butterscotch sweets in a round tin. I also liked the way you put school dramas in perspective by sounding slightly amused or exasperated by some of the more teachery teachers. It gave me the sense that you were absolutely on my side and not theirs. I never doubted that you believed me far more than you would ever believe them. I now see that is unusual and wonderful.
>
> Same at parents' evenings when you would laugh at one of the teachers who terrified me. I would wait expectant in the hall. Always to be congratulated. But never overly. I always knew you counted me higher than any A grade. No pressure at all. Just plenty of space to make my own decisions.

Her father was unaware of what these things had meant to his daughter, and her letter has helped to maintain the close and special relationship between them that has benefitted not only her, but also her husband and children.

Staying in touch

As a married couple, it is important to work out together how to keep in touch with our parents. Regular conversations are of great value, although the habit of talking to a parent on the phone every morning or evening can lead to resentment in the other partner, particularly if such discussions are lengthy or take place when they have just got home in the evening. Make a conscious decision to keep the *best* time for talking to each other. For the sake of your parents, stay in touch. For the sake of your marriage, stay in control.

We must decide together how often to see our parents. If one of us tends to revert to being dependent or is unable to resist unhelpful pressure, it may be better to meet in your own home. If things are strained, shorter and more frequent visits may build the relationship more effectively. A congenial atmosphere can be maintained more easily for short periods; if you stay too long with nothing to do or to say, tension can build up.

One woman told us that she disliked her father-in-law and that spending time with him was very difficult. You cannot change such feelings overnight. But you can use the tools for building relationships described in the first five sections of this book, particularly considering which of the five expressions of love is most important to them. Then, over time, you will start to recognize more of their good qualities, and the relationship will improve as a result. This is a choice you must make for the sake of your partner.

A friend discovered, more by accident than by design, the way to her father-in-law's heart, and her relationship with him changed considerably:

My father-in-law is someone who believes in concepts like duty and effort, particularly in family relationships. I always found this rather annoying, thinking that relationships should be easy, spontaneous, and undemanding. Our relationship plodded on, not disastrous but mediocre. Then one birthday, I don't know quite why, I decided to try to make him a fruitcake. I think it came about as we had no clue what to buy him. He had said that he no longer wanted the gardening magazine subscription that had sustained us through the last three birthdays. I knew that he loved fruitcake. I also knew that I had no clue how to make one. But it dawned on me that even if I bought the best fruitcake in the world, it would not convey the all-important concept of effort.

I struggled and eventually produced a very sad-looking cake. I put it in a tin and, apologizing, presented it to him on his birthday. He was totally thrilled: "It must have taken you so long, and you're so busy in your job?" When we all tasted it, I forced him to confess that it was not the nicest fruitcake he'd ever tasted–and then there was laughter too! And from that day we have laughed, not only about the fruitcake, but about most things.

My father-in-law's love language, I realized when I was doing The Marriage Course, is deeds. If you do something especially for him, he feels loved. It didn't really matter whether the fruitcake tasted nice or not.

So I have learned the importance of love languages (and a sense of humor) not only in marriage but in this complex relationship with our in-laws.

You also need to decide to what extent you are going to be involved with your parents. Many parents are a huge support, particularly when a couple are under pressure with young children. But if you want them to paint the entire house, make all your curtains or look after your children twice a week, you are inviting them to share deeply in your daily life. It would be extremely unloving and manipulative to show interest in them only when they were performing useful tasks. Having thought this through together, you may conclude that it is better to run your lives without their day-to-day involvement. You must maintain integrity with your parents, and you must not exploit their love.

Trying to resolve conflict

Even where there is a close relationship with parents and in-laws, there will always be some differences of opinion. Tense and difficult situations must be resolved with the same principles of talking, apologizing, and forgiving that we looked at in Chapter 12.

We met one woman who had been married for seven years who felt continually undermined by her mother-in-law. They had little in common and conversation was difficult. Her husband, meanwhile, could do no wrong in his mother's eyes. The wife's feelings of hurt were compounded by frequent unfavorable comparisons with the other daughters-in-law. Certain remarks caused a strong emotional reaction within her, way out of proportion to the incident.

However, the relationship was maintained through the husband's understanding and encouragement and through the wife's determination to keep on forgiving and loving. As a result, things have gradually improved over the years, and today, when they are together, the mother-in-law is less judgmental and the wife has more confidence.

It is important to clear up any unresolved conflict from the past, ideally before you get married. If you do not, anger, bitterness, resentment, or guilt will resurface later in some guise or other. Some people get married determined never to act like their parents. They may have had parents who frequently lost their temper, who were uncaring and inconsiderate towards each other, who were emotionally distant, or who had their favorites among their children. Yet after a few months of marriage they gradually start to behave in the same way. This is because they have not dealt with their own feelings of anger and resentment regarding their parents' behavior.

In the analysis of one marriage counselor, whatever we concentrate on in life, we tend to imitate. If we can forgive our parents and move on, our focus on their faults and weaknesses will cease and we will be free to shed any unconscious imitation of them.

If we, as the child, are even partially to blame for a breakdown in the relationship, we will need to apologize to our parents without blaming them or trying to rationalize our behavior. The effect can be far-reaching, as Mary Pytches, an experienced counselor, illustrates:

> I remember being told the moving story of an elderly woman who was dying from cancer. Her son visited her in hospital and then went back home to tell his wife that his mother was dying and that the doctors could do no more for her. On hearing this, the wife suggested that her husband had some unfinished business with his mother that needed sorting out before she died. She then reminded him of a time when he was much younger and he had walked out of his home and had lost touch with his mother for a whole year. "You need to put that right with her before she dies," said the wife. Her husband agreed and went back to the hospital and asked his mother to forgive him for his behavior all those years ago.
>
> She was very moved and willingly forgave him and asked him to forgive her for causing him to be so unhappy that he felt he needed to leave home. They were completely reconciled and the son went home. The following week his mother was discharged from the hospital completely well. She had experienced a miraculous healing. She enjoyed good health for many more years and eventually died of old age.[3]

Considering their needs

While we were young, our parents (or another caregiver) took the initiative in looking after our needs; now we have the opportunity to reciprocate. Children move from a relationship of total dependence upon their parents to an adult relationship of mutual support until, for some, the role is completely reversed and the parent is totally dependent upon the child.

While we cease to be responsible *to* our parents, we continue to have a responsibility *for* them. The fifth commandment, "Honor your father and your mother," does not cease to be relevant for us either when we come of age or when we marry. As parents grow older, their dependence will increase, and we'll have the opportunity to return some of the love and sacrifices they showed towards us. This may include practical jobs around the home, help with finances, or planning for the future. Writer and broadcaster, Victoria Glendinning, describes how much care she receives from her adult son, Matthew, and how much he means to her:

> He always listens carefully, understands what I'm saying, makes measured and enlightening comments, gives himself entirely to the problem, and he doesn't try and hurry me on to something else.
>
> Once, recently, he had already got up to leave when I said something about troubles. "Troubles? What troubles?" And he sat down again at the kitchen table as if he had all the time in the world.[4]

If a parent lives alone, their greatest need is likely to be for conversation and company. Some friends of ours with teenage children have their only surviving grandparent living in part of their house. Not only has this arrangement allowed both the couple and the grandmother sufficient independence, but it has also led to very special friendships across three generations.

Valuing the extended family

Sometimes new couples blindly, unkindly, but rather bravely discard the tribes they came from. Sometimes they have to, because on religious, racial, or class grounds, the tribe is being so foully bigoted about the marriage. More often, I suspect, they do it out of sheer thoughtlessness: moving away, striking out into the wider world together, starting anew.

But with the birth of children comes a time when it is healthy, even pleasant, to let the tribe creep forward again and surround the new family with its old echoes. In other words, however decrepit your family tree looks to you, don't be too cavalier about chopping off the branch you sit on. When you start to be a family, the one which is there already turns out to have all sorts of unsuspected advantages. As well as only-too-well-suspected problems.[5]

Of course, no extended family is perfect; far from it. Yet in the diversity of age, personality, and viewpoint, there is the chance for plenty of color. We live in an age of neat nuclear families, who often close the front door on others of the same surname and lineage. But we easily become one-dimensional, and even claustrophobic, as we do so. Why not get together on special occasions? Libby Purves recommends:

> The family year needs milestones, something on the calendar to look forward to. You can justify them by saying they represent cultural heritage, or religious faith, or you can just take them as a bit of fun, especially at the duller times of year. We have celebrated, in our time, not only all four birthdays and Christmas but New Year, Epiphany, Pancake day, Easter, Harvest Supper . . . Guy Fawkes, May Day, St Nicolas's Day, and Pudding Thursday (a bit obscure that, but all you do is eat Yorkshire pudding). Give me time and I shall devise ways of marking Shakespeare's birthday, Michaelmas, Midsummer's Eve, St Andrew's Day, St Patrick's Day (for the Scottish and Irish connection) and if any American should drop in I will include Thanksgiving and Groundhog Day with pleasure. Celebrating does not have to be expensive: a paper flag or two to paint, a meal around the table, a game if you can.[6]

The gathering together of our extended family has its plus points: we adults get a chance to be mothered and fathered by the older and wiser and we get some living examples of what our children are about to turn into. Children enjoy cousins, especially badly behaved ones, and we all love a doting granny or an eccentric uncle. This is part of the hurly-burly of real life, and it shapes us. If we do not have an extended family, there are other ways of creating the same atmosphere. A friend of ours (a single mother) held a Pancake Party on Shrove Tuesday this year to which she invited twenty colorful representatives of all the generations.

Just as large family events have their place, so too does the nurturing of special relationships across the generations. It is not only we who will benefit from a close relationship with our parents; a grandparent can play a very special role in a child's life too.

Nicky

When I was a young child, I would often go with my mother to visit my grandmother at her home on a Saturday morning. These times have become a special part of my childhood memories. It must also have met the needs of my grandmother, although I did not think of that at the time.

Through maintaining contact with our parents, we enable our children to get to know their grandparents, and we ourselves may come to see our own parents in a new light.

Nicky

I came to appreciate more fully the wonderful qualities of gentleness and humor in my own father through seeing him play with our children. I suppose that I had forgotten these gifts in my own childhood or had taken them for granted. In retirement he had more time to spare and his grandchildren were the main beneficiaries.

Some grandparents can take on a very special role in their grandchildren's lives. And a new baby in the family can mend or cement wider family relationships. Justine, daughter of the founder of The Body Shop, Anita Roddick, writes:

Mum really surprised me because she adored my baby from the moment Maiya was born, and I saw her re-emerge in a whole new maternal way. I had the worst post-natal depression, and I came to Mum: she stayed up all night looking after the baby . . . Now that Sammy [*Justine's sister*] and I have obviously moved away from home, I think Maiya has cemented the family; she's given my mum and dad another bond, so she helps their relationship.[7]

Many grandparents comment on the joy of having grandchildren around them for whom they are not ultimately responsible and whom they can hand back at the end of the day. But grandparents vary. Some would happily give up anything to spend time with their grandchildren. If this is so, grandparents may be involved in frequent childcare and will inevitably have more influence on our children's upbringing. Others are less enthusiastic about prolonged childcare, or perhaps come into their own when the children are older. We must not expect too much of our parents. After all, they are not responsible in the way that parents are.

If our parents have died, or live far away, it is worth trying to help our children make friends with others of an older generation. It is wonderful where we have seen this happening within our church community, leading to great enjoyment for both age groups.

Understanding each other

Even when relationships between ourselves and our parents and parents-in-law are healthy and enjoyable, there is potential for conflict. We are a generation apart, and the gap of two generations between grandparents and grandchildren is yet more gaping. Just as our lives are entering their most intense phase, our parents' lives will tend to be slowing down. We may well need to work hard to understand each other. We may have to face not only the pain of ill health, but also the complicated logistics involved in prioritizing our responsibilities to our children and to our parents.

If at times we cannot understand the attitudes and opinions of parents and parents-in-law, perhaps we should stop trying. Instead, we could relax a little and appreciate them for who they are rather than judge them for who they aren't. They will not be around forever.

British actress and author Sheila Hancock's thoughts on getting to know her mother reflect the kaleidoscope of emotions many experience:

> After my father's death, I brought my mother up to London and she lived in a little flat near me. I had Ellie Jane by then, so there were resentments about her interference between us. There she was in this little place all on her own when she wasn't with us, and I didn't want her with me all the time because I was getting on with my own life. She must have been so unhappy, and I would have been so much nicer to her but she didn't show me she was in pain.
>
> Now I understand what it's like when your children grow up and you feel outside their world. I'm really sorry I didn't put my hand out to her now. I bitterly regret that I didn't know my mother better as a woman. Right at the end of her life, when I was nursing her, I remember washing her, and I said, "You've got a beautiful nose." She said, "I've gone through my life hating my nose. I thought it was so ugly." I was stunned that my mother had any anxiety about the way she looked. I said, "I can't believe that. It is a wonderful nose. Mine's a funny nose. And you're so beautiful." She had no idea that she was beautiful. But I probably never told her that. All I said was, "You're not going to wear *that* at speech day."

I think underneath all that coping was quite an insecure woman, particularly when her uppity girl went to grammar school and became educated beyond her. She was both hugely proud of me, and frightened for me. I think I was extremely unkind sometimes, and I showed off my new knowledge in a way which was not exactly humiliating but extremely upsetting. Intellectually, I began to outstrip my parents, and I didn't, at the time, value the kind of wisdom they had. I certainly do now.

The RADA archive has a letter to the principal from my father saying, "Are you sure our daughter has talent?" My parents were very frightened and hugely ambitious for me. I was very pleased that they saw me beginning to be successful, but they were very overwhelmed by that world—as was I. When I was in repertory, my mother wrote to me saying, "Look after your husband," and things that you wouldn't say to girls nowadays. My girls are ashamed and embarrassed by me in a different way. I'm a bit flamboyant, and I state my views very firmly; I shout when I'm driving, and my language is appalling. When they were at school, I would turn up, dressed wrongly—just like my mother! Now I wish I had valued more how extraordinary my parents were. Similarly, I look back now with such admiration at where my parents came from, and their achievements.[8]

Whether we have happy or sad memories of childhood, whether relationships between ourselves and our parents are peaceful or tense, we share each other's past; we feature on the same family tree; we emanate from the same blood; we share each other's memories. It is natural to want to be part of each other's present: to care about each other's lives, to share each other's failures and successes, to support each other's weaknesses, value each other's strengths and all this is part of healthy family relationships.

Chapter 14

How to Leave Behind Parental Control

When two people together take up responsibility to do what is best for the marriage, love can grow.[1]

Henry Cloud and John Townsend

Laughter, tears, lumps in the throat, anticipation, nervousness, and excitement are all part of a wedding day. This is true for the bride and groom and it will normally be true for their parents also. In the book of Genesis, the significance of the wedding day is put very simply: "That is why a man [and a woman] leaves [their] father and mother . . ." (Genesis 2:24).

We spoke recently to a father the day after his son's wedding. We knew that they were a close family and that he was fond of his new daughter-in-law. We asked if he had enjoyed the wedding day. He hesitated before answering, "It is hard to put into words what I felt—it was more complicated than I had anticipated."

Despite the fact that his son had lived away from home for a number of years, this father had understood that a vital part of the marriage was the *leaving* of father and mother. As a result, the day produced for him a mixture of joy and of loss, of looking forward with pride and back with nostalgia.

> Nicky
> When I am performing a marriage service, there is one particularly poignant moment: when the father of the bride gives me his daughter's hand for me to pass to the groom. This action symbolises that both sets of parents are letting go of their son or daughter, passing them from the parental hands into each other's care. It is the culmination of years of responsibility from their child's conception to their marriage, when a new family unit is formed. The parents of the bride and groom, once the most important people in their child's life, must now for the sake of the marriage take a step back to love and encourage in a new way.

Some parents find letting go of their child the most difficult part of parenting, as Victoria Glendinning recalls:

> I found this process so painful that when Simon, the youngest, left home, and for the first time there was no "child" in the house, I had to write myself a stern memo–I was on a train, I remember, and wrote it with tears trickling down my face–to the effect that I had no rights in them, they were only lent to me, and that if I expected them all to ring me up virtually on a daily basis I was a monster and a fool . . . Some want more contact than others. Some are more naturally communicative. This has absolutely no bearing on who loves whom most.[2]

The need to leave our parents, an essential aspect of marriage, is easily missed today because, in the West at least, most people who are getting married moved out of their parental home some years earlier. Yet the significance of leaving is not so much the *physical* move as the *psychological* and *spiritual* one. For many years the home we were born into was the center of gravity from which we moved out in ever-widening circles of exploration and independence.

But the center remained, the home to which we initially had to return and to which later we would choose to return when comfort was sought, advice was needed, money was short, or the laundry had piled up. The family home was the place of author- ity, provision, and security. After marriage, there is a new center, a new decision-making structure, a new home. Your highest commitment and loyalty must now be to each other. This does not mean you stop loving and respecting your parents, but it does mean the apron strings must be cut.

Even if you have been married for many years, you need to ask yourselves if you have fully left your parents. Consider together the following questions:

- Is one of our parents more important to us than our partner?
- Are we still emotionally dependent on our parents?
- Are they trying to control our lives?
- Do we expect our marriage to be like their marriage?

In this chapter we will look at strategies that will help you to leave behind unhelpful parental control in order to protect and nurture your own marriage.

Recognizing your first loyalty

One woman who was about to get married described her mother to us as "my best friend." She was rightly grateful for a wonderful upbringing, but it was an important development for her to see her husband as her best friend, in whom she could confide and from whom she would receive emotional support. Even if your parents are going through difficulties themselves, your loyalties must change. Author and journalist, Julie Myerson, writes about her own experience:

> My mother had been left by the man she loved, and I'd met the love of my life. Has Jonathan replaced my mother as the most important person? Probably. Jonathan pointed out how I hadn't separated emotionally from her. I had been a fourteen-year-old girl who told my mother everything, and I became a twenty-one-year-old who told her everything. But you have not to do that after a while.[3]

In many marriages this need to change loyalties is never addressed. In some cases, an unhealthy and unhelpful influence continues to exist from parent to child, causing resentment from their partner and placing strain on the marriage. In other families it is because the parents have failed to recognize their child's need to make their own decisions. Insecurity and fear on the parents' part may have led to excessive control. Other parents have sought to hold on to their child in order to meet their own need for affection and support.

Very rarely do parents deliberately try to break up their child's marriage. If they interfere inappropriately with unsolicited advice or criticism, it is most often because they believe they are helping. Your joint responsibility is to resist such interference kindly but firmly.

This will be difficult if you have been compliant all your life, if a parent is controlling and manipulative, or if the culture you live in expects you to continue to obey your parents when you have reached adulthood. Emotional pressure may be brought to bear with the suggestion that you are being uncaring or ungrateful. It may feel like disloyalty not to go along with what your parents want. You have to remind yourselves where your first loyalty now lies.

Making your own decisions

Dr. Xuefu Wang, a family therapist based in Nanjing, China, highlights the dangers of parents failing to give their child sufficient independence to grow to maturity:

> In China, many parents plan things on behalf of their children and are overly involved in their children's marriage relationships. They think, "We have more life experience so, if we make choices for you, they would be the best choices." But the issue is the child then loses the ability to make their own decisions. And this ability is very, very important. It's even more important than always making the right decisions. Because, in life, a person making choices and decisions is a major display of their maturity.[4]

It is crucial to a marriage that issues are discussed and decided upon as a couple. You must make your own decisions, whether big or small, regarding vacations, the use of your money, the decoration and furnishing of your home, your choice of employment, the raising of children, the frequency of visits, and so on.

When Tom and Christine got married, they moved into her home. Owing to a debilitating illness, Tom is only able to work for four days a week and it happens that his parents live close by. We asked Christine how she was finding married life and she told us of a particular incident that had caused friction between them. She returned home on one of the days that her husband was not working to discover that he and his mother had rearranged some of the furniture in their house. It could easily be put back and in that sense was not of major significance. But she felt very upset about it, way out of proportion to what had happened, and it took Tom some time to understand why she minded so much.

We asked her if her reaction was stronger because it had been her house prior to the marriage. She recognized that this had something to do with it. The real issue, however, was that the decision about the furniture had been made, not by Tom and herself, but by Tom and his mother. This may seem a relatively small incident and yet the feelings it caused were very strong indeed. If allowed to continue, this kind of situation can cause serious division between a couple.

Parents will often have valuable advice to offer because of their own experience, and it makes good sense for a couple to listen to it. But it is most important that they are free to take or leave the advice given. You must never make an important decision with one of your parents without discussing it with your husband or wife first. Nor must you give your partner the impression of valuing a parent's opinion above theirs. This will undermine your partner's confidence and lead to tension and conflict.

Even when a couple is being supported financially by parents, they must be free to decide how they use that help. We know of one situation where the husband is American and the wife English. They now live in America in a house built for them by his parents, who live nearby. The wife particularly has felt constrained in her ideas for the decoration of their home, knowing that her parents-in-law have not always approved of her taste. As a result, the couple have found it hard to make their home feel truly theirs as there has always been a sense of control from outside.

This interference in decision-making can often be exacerbated when children are born. Most couples have little or no experience of caring for children before they have their own. Advice from parents can easily be taken as criticism and interference, particularly if the couple are feeling insecure in their new role. There may in addition be some areas where you will decide to bring up your children differently from the way that you yourselves were brought up.

Nicky

Our own parents gave us all the encouragement and freedom we needed to develop our family life in our own way. Yet we have encountered differences of opinion that could have caused difficulties. A relatively trivial example makes the point.

When I was growing up, my hair was firmly brushed from left to right with a straight parting at one side (although over the last thirty years my parting has widened so much that it is now hard to see which side it is).

By contrast, Sila and I took a more liberal attitude towards our children's choice of hairstyle. They brushed it forward. They brushed it backwards. They brushed it upwards. They had center partings. They bleached it. At times they had it longer. At others it was cut to within millimeters of their scalp.

For us this was a way of allowing our children to make their own individual choices and to express their own personality. Our parents, from a more traditional approach, did not always like these hairstyles and usually said as much.

Depending on whose parent made the comment, one of us would be tempted to agree, as loyalty to our parents is deeply ingrained in us. At such times we had to make a conscious decision to stand together on what we had agreed for our own family life.

We heard recently of a marriage that had broken up after thirty years. The reason given was that the wife had never broken free from her very dominant mother. Even after this length of time, parental interference can still be an issue. It cannot be ignored in the hope that it will resolve itself.

Supporting each other

Some friends of ours, soon after having their first child, had a difference of opinion with his parents that precipitated heated emotions. The couple had decided to use a dummy (or "pacifier") for their baby to suck on as a way of stopping his crying. The wife knew that her mother-in-law would strongly disapprove and became increasingly anxious about it, particularly as she was about to stay with her parents-in-law while her husband was away on business. She knew she could not hide it for a whole week. In her own words, "I was terrified of facing her."

When she told her husband of her feelings, he said, "No problem—I'll give her a call and sort it out."

His mother exploded through the telephone, "No child of mine ever had a dummy and no grandchild of mine will ever be seen with one."

After a very heated exchange, the husband finished the conversation by saying to his mother, "That's it. I've said my piece and I don't want to talk about it again."

Even before the wife went to stay with her parents-in-law, her husband's intervention had a powerful effect upon her. She said, "I felt we had made this decision together and he stood up for me—that was all I needed. I didn't care what my mother-in-law said about it after that." In fact, the mother-in-law never said a word about the dummy all week and it has never been mentioned again.

David Mace, formerly director of the American Association of Marriage and Family Counselors, gives this advice:

> When a husband and wife have an agreed policy and stand firmly together putting it into effect, attempts at exploitation and manipulation invariably fail. But any weakness, any crack in the unity of husband and wife enables the in-laws to drive a wedge between them.[5]

You must present a united front. This will mean refusing to take sides with your parents and standing up for your husband or wife against criticism if necessary. Supporting one another consistently over time has a powerful effect, not only uniting us as a couple, but also sending a clear but kind message to parents.

Setting boundaries, if necessary

One couple participating in The Marriage Course told us that the husband's father had been on his own for many years. The father would telephone his son once or twice each day, often just as they were about to sit down for a meal in the evening or were about to go to bed. The husband's mother had died when he was fifteen and, as the eldest son, he had formed a very special and close relationship with his father. This caused no problems before he got married.

Once married, however, it was a big issue for his wife, and she became increasingly upset. As her father-in-law was on his own and the relationship with his son was so important to him, she felt guilty about saying anything to her husband.

Eventually she knew she must tackle the situation and said, "I am finding your phone conversations with your father more and more difficult. The timing of them is bad for us and it makes me feel left out when your dad gets to hear your news first. Then by the time you talk to me, you can't face going through it all again." They discussed the situation and came up with a solution: that the husband would talk to his father once a day at the office.

So the husband said to his father, "When you get up in the morning, give me a ring at the office and I'd love to talk to you then; otherwise this isn't going to work." The father tested it several times over the next few days. Each time he rang in the evening, the husband would say, "Sorry, Dad, I can't talk to you now. Would you mind ringing me in the morning and we can have a really good chat?" But after two weeks, in the husband's words, "He got the hang of it."

The wife said that as a result a lot changed in their marriage. "My husband was putting more emphasis on our marriage, making it the priority, and that made me feel really great." She also commented that both her own and her husband's relationship with his father became closer than before.

In such circumstances, the first step must be to discuss the situation together and to try to understand each other's feelings. This will not be easy. You will instinctively want to excuse your parents or accommodate their wishes, particularly if you have idealized them or if they are ill or on their own. This in turn can cause you to become defensive or dismissive of the other's perspective. You may not even recognize the problem. You need to listen carefully to your husband or wife (as described in Chapter 4) and to acknowledge that there is an issue for them. Sympathetic listening will usually go at least halfway to resolving the situation. You also need to recognize that your partner is not attacking your parents or family but being rightly protective of the marriage relationship. You are then in a good position to work out together what action to take, obtaining outside advice and help if necessary.

A newly married husband and wife spent an hour describing to us the difficulties they were facing with his parents. The parents clearly wanted to continue to control their son's life and they had made no effort to build a relationship with their daughter-in-law. Having listened to and understood each other's feelings, they decided that the best way forward would be to arrange a meeting with his parents. We do not know exactly what they planned to say, but we recommended that they include the following:

- Their appreciation for the ways in which his parents had sought to help and support them.
- Their desire for a close ongoing relationship with his parents.
- An explanation (with some real examples) of why the wife was feeling excluded and why this was putting a strain on their marriage.
- A few practical suggestions as to how they could work together to improve the situation.

They went to see his parents one Saturday and bravely raised the awkward subject about an hour before they had to leave. The atmosphere was tense. The parents were reluctant to listen to what they had to say. However, over the following weeks the couple went out of their way to maintain communication, and the situation steadily improved. The confrontation was painful, but very worthwhile in the long run.

Putting each other first

A Chinese couple in Beijing, called Liu-Lu and Renbo, described what it meant for them to put in appropriate boundaries. Liu-Lu, as an only child, had a very close attachment to her parents. She and Renbo lived in the same building as them but on a separate floor. As they got back late from work, Liu-Lu thought they should go to her parents' flat for dinner each evening. But that left Renbo feeling that he wasn't able to unwind at home after a long day in the office. He felt like he was there as a guest. Sometimes there would be minor conflicts with Liu-Lu's parents, which would build up frustration over time, but instead of expressing his frustration, he would store up resentment inside, which would sometimes erupt and damage their marriage.

Liu-Lu said, "I thought it was a pretty convenient set-up. We can go home and not worry about dinner. What's the problem? Eventually I came to realize that I had this blurred concept of boundaries and an unhealthy reliance on my parents. I realized how that was hurting Renbo. So we made a decision to change and to have our meals separately."

Together they shared their decision with Liu-Lu's parents. Her parents did not find this easy. "For decades we've lived like this," they said. "How come all of a sudden you don't want to eat with us?"

Liu-Lu felt under pressure, but she and Renbo stood by their decision. She said later, "I was so grateful to Renbo, as he was a great support and partner to me. And slowly, after a few months, we all adjusted to the new norm."

Renbo described how the new arrangement has benefitted, not only their marriage, but the whole family: "Now, every week, we invite my and Liu-Lu's parents to come over to have lunch with us. We chat with them; we ask how they have been doing during the week; we ask about their health and we care for them."

When appropriate boundaries are put in place kindly but firmly, the extended family becomes a great strength. As David Brooks writes, "An extended family is one or more families in a supporting web. Your spouse and children come first, but there are also cousins, in-laws, grandparents–a complex web of relationships . . . to share the unexpected burdens."[6]

Chapter 15

How to Address the Effects of Childhood Pain

Love . . . has the power to remake situations.[1]

Alan Storkey

Love grows us.[2]

Sue Johnson

Our past affects the present, which in turn affects the future. Nowhere is this more true than in family relationships–for good and bad. Dr. Sue Johnson, author of *Hold Me Tight*, said in an interview:

> When we haven't had secure connection as children, we're more sensitive; we're more easily hurt; we have more negative expectations of relationships. In the *Hold Me Tight* programme, we call them "raw spots" and we help couples pinpoint and talk about them. I don't want people to feel, if they haven't had any kind of secure connection when they were young, that somehow love is a closed book for them, because it's not true.
>
> Marriage or falling in love is like a new chance. We feel stronger; we're more sure of ourselves; we believe in ourselves;

we're not so scared to go out into the world; we take risks. When you have this connection, your relationship grows. It becomes a safe place; you can support each other; and then you grow.[3]

This chapter is written for those whose childhood and upbringing are casting a shadow over their marriage. They may be struggling to come to terms with a traumatic past or may be unaware of the connection between their experiences then and their behavior now.

Ted's mother was a dynamic and forceful woman. She had boundless energy, which was channeled into pushing her three children to achieve success in everything. She was driven by obsessive ambition, which she had not fulfilled in her own life. Ted's older brother excelled at sports and his sister played two musical instruments to a high standard.

Ted was always expected to follow in their footsteps. "You'll get into the first team, Ted—just like Robert," said his mother. "I've organized two weeks of coaching for you during vacation." Ted's life had been organized and planned for him since the moment he was born. He was never allowed to disagree nor permitted to express his feelings.

When Julia, his wife, suggested that they might go for a biking weekend in the Lake District, his cutting and hurtful reply, "Why are you always trying to control my life?" sparked a heated argument. Accusations flew backwards and forwards, the issue of the biking weekend forgotten in the exchange of fire. Ted had by now perfected the art of finishing the exchange with a sarcastic comment that usually left Julia in tears.

Ted's resentment of his mother's attempts to control his life and his pent-up anger had remained over the years. It poured out, however, not against his mother, but against his wife, Julia. Their confusion about the source of so much conflict in their marriage eventually caused them to seek help.

No parents are perfect and none of us had a perfect upbringing. Sometimes it was not the fault of our parents, and sometimes it was. Unresolved pain or anger could have resulted from death or from long absence abroad. Or it may have stemmed from our parents' divorce, from abuse (either physical or emotional), from excessive control or from the suppression of emotion.

Some people have grown up in a home where the love they received was conditional upon their intelligence, their looks, their abilities, how well they did at school, or how well they behaved at home. The failure of parents to show unconditional love is likely to leave deep wounds. The key is whether our memories of our childhood are happy or painful. For some, these memories are so painful that amnesia has set in and they cannot easily recall anything of what they felt during their upbringing.

As a result of experiences from childhood, we may find that at times we react irrationally towards our partner or another third party. These reactions can be very disturbing for our husband or wife.

Soon after Miranda got married, she began to experience great difficulty in her relationship with her father-in-law. Having had only sons, he was not used to relating to women of his children's generation. The more vulnerable she felt, the more dogmatic he became. On several occasions when they visited Patrick's parents, Miranda ended up in tears, much to Patrick's bemusement. It became so bad that she felt physically sick and full of dread prior to their visit at Christmas. Patrick realized that there was a problem and together they sought help.

It transpired that Miranda's childhood had been traumatic. Her sister had always been treated as the favorite. At the age of eighteen Miranda had been beaten by her father and told to leave her home and family and not to come back. Her parents had subsequently divorced. As Patrick and Miranda talked it through, she realized that her difficulties in relating to her father-in-law were an overreaction as a result of her own deep pain from the past.

In a loving marriage, hurt such as this can be healed. Looking for a quick cure is unhelpful but, over time, feelings can be changed and our ability to relate intimately can be restored.

We should be aware of two dangers with regard to childhood pain. One is a sense of hopelessness in the person who has been hurt. They might say, "I cannot help behaving and reacting the way I do. I'm a victim. It is just the way I am, and it is my parents" fault.' We must not abdicate responsibility like this. At any moment, even while carrying hurt from the past, we can choose to look outwards to the needs of others, including those of our husband or wife.

The second danger is a lack of understanding by their partner, who may blame them rather than seek to help. Their partner needs to understand that, while healing is possible, it often takes time. Those who have been deeply hurt may need the help of an experienced counselor. During the process of healing, they can be supported greatly by the love, encouragement, and prayers of their partner walking beside them on their journey to emotional confidence and well-being.

If you have particularly painful memories of childhood that may be affecting your marriage, we would encourage you to talk about the following points together. If you get stuck at any stage or encounter feelings that seem uncontrollable and dangerously strong, it is wise to seek professional help.

Recognize the source of the pain

At the start of the last chapter, we looked at the role of parents in providing for the physical and emotional needs of their children. Ask yourself if your parents, or any others who took care of you, met these needs in your childhood.

It can be hard to face the situation honestly. For most people there is a sense of deep loyalty to their parents and they do not want to appear ungrateful to them. Those with unmet childhood needs easily think it was their own fault that they were not shown love. They assume that they could not have been lovable or worth bothering with and that is why their parents did not affirm them. It is important to take an honest look at what was lacking and the consequences this is having on your relationships now.

You should not be surprised if, as you do so, you encounter a strong sense of anger or other emotions such as sadness, rejection, fear, and shame. These emotions will have been suppressed over a long period. A young woman who participated in The Marriage Course, who has had a difficult relationship with her mother, described how she spent an evening throwing shoes around her bedroom. She had not previously recognized the buried anger.

If we experience such emotions, we can always tell God what we feel and look for his comfort. The more honest we are in prayer the better. The Bible uses imagery that portrays God as father and mother, full of compassion towards us and encouraging us to bring every need to him. The psalmists were able to express to God the whole range of human emotions—anger, frustration, pain, regret, as well as gratitude and joy—and so can we. In the words of the apostle Peter, "Cast all your anxiety on him because he cares for you" (1 Peter 5:7).

Grieve with each other

Unmet childhood needs constitute a type of bereavement or loss. If a husband or wife can talk about what was lacking in the past, their partner can seek to provide emotional support through their willingness to listen, without trying to explain away the feelings or minimize the effect. The Bible tells us to "mourn with those who mourn" (Romans 12:15). This very process of speaking openly of the sense of loss to someone who cares brings healing and assists the grieving process.

If your partner recalls a lack of affection, affirmation, or support in their childhood, you must be particularly careful not to compound the pain by ignoring these ongoing emotional needs within your marriage. Those who lay bare their childhood pain need to receive comfort, without demanding it, from their partner.

Forgive those who have caused the hurt

In Chapter 12, we wrote about the process of forgiving. Here are the main points again. First, to forgive is an act of the will. You must forgive those who have hurt you even when you do not feel like doing so. For some, childhood experiences will have become a "no-go area." We received a letter from a woman called Jennifer who, while attending The Marriage Course, had realized that she needed to forgive her stepfather. She wrote:

> I had a stepfather named John. My mother married him when I was seven and divorced him when I was fifteen. The application for divorce was made on the grounds of "mental cruelty." My childhood was a nightmare. My biggest wish was to grow up as quickly as possible to get away from the situation.

I am now thirty-three. I have carried the burden of these memories and the hate around for eighteen years, despite becoming a committed Christian two years ago. It was the one part of my life that was simply a no-go area. I was desolate. How could I possibly "forgive" John for what he had done? Where would be the justice in that? I was a child. I was the victim. I haven't seen him since I was fifteen–he wasn't even asking (I would have preferred begging) for forgiveness.

The combination of The Marriage Course, Philip Yancey's book *What's So Amazing About Grace?*, and God's work in my life enabled me to see clearly that I needed to deal with this once and for all–unless I wanted eighteen years to turn to twenty-eight, thirty-eight, forty-eight . . . with no end.

I prayed, lay awake for several nights, cried, and prayed some more. Then I wrote John a letter, forgiving him for the hurt and anguish I had experienced as a child in his care. As I wrote, I had no idea if he was even aware of the impact that that part of his life had had on mine–I decided to leave that part up to God. But I knew as I mailed the letter that I had been set free.

We subsequently heard that Jennifer's stepfather made contact with her. He was unable to see the damage that he had caused or why he needed her forgiveness. Despite his response, Jennifer still experienced complete freedom from the pain that he had caused her.

Forgiveness is first an act of the will. Second, it is an ongoing decision. Where we have been deeply hurt, we will need to keep on deciding to forgive, even on a daily basis, for the same offence. When we forgive as a conscious act, like Jennifer, the feelings will follow.

Third, as we saw in Jennifer's story, your forgiveness is not to be conditional either upon your parents' (or step-parents') understanding of where they have failed you or upon a change of attitude in them. Forgiveness means giving up both the desire to repay and the expectation that your parents will now meet your needs. This is part of letting go of your dependence upon them.

It will not always be advisable or indeed possible to express forgiveness directly to those who have hurt you. If both parents are dead or all contact with them has been lost, you still need to let go of any anger towards them, and we suggest on the next page the outline of a prayer that could help you release those feelings to God.

Seek God's love

We can ask God to heal our sense of loss, inviting him as the perfect parent to give us the security that we did not receive from our parents. His promise to us is this: "I have loved you with an everlasting love; I have drawn you with unfailing kindness" (Jeremiah 31:3). His love, therefore, is able to meet our deepest needs for acceptance, security, attention, encouragement, and so on. Parental love even at its best could only ever be a pale reflection of the strong, steady, and unconditional love that God has for us.

God invites us to become part of his family and to experience him as Father: "Yet to all who did receive him [Jesus], to those who believed in his name, he gave the right to become children of God" (John 1:12). When we put our lives into God's hands, he gives us his Spirit, who fills us with the assurance of his love: "God's love has been poured out into our hearts through the Holy Spirit, who has been given to us" (Romans 5:5).

Below is a suggested prayer that you might like to use if you are carrying hurt from your upbringing:

Lord, thank you for your unconditional love for me and your willingness to forgive me freely. Thank you for the good things my parents gave me. [Here put some good memories into words.] I now bring before you the ways they failed me and ask you to help me to forgive them.

My father/mother (or whatever term you normally use) caused me to feel like this through failing to . . . [name the unmet childhood needs] . . . but I choose to forgive them.

Lord, thank you that you are a perfect Father. Please fill me now with your Holy Spirit that I may know your love in my own experience. Thank you for your promise to give your Spirit of love to all those who ask you. Amen.

We have listed at the end of the chapter some of God's promises on which it will be helpful to meditate. Dare to believe God's unconditional love for you. As you do so, God will gradually replace the pain of unmet childhood needs with a sense of security and comfort.

Move on

As you forgive your parents, you may become aware that, because of the unseen motive to satisfy childhood needs, you have acted irrationally and upset others, especially those you love most. There may have been angry explosions at your husband or wife for no obvious reason, or denial, self-hatred, and the pushing away of those who try to love you and get close to you. You may have visited and phoned your parents too often, telling them of your achievements and longing to hear the "well done" that was absent in your childhood. Though at times it may feel impossibly difficult, with God's help and the encouragement of your husband or wife, and others if necessary, you can leave this behavior behind.

Change, however, makes us feel insecure. Viktor Frankl describes the liberation of surviving Jews from the concentration camp, Dachau, at the end of the war. The prisoners walked out into the sunlight but were so dazzled by it that they went back into their cells.[4] Sometimes we would rather return to the familiarity and safety of our obviously imperfect relationships and old patterns of behavior. As we move on, we may well feel exposed and need reassurance. We should not be surprised or put off by this.

If one partner has had to bear the brunt of some irrational behavior, they should not expect changes to be instantaneous. It takes time for old ways of responding to be replaced with new ones. Be gentle, patient, and encouraging.

Take hope

We have written this chapter not for everyone, but for those whose unresolved pain and anger from their childhood have put great strain on their relationship. If this chapter has relevance in your life, we would encourage you, for the sake of your marriage and despite the emotional energy required, to work through these painful issues together and with professional help if necessary. Attempts to restore relationships with the wider family may or may not be reciprocated. It is still worth it for the sake of your own marriage.

In God we have a perfect father, "slow to anger and abounding in love" (Jonah 4:2), always ready to listen, to comfort, and to help. If our own parents failed to love us, we may find this hard to accept at first. The well-known words from 1 Corinthians 13:7 that love "always protects, always trusts, always hopes, always perseveres," are an inspiration and encouragement to see the process through.

We have written here a selection of God's promises of love which many have found reassuring.

In a desert land he found him,
in a barren and howling waste.
He shielded him and cared for him;
he guarded him as the apple of his eye,
like an eagle that stirs up its nest
and hovers over its young,
that spreads its wings to catch them
and carries them aloft.

(Deuteronomy 32:10–11)

But while he was still a long way off, his father saw him and was
filled with compassion for him; he ran to his son, threw his arms
round him and kissed him.

(Luke 15:20)

As a father has compassion on his children,
so the LORD has compassion on those who fear him.

(Psalm 103:13)

So do not fear, for I am with you;
do not be dismayed, for I am your God.
I will strengthen you and help you;
I will uphold you with my righteous right hand.

(Isaiah 41:10)

Because you are his sons, he sent the Spirit of his Son into our
hearts, the Spirit who calls out, *"Abba*, Father."

(Galatians 4:6)

And so we know and rely on the love God has for us.

(1 John 4:16)

Section 6 –
Parents and in-laws

Conclusion

This is the experience of one married woman's relationships with her wider family:

> As I listen to friends struggling with manipulative mothers and cold, distant fathers, interfering grannies and obsessive grandpas, I find myself wondering if my upbringing was boringly simple. But I now see that it must, at times, have been mind-stretchingly complex.
>
> Mum and Dad provided my brother and myself with a very real, normal family life. We all argued from time to time, of course, my brother and I hourly between learning to walk and learning to drive (according to my mother).
>
> But through the highs and lows of family life (and despite all of our imperfections) we always communicated—and we still do. We sat down virtually every evening to supper and we discussed our respective days, asking everyone's advice and minding about everyone's struggles.
>
> My first boyfriend arrived one evening on his motorbike dressed in full leathers. He was instantly invited to join us for supper with absolutely no fuss, whispering or raised eyebrows.

It all carried on exactly as normal, apart from my father saying, "Why don't you take your jacket off? The tassels are dragging through the creamed leeks."

And so it went on.

And then I got married, and the relationships grew between Tim, my husband, my brother and of course my parents. My own relationship with them expanded to include Tim and it must have changed too—but I've no idea how.

I guess that without really thinking about it, we allowed ourselves to regroup and to rearrange ourselves into our new roles. Then we had children and we probably rearranged again.

We chat on the phone; we ring to find out how many times you can reheat mince; we ask Dad how to build shelves and hope he might offer. We meet for lunch and supper. They sometimes have the children and we escape. They are incredibly busy. So are we. We had to live with them for a while between houses with an eighteen-month-old son with a tendency to empty cupboards and wake at dawn. But that's another story. Yes, the whole thing is spectacularly underwhelming. And I love the lot of them—absolutely.

While the members of that family were far from perfect—indeed, they would stress their many imperfections—they experienced firm foundations upon which to build their own marriages.

Where your past has been painful or you have had no first-hand experience of what a healthy marriage relationship looks like, your own marriage need not be jeopardized. Indeed, marriage itself can be a healing relationship. A friend of ours told us the other day how painful she had found it as a child to discover that she was adopted. She could not accept that she had no known blood relation. When she became pregnant and started her own family, she found her pain was healed. The healing came through her marriage and her experience of family life.

Another man, who had a difficult relationship with his own father, spoke of the thrill of forming a healthy and loving relationship with his father-in-law. It convinced him finally that there was nothing wrong with him. He was an acceptable man.

Those who had neglectful or cruel parents sometimes worry about their own ability to be a good parent. But as they discover the joy of having and loving their own children, again the past can be healed. Victoria Glendinning writes:

> I had a difficult childhood myself. I rewrote it, in happiness, through my children's childhood.[5]

For all of us, marriage can be a healing relationship. It is the place where the insecurities and self-doubt that we carry with us from the past can be revealed and reversed. Through God's love, and the love of our husband or wife, the gaps can be filled, the hurtful words repealed, and our confidence in who we are rebuilt.

Sixth golden rule of marriage

Honor your parents but do not be controled by them.

Section 7

Good Sex

Chapter 16

Sex–What is it All About?

My beloved spoke and said to me,
 "Arise, my darling,
  my beautiful one, come with me.
See! The winter is past;
  the rains are over and gone.
Flowers appear on the earth;
  the season of singing has come,
the cooing of doves
  is heard in our land.
The fig-tree forms its early fruit;
  the blossoming vines spread their fragrance.
Arise, come, my darling;
  my beautiful one, come with me."

Song of Songs 2:10 13

Sex is the greatest natural intimacy builder. We have left the subject until now, not because it is an unimportant part of marriage, but because every other part of our marriage affects our lovemaking and our lovemaking affects every other part of our marriage. When our sexual relationship is a vital expression of our love for each other, we experience a togetherness that permeates every level of our being.

God loves sex. He invented it. We are designed to revel in the attraction we feel towards our husband or wife. The ability to express love through the joining of our bodies is a gift from the one who is pure love. He intends us to enjoy it to the full within the loving commitment of marriage where there is nothing to hide or hold back from each other. Mike Mason describes this act of "total nakedness":

> To be naked with another person is a sort of picture or symbolic demonstration of perfect honesty, perfect trust, perfect giving and commitment, and if the heart is not naked along with the body, then the whole action becomes a lie and a mockery. It becomes an involvement in an absurd and tragic contradiction: the giving of the body but the withholding of the self. Exposure of the body in a personal encounter is like the telling of one's deepest secret: afterwards there is no going back, no pretending that the secret is still one's own or that the other does not know. It is, in effect, the very last step in human relations, and therefore never one to be taken lightly. It is not a step that establishes deep intimacy, but one which presupposes it.[1]

Your perception and experience of sex may well be very different. In the twenty-first century, sex has been overused, over-portrayed, and sometimes over-emphasised. We see references to it everywhere, at times cheapened, at times sentimentalized, at times idolized, but nearly always outside the context of marriage. Some have become addicted to it. Others have got fed up with it, such that a national newspaper headline declared: "Why sex just isn't sexy any more!"[2]

Many people (us included) learned about sex from their peer group, who seemed at an incredibly young age to be a great authority on the subject. Later it emerged that they were equally ignorant or misinformed.

Historically, the church must bear some of the blame for a false understanding. The Bible is clear that sex within marriage is good, but the church has not always reflected this teaching accurately. In the fourth century, Augustine spoke of "the shame that attends all sexual intercourse."[3] Other theologians went farther. Some warned married couples that the Holy Spirit left the bedroom when they engaged in sexual intercourse. Therefore the less sex, the better.

But perhaps the greatest influence on the shaping of our attitudes is our parents' view of sex. In some homes the subject is never discussed openly, or it is talked about inappropriately–in cheap jokes or bad language. For others, their parents' fear and over-protectiveness have caused false guilt and left them feeling that all sex is dirty. Tragically, some people struggle with a distorted view of sex, having suffered the horrors of sexual abuse, while others bring the painful consequences of past sexual relationships or an addiction to pornography into their marriage.

There is supposedly great openness about sex and sexuality today, yet many people are still embarrassed to talk honestly with their partner about sex in their marriage. This is a strange paradox: sex is bandied about in society, but privately we don't mention it, especially if we have problems.

Before we discuss sex at a practical level, we will outline four biblical principles that provide the setting for a fulfilling sexual relationship within a loving and lifelong marriage.

Sex—a powerful force

> The man said,
> "This is now bone of my bones
> and flesh of my flesh;
> she shall be called 'woman',
> for she was taken out of man."
> That is why a man leaves his father and mother and is united to
> his wife, and they become one flesh.
>
> (Genesis 2:23–24)

The modern equivalent of Adam's words when he first set eyes on Eve might start with a long, drawn-out, "Wow!" God's great plan for marriage is that the longing that a husband and a wife have to be together culminates in the sexual union. When practiced lovingly, it both expresses and creates oneness.

This is why casual sex ends up being damaging and leaves people feeling hurt. The joining of a man and a woman sexually will always be more than a temporary physical bond. Whether we intend it or not, it affects us at a deep emotional, psychological, and spiritual level. The two sheets of paper that we spoke of in Chapter 1, glued together to become one sheet, cannot be torn apart without damage to both.

Sex is designed by God to be an expression of the exclusive and committed relationship between a man and a woman. Each time we express our love for each other through this physical joining of our bodies, the bond between us is made deeper and stronger.

Sex—a lifetime of discovery

The second principle is well-illustrated in the Song of Songs. In the middle of the Bible there is a beautiful, erotic love poem describing the passionate relationship between a lover and his new bride. The writer unashamedly celebrates the mysterious power of God's gift of sexual love. The poetic imagery, although obscure at first reading, leaves us in no doubt that God intends us to enjoy exploring each other's bodies and delighting in our mutual attraction, arousal, and climax. There is no hint of shame, guilt, or embarrassment.

Eat, friends, and drink;
drink your fill of love.

(Song of Songs 5:1)

The lovemaking in the Song of Songs gradually matures over the course of the poem as the couple's relationship develops. Perhaps this gives a further glimpse into why God's purpose is for sex to be kept for a lifetime's enjoyment within marriage.

By contrast, the impression given by countless films today is that sex is most exciting when a relationship is new or adulterous. This myth causes many to assume that, as a husband and wife grow familiar with each other, the excitement will inevitably wane. Only the adventure and secrecy of an affair can produce the sexual high again.

But this is not the way God designed sex to be. It is rather that, as we grow in understanding how to arouse and bring pleasure to each other, our sexual relationship develops and the enjoyment increases with the years, nourishing the entire marriage as we express and receive love. This conviction led the writer of Proverbs to state with such feeling, "may you rejoice in the wife of your youth . . . may her breasts satisfy you always, may you ever be intoxicated with her love" (Proverbs 5:18–19).

A couple in their eighties wrote about their own experience after fifty-eight years of marriage:

> There's a sort of a skin hunger that is really significant to human relationships, particularly intimate relationships. While some things change, the tactile dimension is always there.

When a husband and a wife take a long view, they will be amply rewarded. The Christian author and psychiatrist, John White, comments:

> The communion (the closeness, the intimacy, the knowing-and-being-known, the loving-and-being-loved) is a complex living structure that takes years to grow. It begins as a delicate and beautiful plant, vibrant with life. It grows into a sturdy tree with deep roots to sustain it through drought and storm.[4]

Because of the power of sex to create pleasure and intimacy, the passionate sexual imagery of the Song of Songs is also used as a metaphor for the close personal relationship God desires to have with us.

Sex–an essential ingredient

The third principle is expressed in St. Paul's first letter to the church in Corinth, a city noted for its sexual license and red-light district.

> The husband should fulfil his marital duty to his wife, and likewise the wife to her husband. The wife does not have authority over her own body but yields it to her husband. In the same way, the husband does not have authority over his own body but yields it to his wife. Do not deprive each other except perhaps by mutual consent and for a time, so that you may devote yourselves to prayer. Then come together again so that Satan will not tempt you because of your lack of self-control.
>
> (1 Corinthians 7:3–5)

These verses have historically been misused, particularly by husbands making demands on their wives to satisfy their every sexual whim and wish. This contradicts the main point of this passage, which is to remind husbands and wives of their *duties* towards each other rather than of their *rights*. Neither a husband nor a wife is to withhold physical lovemaking except by mutual agreement for a limited period. Both need to recognize that their sexual relationship is not the icing on the cake of their marriage but an essential ingredient of the cake itself.

As we saw earlier, Roman law gave a husband absolute rights over his wife. St. Paul's teaching about this mutual giving of a husband's and a wife's body to each other was therefore revolutionary in the first century. Today it is just as relevant.

An article in *The Sunday Times* reporting on the British National Survey of Sexual Attitudes and Lifestyles showed that, while outside marriage sex is widely regarded as a normal part of relationships, within marriage thousands of couples "have spurned sex in favour of chastity . . . Research reveals that up to one in thirty of all couples are opting for celibacy in their relationships because they have neither the time nor inclination for sex."[5]

It is widely assumed that sexual relationships have a natural lifespan. Liz Hodgkinson, author of *Sex is Not Compulsory*, writes, "For some that may be a week, for others it could be twenty years. But if you try to extend your sexual relationship beyond its natural life, then you are asking for trouble because then it no longer becomes spontaneous or enjoyable."[6]

This is a sad misunderstanding about the way sex works. God designed sex for a lifelong marriage relationship and intended it to be fulfilling (although changing) throughout our lives. As we get to know each other more deeply over the years, the potential for intimacy and joy through the sexual bond increases—not decreases. Far from giving up when sexual desire diminishes for a while, a couple needs to discover new ways of arousing and satisfying each other.

If we neglect the biblical command and withhold ourselves from regular times of making love (except for reasons such as ill health or recovering from childbirth), we become separate at every level. Lack of lovemaking in a marriage must be taken seriously. It can lead to feelings of isolation and aloneness. And when we feel lonely, we are vulnerable to temptations from elsewhere.

Sex—an act of giving

The fourth principle comes from the fullest teaching about marriage in the New Testament. It is not exclusively about the sexual relationship but certainly includes it:

> Submit to one another out of reverence for Christ.
>
> Wives, submit yourselves to your own husbands as you do to the Lord . . .

Husbands, love your wives, just as Christ loved the church and gave himself up for her . . . In this same way, husbands ought to love their wives as their own bodies. He who loves his wife loves himself. After all, no one ever hated their own body, but they feed and care for their body, just as Christ does the church—for we are members of his body. "For this reason a man will leave his father and mother and be united to his wife, and the two will become one flesh." This is a profound mystery—but I am talking about Christ and the church. However, each one of you also must love his wife as he loves himself, and the wife must respect her husband.

(Ephesians 5:21–22, 25, 28–33)

Good sex requires both husband and wife to think how best to give each other pleasure through their lovemaking. Much of the stimulation and satisfaction of sexual desire today has become self-orientated. The emphasis is upon *my* right to satisfy *my* desire in the ways that *I* choose. Sex, however, is not a gift for self-gratification. It is a way of giving ourselves to one another, submitting to each other's needs and desires.

Sexual intercourse is the most intimate way of showing our love to our husband or wife, and it involves making sacrifices for each other. Every couple needs to learn how to give to one another. At various times and for various reasons we will each have a different level of sexual desire, especially during periods of stress or with the arrival of a child. For one, sacrificial love might mean showing restraint. For the other, it might mean making love despite tiredness.

The concept of giving through sex can be difficult to grasp. We are so easily preoccupied with getting rather than giving. Many people grow up thinking that sex is something to take, to earn, or to manipulate. The art of giving oneself to another person can therefore feel foreign at first, but this art must be cultivated in every area of marriage, not least in the area of sex.

Chapter 17

Six Qualities for Great Lovers

[Sex] celebrates what is happening in the rest of the couple's life.[1]

Alan Storkey

The most basic yet most important fact to grasp about our sexuality is that men and women are made differently. Someone described the differences this way:

Men are like gas cookers: they heat up instantly and cool down rapidly. Women are like electric cookers: they take time to heat up but stay hot for much longer.

Sex and relationship therapist, Emma Waring, summarizes the difference between men and women in their typical sexual responses: "The man has the spontaneous desire, and then he gets aroused. The woman gets aroused, and then the desire kicks in."[2]

God designed men and women to be aroused in different ways, and it is the combination that can produce a long and fulfilling sexual relationship. If women were made like men, it could all be over in thirty seconds and sex would not be the great intimacy builder God intended it to be.

Both husbands and wives have to understand and enjoy these differences, otherwise they can seem like insurmountable problems. A husband has to learn to be gentle and patient and give time for his wife to be aroused. Meanwhile, a wife needs to understand her own as well as her husband's sexuality. For her, the process of arousal is generally more complex than for her husband and sex may not be so easily divorced from the rest of life. These differences in our sexual responses often lead to misunderstanding and conflict, which will affect the whole marriage for the worse.

One couple, called Emerson and Christina, described their journey of growing in their understanding of how each other is wired sexually:

Emerson: I expected her to respond the way I respond.

Christina: Men don't need to connect to *go there* and women do. You can't be mad at me all day and then say, "Let's go!"

Emerson: I've had to deal with that, because a man hears a "No" and feels like you don't love me any more. I've realized it's not about love. She does love me. She's just not where I'm at. How do I take her there? It's almost like she's a Ferrari that I don't understand. She's an amazing species that's different. I've learned to take out the trash, to clean the house, to do acts of service, because that's what turns her on. That's what triggers her feelings, to know that I care.

What follows is the first of six important qualities that will enable your lovemaking to develop.

Speaking to each other

The whole subject of sexual intimacy is deeply private for many people. However, if you can be open and honest with each other, it will greatly strengthen your mutual trust and your closeness.

A couple who attended The Marriage Course described the effect of talking more openly:

Carol: Before we did The Marriage Course, for me our sex life was fine. I thought my husband had all the problems and I didn't have any. I was quite happy with the way things were.

Richard: If you had said, "Do you have any problems with your sex life?" I would probably have said, "No." But there was an issue for me. I always seemed to be having to ask, "Do you feel like it?" I felt helpless. There seemed no way in which I could influence Carol's response.

Carol: During the course we had to write down a score to assess the friendship, spiritual intimacy, and physical intimacy in our marriage. It came as quite a shock to me when my husband showed me what he'd put; out of twenty, our friendship was eighteen, our spiritual relationship was nineteen, and our physical relationship was two! Really it was like that! Then when we talked together, for the first time I actually listened to Richard and tried hard to understand what a problem it was for him. I took it seriously. Until then I thought that he was always demanding and that he didn't understand me, but now I began to realize how important this part of our marriage was to him.

Before The Marriage Course I had never really understood the Christian view of sex and I hadn't seen what a crucial role sex plays in a marriage. I thought we were great friends, that we were spiritually aligned, and that if our sex was not very good, it didn't really matter. During the course I realized that I was suffering from certain hang-ups and these were preventing us being free with each other sexually.

When I was twelve years old, I walked into my parents' bedroom while they were making love. Nobody, including my parents, had ever talked to me about sex. I had no understanding of what they were doing but it didn't sound as if it had anything to do with love. I was so embarrassed by the incident that I went to school the next day before my parents were up. That evening they sat me down and, looking extremely awkward, they tried to explain. From that day, sex became a highly embarrassing subject for me. A few years later I discovered that my father had been unfaithful to my mother and deep down I started to believe that it was impossible to trust men sexually.

I had not told Richard about any of this before The Marriage Course, but he was living in the shadow of its effect upon me. When I told him one night, in the dark, feeling a mixture of shame and embarrassment, he was so kind and gentle. I then spent some time talking and praying about this with one of the leaders of the course and, with Richard's love and support, it was resolved.

Richard: It was so good for me to be able to be honest and give us a two. The best part was to be listened to and taken seriously, rather than feeling like a whining sort of animal, which is how I felt treated before. The second thing was that I decided to cool down a bit and we started experimenting with making agreements. We agreed to make love once a week. Meanwhile, I would try to be more romantic.

Holding a Christian perspective is really great because it means that sex is more than an instinctive physical process. It has become something that is part of our intimate relationship. Also, I realized I had been behaving like a victim and not being straight over my requests.

Carol: Since we completed The Marriage Course, I have discovered how wonderful sex can be. Now that our physical relationship is no longer something separate, our growing together has suddenly become a reality. I used to think that if we talked about everything, our marriage would be fine. Now I see that our sexual relationship is a way of communicating in marriage, that is as important as the words we say.

You need to learn to be open with each other, telling your partner what you enjoy or do not enjoy, expressing your desire to make love. Assumptions about one another or generalizations about gender are unhelpful. No couple is a stereotype. We all differ in the peaks and troughs of our sexual desire. Listening to each other and expressing your feelings about sex is as important as any other area of communication in your marriage.

During lovemaking, wives need to tell their husbands what arouses them and when they are ready for intercourse, while husbands need to tell their wives what *not* to do if they are struggling to delay orgasm. The more you discover about one another, the more you will enjoy making love. Any embarrassment quickly disappears once this kind of communication has begun.

Past sexual experiences can affect you deeply: there may be a reluctance to give yourselves for fear of being hurt again or flashbacks that inhibit your freedom. It is important to expose your deepest fears to each other in this complex area of your personality. For it is as you communicate verbally (often with painful feelings of vulnerability) that your husband or wife is able to comfort and encourage you and your feelings of rejection and estrangement will be replaced by warmth and welcome. And this acceptance can then be expressed through a loving sexual relationship. The issue thus becomes a virtuous circle: as you make love, you heal the bad memories, which in turn leads to less fear and more desire.

You may in addition need to seek professional help to work through the consequences of an abusive sexual relationship in your past in order to find freedom with your partner.

Tenderness

A number of women were asked what makes a man a good lover.

Their replies revealed that it is neither athletic prowess nor the size of a man's muscles nor the size of anything else, but rather tenderness. This was put far higher than physical technique. Sexual love cannot work against a background of selfishness, exploitation, criticism, or harshness.

Sexual intimacy arises out of tenderness: they are two sides of the same coin. Tenderness is a vital aspect of our relationship, and lovemaking will feel empty and one-dimensional without it. Tenderness involves taking time over making love. Time to unwind from the pressures of the day. Time to build romance and desire. Time to enjoy being physically close. Time to love each other with your words: kind, tender, affirming words. It does not matter if the same words are used again and again if you really mean them.

Just as an orchestra starts with the oboe and then the other instruments in the orchestra tune to it, so tenderness means tuning in to each other's emotional needs. If you do not take time and are looking only to achieve orgasm, sex will be mechanical.

Some husbands only touch their wife when they want sex. This sends terrible signals to her. Indeed, it can lead to a marriage with no physical contact at all as the wife backs off, resenting her husband's attitude and intentions. If she feels in any sense *used*, her body will shut down. For a woman to give herself to her husband, she must feel safe. She needs to feel loved. She must feel special. We are not suggesting that tenderness and passion are mutually exclusive but, for a woman particularly, the emotional fulfillment can be as satisfying as reaching orgasm.

According to the UN, violence against women currently affects one in three women worldwide.[3] And most terrible of all is that some of that takes place in the bedroom. That is a terrible reversal of those words in Ephesians that we referred to in the last chapter: "Husbands, love your wives, just as Christ loved the church" (Ephesians 5:25). In one tradition in a Jewish wedding ceremony, instead of putting a ring on his wife's finger, the man takes off his coat and puts it around her as a symbol of his promise to protect her.

When a woman feels safe, special, and beautiful, her mind and body will respond sexually towards her husband, and this will enhance their mutual fulfillment. The bedroom should be the place where the wife knows, "I am cared for, loved, and cherished. In a world that may undervalue, scorn, or ridicule me, there is a man who knows me like no other and is tender towards me."

Responsiveness

Many husbands, like Richard earlier, if asked about sex in their marriage, would reply that their wife is not very responsive, but this is neither in line with the biblical portrayal of the potential for their sexual relationship nor of a woman's sexuality. The Bible speaks of a woman as a secret garden, "a garden locked up . . . a spring enclosed, a sealed fountain" (Song of Songs 4:12).

Sila

There is an old and beautiful English garden that I know and love. In front of the house are herbaceous borders. As you turn the corner, stretching away beside a long lawn is a yew hedge, broken by an arch. Through the arch you walk down some steps into a hidden sunken garden. On the far side is an opening in an old wall which leads through to a small and intimate rose garden with a circular pond in the middle. Beyond this, past climbing wisteria, roses, and clematis, you come upon a large walled vegetable garden. In summer there are beds of pink, orange, and red poppies, mixed together. The garden leads on into an orchard full of apple, plum, and damson trees with a gate at the far end out into the fields.

Whatever the weather, whatever the season, this garden excites curiosity and invites exploration, always offering some new discovery in a hitherto unseen corner. It is in this sense that the Song of Songs uses a garden as a picture of a wife's sexuality; there is enough to discover and delight in over a lifetime.

The imagery in the Song of Songs resonates with pleasure and delight for both lovers. This woman is aware of her own sexuality and is wonderfully untainted by self-consciousness or restraint. She takes the initiative in welcoming her husband into the garden: "Awake, north wind, and come, south wind! Blow on my garden, that its fragrance may spread everywhere. Let my beloved come into his garden and taste its choice fruits" (Song of Songs 4:16).

Knowingly or unknowingly, the wife holds the key to unlock the garden. She must choose to explore it together with her husband. Some women, however, do not know that the key, or indeed the garden, exist; others fear what lies beyond the gate; for others, their past experience of the garden has been negative and traumatic. Within the safety and commitment of marriage, these issues can be dealt with. A wife needs to believe in the possibility of pleasure and fulfillment through the act of lovemaking. In some cases, this will take great courage and she will need patient and sensitive support from her husband if she is to give herself freely to him. Only in this way will a climate of trust be built between them.

One wife, who had suffered sexual abuse in her childhood and had been through two years of counseling, said to us, "There were times, particularly at the beginning of our marriage, when I'd say, 'I just can't,' and I had to work very hard on saying to myself, 'He's my husband; he loves me; he's going to care for me; he's not going to hurt me.' It was like I had to train myself in that way.'"

The ideal is that the husband and wife enter the garden, hand in hand, and start to explore and enjoy it together. Later in the poem, the bride says, "Let us go early to the vineyards . . . there I will give you my love . . . at our door is every delicacy, both new and old, that I have stored up for you, my beloved" (Song of Songs 7:12–13). A wife's responsiveness can be the secret to her husband's emotional well-being. A wife can all too easily interpret her husband's desire for sex either as a purely physical desire or an insensitive demand. A husband needs to know that his wife finds him attractive. He needs to know how much his wife desires his love. He needs to hear his wife say how special (in physical as well as in other ways) he is to her. A husband needs to sense the excitement and anticipation of his wife's desire and all the delights that she wants to share with him. As one husband said, "When she says no, I feel that I'm rejected. No is not no to sex, as she might feel. It is no to me as I am. And I'm vulnerable as I ask or initiate."[4]

For most women, as for a significant number of men, sex starts as a decision and then arousal follows. Being responsive may well involve making a deliberate choice to be in the right frame of mind. Emma Waring explains:

> If we're intentional about having sex and we've planned it in with our partner, then it can be something that is in our mind. Rather than suddenly finding ourselves in a situation where we're

expected to be responsive, there's an expectation in ourselves and we take ownership about what will help us to enjoy that experience. How are we going to be fully engaged? What do I need to do in the run-up to get myself in the right frame of mind?

And if we're fully invested, we're much more likely to enjoy it because the arousal circuit will be connected; we will be connecting our head with our body.[5]

Romance

Romance has the potential to draw you into a world that belongs only to the two of you: a world in which your imagination is awakened and your senses stimulated. It stops sex from becoming mechanical and routine. Romance creates the setting for lovemaking that involves every part of your being and draws you together, and typically plays a bigger part in sexual arousal for women than for men.

Nicky
One Mother's Day I decided to make a special supper for Sila. I then asked her what she would like to do for the rest of the

evening. She had earlier watched the first half of Jane Eyre on television with our children and had recorded the rest. She suggested that we watch it together. Not an inch of bare flesh below the neck was revealed throughout the film yet I could not believe how arousing this romantic love story was for Sila!

If romance is neglected and your marriage revolves around doing the chores and paying the bills, you can end up as teammates rather than lovers. There may even be an awkwardness between the two of you regarding sex, inconceivable as that would have seemed at the start.

Husbands and wives can create romance for one another. This need not involve great expense. You just need to do something different from the normal routine: a walk along the river, a picnic in the park, or a trip to the cinema. If you can get away together for a weekend, a change of environment often creates feelings of romance.

Nicky

I have made various attempts at romance over the years, not all of them successful. One particularly uncomfortable memory is a visit to the theater to see the musical *Les Misérables* on our tenth wedding anniversary.

I had hoped, somewhat naively, to combine it with a picnic in a park halfway through. Not only was there no park in sight and an impossibly short interval but, owing to the exaggerated size of my romantic picnic, I had to spend the entire evening with a very large basket digging into my knee.

Sila

Nicky was determined to see his plan through and not to let the romantic picnic supper go to waste. We ended up spreading out our rug on the stairs between the upper circle and the grand circle. I sat down on one side of the narrow Edwardian stairway while Nicky sat on the other, passing me a red rose to accompany a glass of champagne and a plate of delicious cold food, while people cast us curious glances as they went up or down the stairs.

It was a memorable evening (in fact, I shall never forget it!), although I was very glad not to have recognized anyone in the audience or, more particularly, on the stairs. And Nicky's intentions meant a lot to me even if the evening didn't quite work out as he had planned.

Anticipation

One of the secrets to good sex is realizing that your mind is your most important sexual resource. In a healthy relationship, anticipation builds desire, which then leads to the most satisfying lovemaking. As one husband put it, "The best sex starts at breakfast."

Some couples develop a secret code to create anticipation. One wife told us of an evening that she and her husband had set aside to spend together. They were about to go upstairs to bed when a friend rang to say she was bringing over some food for a party the following day. Thinking quickly, the wife asked her to leave the pasta on the doorstep. Since that evening, the phrase "pasta on the doorstep" has become part of their vocabulary with a whole new meaning.

Because of the importance of your mind for lovemaking, a couple must keep their sexual thoughts exclusively for each other. With its easy accessibility online today, most people at some point in their lives, often during their school days, have been exposed to pornography. One of the main dangers of porn is that you can so easily become addicted.

Psychologist and author, Henry Cloud, explains the process and the consequences:

> When somebody has a pornographic experience, it's a good experience. It feels good, and that in itself is reinforcing. It goes to pleasure centers in the brain where certain chemicals are released. Then it starts to become a track that you run down; it becomes a neural pathway that drives behavior.
>
> That is really problematic for a number of reasons. One is that you need more; there are diminishing returns. But another is that you're using a fantasy object as a sex object, as a love object. You've separated your orientation in your wiring towards love, towards satisfaction, towards fulfillment; you've compartmentalized it away from a real human being. If you're having another relationship that's a fantasy, one that you're in control of, you'll never get to the place where you as a couple can have everything that marriage was designed to provide.
>
> So, if you're going to have fully fledged intimacy with a real person, it's really important that you deal with this and get it out of your life.[6]

Pornography dehumanizes you and can rob you of true sexual fulfillment. Other people become objects to arouse and then satisfy sexual desires, and it will be felt at some level by your partner, even unconsciously, that there is a moving away from the relationship.

Henry Cloud continues:

> Sometimes the person using pornography says, "Oh no! It has nothing to do with you. This is just something that I enjoy." But in an integrated, intimate relationship those things are felt, and they

drive wedges. You're truly abandoning your spouse and some-times, when that gets discovered, one of the biggest cries we hear from spouses is that you're having an affair. That's how it feels, that you prefer this fantasy world to me. There's a sense of rejection and abandonment.[7]

In today's culture, it is difficult to avoid some degree of arousal through what is displayed on advertizing billboards, on maga-zine covers, online, or in films. For the sake of your marriage, it is vital that any erotic thoughts are directed towards your partner.

You may, in addition, need to find ways of protecting your-selves. For those who are required to travel and stay in hotels alone, the TV can be a snare, especially where pornography channels are available. You will be especially vulnerable if you are tired and missing the close companionship of your partner. A friend of ours gives the TV remote control to a somewhat bemused hotel receptionist so as not to be tempted to scroll through the channels late at night.

Many people today choose to have protective software on their computer to block pornography from their web browser. Self-imposed boundaries like this are not a sign of weakness but rather of wisdom, and the marriage relationship will be the stronger for it.

Sila

For many women, the biggest danger is fantasizing. One famous actress being interviewed for a Sunday paper spoke candidly about her sexual relationships and told the journalist that she would regularly think of other men when making love to her husband. This may have increased her sexual desires, but it would not have helped her marriage.

A woman can become addicted to fantasy through what she reads or sees, making real life seem by comparison dull, routine and empty of the love and intimacy she craves. Many popular novels encourage such fantasizing. But seeking to escape from reality on a regular basis through what is often regarded as harmless entertainment can be dangerous for our marriage.

The New Testament emphasizes the need to discipline our minds: "Finally, brothers and sisters, whatever is true, whatever is noble, whatever is right, whatever is pure, whatever is lovely, whatever is admirable—if anything is excellent or praiseworthy—think about such things" (Philippians 4:8).

If a husband or wife has a problem with pornography, as well as asking for God's forgiveness and help to break free from the addiction, we strongly suggest finding another person, or a group of people, of the same sex in whom you can confide that you are struggling. Breaking the shame is so important. Shame isolates people, which then exacerbates the addictive behavior. It will be important to remain accountable to someone in the future, allowing them to ask at regular intervals how you are doing. A husband, who had a porn addiction that he eventually confessed to his wife, talked about his journey to freedom:

I had started a job that demanded so much of my time that I was basically isolated. There are so many lies that go on internally: "You're alone in this." "This is not something that anyone else struggles with in this way."

But then, talking to people and being honest with other people was really the key to moving forward and to becoming free. The more you bring people in, it isn't the more exposed you feel, it's actually the safer you feel and the more likely you are to come out on the other side doing really well.

Variety

The sixth and final quality essential for good lovemaking is creating variety. All of us tend to take extra care of new things. We once bought a brand-new car and we treated it with kid gloves. In the early days the children were not allowed to eat anything in the back; but a few years later we thought nothing of consuming a three-course McDonald's meal, complete with ketchup, drinks, and melting ice cream. Our attitude had totally changed. We take less care of something when it is no longer new. Familiarity produces complacency.

It is at the point of familiarity in your sexual relationship that the thought of an affair can seem appealing. A good sex life needs creativity, thought, and variety. Some of the following sugges tions may seem impractical, but it is amazing how much effort people put into conducting an affair. You need to use a similar amount of imagination, and more, in your marriage.

- Vary the place you make love. It doesn't always have to be in the bedroom. What about on the sofa, in the shower, or in front of an open fire? If there are other adults living in your house, it is worth making one night a week your own particular evening in! You can be clear about the time you need alone.

- When children are around, the options are more limited. Having a discreet but efficient lock on the bedroom door when children are old enough to wander in is important both for the children's sake and to make it possible for you to be totally relaxed. Relaxation is essential for good sex.
- Planning a night or two away in a different setting can be a great antidote to boredom and over-familiarity. This does not need to be expensive. Once or twice a year you could ask friends to look after your children, or even swap houses, as we suggested in Chapter 2.
- Try making love before eating. Neither men nor women are at their best sexually after a huge meal, especially if it is eaten late. Alcohol can also have a detrimental effect. Two or three glasses of wine can impair a woman's ability to have an orgasm and a man's to maintain an erection. Some changes in your eating and drinking habits may regenerate the quality of your sex life. Setting aside time to make love is as important as making time to go out together.

"Can you smell burning?"

- Vary the atmosphere. For example, put on some music or try different lighting. Making love under a 100-watt bulb does not create the most romantic atmosphere. Experiment with candlelight, darkness, moonlight, or firelight. In the Song of Songs, the lovemaking involves each of the five senses being evoked and enjoyed. As one woman put it, "Lovemaking is at least seventy-five percent sensuality and, at most, twenty-five percent sexuality."[8] Sensuousness stimulates the imagination and enhances the enjoyment.

- Vary the routine. You can so easily fall into a pattern of always making love the same way, because it works. You get comfortable with what you know and are used to. While being sensitive to each other's enjoyment, be creative. Vary which of you initiates things. Variety and romance help to put proper erotic thoughts and desires into each other's minds and increase your passion for each other.

- There will be times, however, when too much experimentation is inappropriate, particularly for a woman who has just given birth and may be nursing a baby.

People sometimes ask us what the Bible *allows* in terms of sexual practice in marriage. It is not specific about details, but there are certain principles that act as safe boundaries, the most important of which is that whatever you do must be mutually agreeable and show respect for one another's dignity. Ask yourselves: does this practice bring enjoyment and satisfaction to both of us? Or does it make your partner feel uncomfortable, embarrassed, or used? Could it lead to mutual orgasm? Does it cause you to focus your thoughts exclusively on your husband or wife?

God intended you to love one another through sexual intercourse within marriage—he is not surprised or shocked by your enjoyment of it. It was his idea. He made you spiritual, emotional, and sexual beings. He intended that your bodies should be desirable and pleasurable to each other, and he deliberately created the sexual union, a lifetime of exploration and possibilities.

Chapter 18

Protecting Your Marriage

Place me like a seal over your heart,
like a seal on your arm;
for love is as strong as death,
its jealousy unyielding as the grave.
It burns like blazing fire,
like a mighty flame.
Many waters cannot quench love;
rivers cannot sweep it away.
If one were to give
all the wealth of one's house for love,
it would be utterly scorned.

Song of Songs 8:6–7

Marriage should be honored by all, and the marriage bed kept pure.

Hebrews 13:1

None of us is exempt from the danger of an affair. We are all capable of being attracted to another person, sometimes when we least expect it. King David, one of the most famous Old Testament kings, succumbed one evening as he walked on his palace roof: "From the roof he saw a woman washing. The woman was very beautiful, and David sent someone to find out about her" (2 Samuel 11:2–3). The woman, named Bathsheba, was the wife of a loyal soldier in David's army. Already it was too late. Even before he summoned her to his bed, David had gone too far. By the time he had allowed himself to entertain thoughts of adultery, he had set the direction for his actions, which were to have terrible consequences for him and for his family for many years to come.

The prevalence of affairs and their wide acceptability today does not lessen the pain that they cause for each individual involved. This story about a teenager called Judy appeared in a national newspaper:

> Judy thought her parents' twenty-three-year marriage was unshakeable but on a dull afternoon eighteen months ago, her father told her that he had been having an affair for two years with a family friend. She described her feelings of betrayal, hurt and anger at her father's infidelity, "I don't know if I can forgive him . . . Friends say to me, 'He is your Dad. Look at all the things he did for you', and I think, 'Well, sure, he read me bedtime stories but it does not excuse what he has done.' It is one of the most selfish things you could ever do. We were the typical happy family, three kids, two cats and a dog. I feel sorrow, real sorrow, that my Dad did this and thought that it would all work out. My only contact with him now is the money he pays into my account every month."[1]

Affairs are easily entered into, but the ensuing hurt and damage are not so easily repaired. A marriage is built on trust and, once abused, the re-establishment of trust is a slow and painful process. An affair appears alluring in the short term, promising emotional closeness, intimate conversations, and exciting sex. But in the long term it leads to many regrets when a marriage is broken and family life is destroyed.

In the Christian wedding vows, we echo Scripture as, in the presence of our family and friends and in the sight of God, we vow to "be faithful . . . forsaking all others." When a husband or a wife breaks that vow, their partner (and their children, if they have any) face a terrible sense of betrayal.

Be wise

An affair is not usually premeditated. Catherine, a married woman who felt herself being drawn towards a relationship with another man, spoke to us of her experiences. She was taken by surprise by the suddenness and strength of her emotions. Because the attraction was not sexual, it felt "pure and good" to her, at least initially. She had been married for seven years when she found herself strongly attracted to Rob, a colleague at work. She struggled privately with her feelings for six weeks.

Then one evening she went out with a group from work, including Rob. After a few drinks she found herself telling him about her feelings. He was keen to pursue the relationship. For Catherine, the draw was the sense of closeness to a man who listened to her and seemed to understand her. His desire was for a sexual relationship with a woman he found attractive.

Catherine told us that two realizations saved her from starting an affair. The first came through a Christian book on marriage, which enabled her to distinguish between the initial attraction, for which she was not responsible, and the choice to pursue those thoughts, for which she was.

The second realization was that she was not strong enough to deal with the temptation on her own. She cried out to God, asking for his forgiveness and help. She then confided in an older woman whom she could trust, seeking her support and advice. Having poured out her inner turmoil, she felt no longer alone in the struggle and could see the issues much more clearly. Catherine then determined to put boundaries in place to avoid being unfaithful. As her work forced her together with Rob, she was prepared to change jobs if necessary, although, as it happened, he was transferred to another office.

Meanwhile, as she had kept these thoughts secret from her husband, Simon, a distance had grown between them. He had felt her shutting down deep communication without knowing why. Having started to take action to prevent an affair, Catherine felt able to tell him the reason for the change in her. She then asked for his forgiveness.

Since bringing it out into the open, Catherine has determined to focus her thoughts on her husband and on all that is good about their marriage. Simon has taken more care to listen to her and to encourage and affirm her. Not only has their marriage been saved, but they have also grown closer as a result of this near-crisis. Indeed, friends who knew nothing of these events have commented spontaneously that they look like a couple who have just fallen in love.

Invest time and energy into the marriage relationship

Almost always, the root cause of an affair is a lack of intimacy in the marriage. For a while at least, the affair meets a dissatisfied husband's or wife's longing for attention, respect, affection, or excitement. The best protection against unfaithfulness is therefore to take care of your marriage so that your relationship grows in strength, closeness, and depth. Charlotte, mother of two and a banker in the City of London, describes what can happen:

Although I didn't realise it at the time, when I married John my attitude to him changed and I began to take him for granted. He'd been looking forward to the togetherness of marriage but I still wanted to be a girl about town–so I'd go out playing all the time, safe in the knowledge that I had my husband's support at home. We carried on leading separate but perfectly happy lives until we had our first child. I adored being a mother but I still tried to go out as much as I could. That's when things went badly wrong between John and me, because we just didn't have time for each other any more. I never stopped loving John but I became more and more irritable and bad-tempered with him. I had no idea he was becoming less and less enamoured with *me* but the resentment was building up and by the time our second child was born he was having an affair.[2]

By failing to work at their relationship, Charlotte and John grew apart. They had failed to grow roots that intertwined.

If you do not spend time together, do not have fun as a couple, do not communicate deeply, do not make love, do not resolve your hurts, your relationship will have a weak foundation. And if your love is only surface deep, you will be more prone to temptation, more critical, less understanding, less forgiving. You may struggle to accept the changes brought about by age or the arrival of children. You may idealize other people's relationships and fantasize about other men or women. Like a rootless tree, you will not withstand the storms.

And you also miss your opportunity. Joy is not found in a new and shallow relationship, not in hotel rooms with false names, nor on guilty getaways. Real joy is found in "the beauty of those hands, recognising the sound of the footsteps on the pathway or looking at the face which you can read down to the last milli-metre of muscle movement."[3]

Set boundaries

Infidelity starts or stops in the mind. This was true for King David. It was true for Catherine. It has been true for everyone down the ages irrespective of age, culture, or gender. You cannot always prevent yourself from being attracted to someone, but you can decide whether or not to control such thoughts. For the sake of your marriage, these thoughts must be put out of your minds before they are allowed to become habitual. Jesus' teaching sets in place boundaries that protect our hearts and our minds:

> You have heard that it was said, "You shall not commit adultery." But I tell you that anyone who looks at a woman lustfully has already committed adultery with her in his heart.
>
> (Matthew 5:27–28)

Jesus' point applies equally to a woman thinking lustfully about a man. When we are aware of a growing attraction, we have to determine not to spend time alone with the person concerned or sometimes not to see them at all. An invitation to have lunch alone together has to be refused. Saying no early on can avoid many problems later.

Many affairs begin not with immediate sexual attraction but through intimate conversation. When a person of the opposite sex allows you into the private world of their thoughts and emotions, a dangerous (and alluring) closeness is created. As you are drawn farther in, you may start to feel better understood or more needed by them than by your husband or wife. If you ever sense that you may have (even slightly) overstepped this boundary, the best course of action is to tell your husband or wife as soon as possible about the contents of the conversation.

Talk to someone about the feelings

Where strong feelings have been allowed to develop or have taken you by surprise, talking to someone else will often rob them of their power over you. One couple told us that in their first year of marriage they both found themselves at different times strongly attracted to other people. The longer they kept their thoughts secret, the stronger the attraction became. Only when they confessed their feelings to each other did the bubble burst and the infatuation quickly die down. If talking to your husband or wife seems impossible, you need to find someone you trust and confide in them.

The longer unfaithfulness continues, the harder it becomes to turn back. People who have started down the road of infidelity often speak of the power of what they feel. They say that they have never before experienced such intense emotions for another person, and that these emotions seem authentic and good. They sometimes maintain that they feel alive for the first time and that this may be the only opportunity they have in their lifetime to experience such "love." They feel that they are being swept helplessly away to a future of freedom and happiness.

Such feelings are highly unreliable. A long-term perspective is needed: in due course this infatuation (like any other) will wear off, at which point their marriage partner will not seem so inadequate and they will frequently look back with deep regret on the marriage and family life they have abandoned. Although the ending of an affair may be the hardest decision they ever make, in years to come they will look back and see it as the best.

Take a firm stand

What should you do if you discover that your partner is having an affair? Are you required to forgive and to carry on loving in the hope of winning him or her back? Certainly, both forgiveness and love are essential. But that does not mean condoning a partner's behaviour when it is destructive to the marriage. There are times when to act most lovingly requires to be tough and to take a firm stand. Gary Chapman gives the following advice:

> Some things are not permissible in a marriage. When physical abuse, sexual unfaithfulness, sexual abuse of children, alcoholism, or drug addiction persist in a marriage, it is time to take loving action.[4]

Such attitudes and actions, if left unchecked, will destroy both of you and your marriage. Love requires you to forgive, but also at times to confront.

Lisa had never stood up to her husband Martin's bullying tactics. He always got his own way and she lost all confidence in herself. After eight years of marriage, she discovered that he was having an affair with a neighbor. He promised that he would break off the relationship for the sake of their marriage and three children. But on three further occasions she discovered that the affair was continuing. Each time he assured her that it would end. Finally, on the advice of a friend, she took action.

She told him that he had undermined the trust in their relationship and that he must move out. If he persisted in being unfaithful, the marriage would be over. If, however, he proved with his actions as well as his words that he wanted to come back, there was a chance that their marriage could be saved. For the first time in their marriage, Lisa stood up for what she knew to be right.

We met them when they had been separated for several months, by which time Martin was wanting to return home. His respect for Lisa had grown since she had drawn a line over his behavior. He realized that he could not have it all his own way. He had to make a choice between the affair and his family. Lisa's firm stance was more loving than her previous acquiescence because it gave the most hope for them to get back together and for their marriage to be restored.

Do not give up too quickly

Charlotte, the city banker we quoted earlier, did not give up hope of her husband, John, returning to her. Eventually he told her that the affair was finished and he agreed to come home. Charlotte explains:

> He made the commitment to stay, but it took another year for him to be happy at home and during that time he wouldn't touch me in bed, barely talked to me, seemed furious to be back and kept telling me he was still in love with this other woman.
>
> The summer after he came back I went on holiday with one son, leaving our other son with John. It was a wonderful holiday and I didn't ring John once. On the fifth day he rang me, though, saying how much he was missing us. That was the turning point. Two years exactly from the time he'd moved out, he came back to me.
>
> Slowly we began to rebuild our marriage.[5]

If either you or your partner are or have been engaged in an affair and are struggling to rebuild your marriage, it is important to recognize that it takes time for trust to be rebuilt. An unfaithful husband or wife cannot expect their partner to act as though nothing has happened. They will need to be sensitive and patient, understanding the range of emotions from anger to fear that their partner will probably go through. For some couples, seeking professional help will be important to process the strong emotions and to rebuild trust.

Forgiveness will often need to be a daily decision. One man, whose wife recently had an affair, told us that each time they have an argument, he thinks, "What right does she have to disagree after what she's done?" But he knows that forgiveness means not holding the past against her. He must allow her and their relationship a new start. Meanwhile his wife has had to learn how to be free from constant guilt through believing that both God and her husband have forgiven her past behavior and that this is a fresh beginning for their marriage.

Chapter 19

Keeping Sex Alive

Sexual union says truthfully, "I love you," and the message bears much repetition.[1]

Alan Storkey

A failure to address any one of the areas raised in this book can open a marriage to the risk of an affair, but a failure to develop your sexual relationship makes you especially vulnerable. Our sexual desires and responses are complex. Even the strongest marriages have their seasons when desire wanes and difficulties arise. Our encouragement is not to let this become long-term. If sexual intimacy is allowed to exit quietly from your marriage, your relationship will lose its special quality.

There are some couples who find sexual intercourse difficult or impossible because of a disability or a debilitating illness. But the sexual dimension of their relationship is still vital and there are means other than full sexual intercourse by which you can meet your partner's need to be loved and cherished in a sexually fulfilling way.

This section is not a comprehensive guide to every sexual difficulty. We will not be dealing with the painful area of sexual abuse or trauma from the past. Nor will we be looking at the consequences of infertility, miscarrying a child, or terminating a pregnancy. These may leave emotional scars, suppressed grief, nagging guilt, and feelings of fear or despair surrounding sex.

We would recommend talking in confidence to a doctor or church leader, who can then refer you for professional help if necessary. If you identify with one of the issues above, do not give up. We know many who, through a new discovery of the love and power of God, have found healing for their past and hope for the future.

Most marriages will be susceptible to difficulties at some time or another. Some couples remain stuck in a passionless rut, either because they do not know how to resolve the difficulty or because they have let it go on so long that they are no longer close enough to face it together. We have seen couples get out of the deepest ruts simply by facing their situation, talking together, and being willing to change.

What follows are five common reasons why the sexual relationship in a marriage can run into difficulties, fizzle out, or never get going. They can all be addressed and rectified.

Low self-esteem

Our self-esteem and our attitude to our body have a profound effect upon our sexual desires. In the Song of Songs, the "lover" and the "beloved" speak explicitly about the physical attributes that attract and captivate them (see Song of Songs 1:15–16; 4:1–7). The biblical perspective is a liberating acceptance of our own body and of our partner's body. God did not create us all with bodies like supermodels or athletes. He made each one of us unique, and there is infinite variety. Today, the media dictate to us what it means to be beautiful. The pressure to conform to a particular shape may be felt particularly keenly by women. According to one survey, over one third of adults in the UK said they have felt anxious or depressed about their body image.[2] However, we can choose to help ourselves and each other. We must not compare our partner's body or our own to the current fashion. For a woman especially, sexual enjoyment is profoundly affected by how she feels about herself. Poor body image and feeling self-conscious will short-circuit her ability to be aroused and to reach orgasm.

Each one of us can build up our husband's or wife's self-esteem through telling them on a regular basis how attractive and beautiful they are. (If we don't, they are likely to listen to someone else who will, and we open our marriage to the danger of an affair.) There needs to be an unspoken rule between us never to criticize or to have unreasonable expectations of each other's body.

At the same time, it is important to recognize that we need to continue *within marriage* to make an effort with our appearance for one another, as we did when we first went out together. Otherwise we can easily find ourselves in a vicious circle. We think, "My partner is not interested in how I look any more," or, "He never says how attractive he finds me," or, "These days she never tells me that I turn her on." And then we lose the confidence and the motivation to try to be attractive for each other any more: it is too awkward and it seems unnecessary.

But our partner was almost certainly physically attracted to us when we got married, and there is much we can do to make that continue. One husband, married for eighteen years, said, "What we did to get each other, we continue to do to keep each other. We try to be fit for one another."

His wife responded, 'That's true for everyday situations and then, if we're going out on a date, we amp it up. It's a core value for us.'

As you make love, verbally and physically, tenderly and passionately, you need to bring out the beauty inherent in each other. We have often noticed that when someone *knows* they are loved their beauty increases. An inner beauty shines out of them, and in subtle ways this can lead to a change in their physical appearance. Beauty grows in a culture of love.

Unresolved emotions

Sex should never be used as an alternative to resolving problems or conflicts. Unexpressed feelings, such as anxiety, mistrust, or resentment, all affect our sexual intimacy. Typically, a man may use sex as a temporary escape from pain or anger, whereas negative emotions will often cause a woman to withdraw and shut down.

Lack of desire for sex, or the inability to give ourselves a hundred percent, can be the result of unresolved hurt within the marriage, from previous sexual relationships or even from our upbringing. If necessary, refer to Chapter 12 again for the process of talking through ways you have hurt each other, and to Chapter 15 for ways of addressing pain from childhood. Many couples have spoken to us of the benefit to their lovemaking when they have faced these issues together. New energy is released and a new level of intimacy is experienced.

Physical problems

There are a variety of common physical problems that a couple may encounter, such as a failure to reach orgasm, dispareunia (painful sex), early or delayed ejaculation, or erectile dysfunction (failing to get or keep an erection). These are not hopeless conditions, and sexual difficulties can usually be resolved with the right help and information from a doctor, a specialist, counselor, or even a good book.

One such book, written from a medical and a Christian perspective, is *Seasons of Sex and Intimacy: For a Husband and Wife in Marriage* by Emma Waring.[3] As well as general advice on how to develop the sexual relationship, the book contains detailed descriptions of ways to help each other through sexual difficulties. One of her core messages is that, in order to nurture lifelong desire and work through any sexual problems we come up against, we have to work together as a team, nurturing open and honest communication and emotional connection, and committing to making our marriage our highest priority.

Tiredness

Tiredness is probably the most common factor that disrupts a couple's sex life. This can happen at any stage of a marriage, whether in the early months, a few years on when children arrive, or as a career becomes increasingly demanding. Whatever the pressure, physical and mental exhaustion usually result in our sex lives being the first casualty. The neglect can be imperceptible at first, but, if allowed to become a pattern, sex can all too easily become non-existent.

Tiredness often means that the easiest thing to do in the evenings is to flop down in front of one or more screens and cease to communicate either verbally or physically.

There is no easy remedy. Being aware of the danger to your sexual relationship is half the battle. Some changes in your lifestyle can also help. Strangely enough, more exercise can make you less tired. Many of us do little or none. We sit in the car or at a desk or at home all day. Exercise is beneficial to your health in every way (unless it becomes obsessive), and especially to your enjoyment of sex. You feel more energized. It is worth finding a form of exercise that works well for you, maybe an online exercize class you do in your home, perhaps twenty minutes of fast walking a day or cycling to work.

For others, clearer boundaries have to be made concerning work and home time. Creating times of relaxation and romance together and planning a weekly date will help to prevent exhaustion.

In the long term, despite feeling tired, less sleep than you might like, or think you need, is worth the sacrifice if it means that this essential dimension of your marriage remains alive and active.

Adjustment and change after childbirth

During pregnancy and around childbirth a woman is at her most vulnerable. Inevitably there is a dramatic change in a couple's lovemaking. A husband needs to be at his most sensitive, caring, and protective. There *is* life after birth (sexually), but unselfish love and understanding are required from both husband and wife.

A husband must appreciate fully the physical changes that occur for his wife before, during, and after giving birth. He can then show the necessary tenderness and be guided by her as to when they can resume lovemaking. The change in shape of the vagina, the tendency for it to be less well lubricated, and the possible scarring caused by tearing all need to be taken into account.

A husband has a delicate road to walk between the two extremes of being over-anxious about touching his wife for fear of hurting her and being over-enthusiastic to resume their sexual relationship before she has healed physically.

Each couple must work out what is right for them. This requires openness and honesty, particularly by the wife as she explains how she is feeling physically and emotionally. Breastfeeding and the accompanying tiredness affect a woman's libido. Don't despair! The hormones can take many months to return to more normal levels. Time and more sleep bring healing, and desire will usually return. In addition, pelvic floor exercises help to ensure that a woman continues to enjoy fulfilling orgasm. (There are helpful websites with more details on these.[4])

In the short term, a new mother will often go off sex as she bonds with and nurtures her new baby. This is natural. What is unnatural is when this is used as an excuse for continuing to be "off sex" for many months or even a year. A wife has to understand the difficulty her husband experiences as he sees her role change from being wife and lover to wife and mother. Her breasts, which have been a source of pleasure only for him, are now apparently monopolized by someone else. A wife needs to help her husband to adjust to the new situation and to recapture his image of her as a sexual being.

The more involved a husband and wife are together with the baby they have created, taking joint responsibility and both learning as they go along, the closer and more attracted they will feel to each other. If the husband carries on as though nothing has changed, isolation and separation can easily set in. For a wife, the most desirable husband is one who is with her in the whole experience. She sees him in a new light, and that creates intimacy and sexual attraction. More than at any other time, a couple must realize what it means to give themselves to each other in caring, cherishing ways. It is not unusual for a woman to take a year before she feels normal about sex again.

Finally, you need to be careful about having a child with you in your bed. Patterns are hard to change in young children, and trying to do so with a child of eighteen months can be traumatic for everybody. A child in your bed will seriously damage your sex life! Our suggestion is not to let a habit develop in the first place. This will not interfere with the important bonding process between the parents and their baby.

The birth of a child should not lead to a decline in sexual enjoyment—indeed, quite the reverse—as a couple take in the miracle of creating a new life through their lovemaking.

Even if you are doing [everything you can] to stop another miracle happening just yet, that feeling remains: the miracle of Life trying to happen. And the extraordinary fact is that sex is actually better—if different—on the far side of childbirth. Men and women who understand this stay together. The ones who don't–the women who cool off entirely, or grant themselves grudgingly as a favour, the men who see no difference and grumble at the roundedness and tiredness of the maternal woman–are most likely to fall into the miserable chaos of affairs and estrangements. Take your pick. Be prepared to accept change, as spring turns to summer and later to autumn. As in so many areas of family life, you can't have everything; but you can, with patience and humour, get a great deal of it.[5]

Section 7–Good sex

Conclusion

Our culture bombards us with much misinformation about sex. "Do it with lots of different partners; you will become a more mature person and a better lover." "Sex is just one way of enjoying yourself. If it feels good, do it!" "If you love each other, have sex. There's no need to wait until you're married."

And then there are the lies about sex within marriage. "Marry someone you're physically attracted to and sex will be instantaneously wonderful." "Don't expect to be sexually fulfilled with one man or woman your whole life. Experiment! Fantasize! Flirt with others! Be realistic. Sex always peters out in a long-term relationship."

It is easy to be deceived and confused. The truth is that God gives us sex as a gift of love. Countless thousands of couples have discovered that the best sex is experienced within a loving marriage. Such sex goes way beyond physical gratification. It creates a deep emotional, psychological, and even spiritual bond, which has the power to communicate love in a way that transcends words. Our sexual relationship can express our love for each other tenderly, regularly, and passionately over years of married life.

When wrongly used, sex has the power to plunge us into the depths of pain and isolation; but, when rightly used, it can lift us up to the heights of togetherness and ecstatic joy.

Seventh golden rule of marriage
Do not neglect sexual intimacy.

Section 8

Epilogue

Chapter 20

The Opportunity of a Lifetime

A cord of three strands is not quickly broken.

Ecclesiastes 4:12

An elderly couple were celebrating their platinum wedding. A radio reporter was sent to cover the story and did his best to make the old man (who was very deaf) understand his questions. "Seventy years is a long time," he shouted in the old man's ear. "Have you ever contemplated divorce?"

The old man toyed with the question. Then he replied, "Divorce? No, I can't say I have. Mind you, I've considered murder, several times!"[1]

The secret of a long and happy marriage is found, in the words of the psalmist, where "Love and faithfulness meet together" (Psalm 85:10). You will, we hope, know couples who have been married for twenty-five years or more, whose lives have been woven together into an intricate interdependence. Over the years, they have developed a deep understanding of each other's needs and desires; their love has matured and grown steady with the passage of time; together they have weathered the storms of life's disappointments and tragedies; they appreciate each other's strengths and accept each other's weaknesses; they have learned to apologize for their own acts of selfishness and to forgive each other's; if they have children, they have supported one another through the physical strain of parenting young children and the emotional exhaustion of guiding teenagers; they now relish the new opportunities of togetherness presented by the "empty nest."

In such a marriage, love and faithfulness have met together, and it was for this that God gave marriage to be a great blessing to humankind. Indeed, this is the potential for your marriage and ours. For we have been created for love by the God who is love. We are capable of friendship, companionship, romantic love, and sexual love. We were created to feel loved and to give love. Besides this, we have been created for faithfulness by the God who keeps his promises. We are capable of commitment and are able to choose honesty and loyalty.

Again, in her book *Becoming*, Michelle Obama writes about her own marriage and the significance and the effect of the commitment she and Barack made to each other:

> It sounds a little like a bad joke, doesn't it? What happens when a solitude-loving individualist marries an outgoing family woman who does not love solitude one bit?

Love with faithfulness is the most powerful force for good in the world, and God planned it to be at the heart of the marriage relationship. Despite his own failings in this area, Martin Luther King recognized that this kind of love "is the most durable force in the world. It is the key that unlocks the door to ultimate reality."[3]

Many people are asking why marriage is in such trouble today. The overwhelming reason is that love and faithfulness have been torn apart. Commitment has gone out of fashion. Love *without* faithfulness is fickle, damaging and painful–it is at best no more than a physical infatuation that departs as randomly as it arrived, evaporating like the dew.

Behind all the humor (and despite the various weddings), the climax of the film *Four Weddings and a Funeral* is an accurate reflection of our Western society's fear of commitment. Early on in the film, the main character, Charles, begins his speech at his best friend's wedding, "I am, of course, in bewildered awe of anyone who can make a commitment like this." The film concludes with him making a somewhat lame non-proposal to the heroine, Carrie. The final pictures create the impression that they then lived happily ever after.[4]

The problem is that, in real life, close relationships are built on commitment. Tom Marshall, in his book *Right Relationships*, says, "because intimacy produces vulnerability it requires commitment for its security . . . The tragedy today is that people are so hungry for intimacy yet so afraid of commitment that they seek intimacy in uncommitted relationships and time and again reap devastating hurt."[5]

Marriage, in biblical terms, is a covenant in which a man and a woman make binding promises to each other. Some couples who cohabit assert, perhaps correctly, that they are more committed to each other than some married couples they know. Certainly, being committed eighty percent is better than being committed sixty percent. But that is not the point. Marriage is about a hundred percent commitment to each other, knowing that your husband or wife is not going to walk out if the disagreement is too serious or the lovemaking not good enough. That is the only way for real trust to be built.

Within such a covenant there is safe ground on which to build a strong and intimate marriage. Without such commitment, each partner inevitably holds back for fear of disappointment. Commitment provides security and trust: there is no issue that will not be faced and worked through.

Faithful love requires you to go against the contemporary culture. The long-term building of relationships carries a higher cost than the short-term fulfillment of your desires. For some couples, the first year, even the honeymoon, is agony. Each day the painful adjustments tempt them to look back over their shoulder, questioning their decision. Mike Mason paints a realistic picture of what is involved:

> A marriage . . . may be compared to a great tree growing right up through the centre of one's living room. It is something that is just there, and it is huge, and everything has to be built around it, and wherever one happens to be going–to the fridge, to bed, to the bathroom, or out of the front door–the tree has to be taken into account. It cannot be gone through; it must respectfully be gone around. It is somehow bigger and stronger than oneself. True, it could be chopped down, but not without tearing the house apart. And certainly it is beautiful, unique, exotic; but also, let's face it, it is at times an enormous inconvenience.[6]

Faithfull love means that you must be prepared to change and adapt yourselves to each other. A father whose daughter played the violin spotted an expensive instrument in a junk shop at a very cheap price. He was delighted–until he discovered that the tuning knobs were immovable. Someone had glued them in place. But, of course, the violin had not stayed in tune. Tuning up is an essential routine for every musician. So it is in marriage. There needs to be frequent adjustments.

For many people, the most significant achievement of their

lives will be the building of a loving marriage. Their children will benefit from the security of a loving and stable home. Their friends will enjoy the overflow and warmth of their love. Their society will be the stronger and healthier for their contribution. Barbara Bush, former First Lady of the United States, said in her address to students graduating from Wellesley College:

> As important as your obligations as a doctor, lawyer or business leader will be, you are a human being first, and those human connections–with a husband or wife, with children, with friends–are the most important investments you will ever make. At the end of your life, you will never regret not having passed one more exam, not winning one more verdict, or not closing one more deal. But you will regret time not spent with a husband or wife, a child, a friend, or a parent . . . Our success as a society depends not on what happens in the White House, but on what happens inside your house.[7]

Building a strong marriage not only yields the highest rewards but also fulfills a noble and holy place in the purposes of God. Dietrich Bonhoeffer, the German pastor executed during the Second World War for his opposition to the Third Reich, wrote a letter from prison to his niece on the eve of her wedding:

> Marriage is more than your love for each other. It has a higher dignity and power for it is God's holy ordinance through which he wills to perpetuate the human race until the end of time. In your love you see only your two selves in the world, but in your marriage you are a link in the chain of the generations, which God causes to come and to pass away to his glory, and calls into his kingdom. In your love you see only the heaven of your happiness, but in marriage you are placed at a post of responsibility towards

the world and mankind. Your love is your own private possession, but marriage is more than something personal—it is a status, an office.[8]

The Bible sees marriage as a commitment to give your life away out of love for another person, "just as Christ loved the church and gave himself up for her" (Ephesians 5:25). His example of loving us is our model for loving our husband or wife.

> When we get married we are giving ourselves away lock, stock and barrel to each other. Making love, which is the central act of marriage, is simply another form of giving ourselves away. The total abandonment of it all is the nearest thing this side of heaven to the spiritual ecstasy and intimacy we will one day have with God. *That* is how Christ loved us. He lavished himself upon us and gave himself completely. There was no holding back.[9]

On your wedding day, the two strands of your separate lives are knotted together, and during your marriage those strands wrap themselves around each other, twisting together into oneness. But how can they be held together in harmony without unravelling, fraying, or even breaking? What are you to do in the harsh reality of day-to-day life when love seems to run out or dry up? What if you can't find the resources or the will to go on loving your husband or wife? Are there any answers?

We believe that the only certain answer lies outside ourselves: "A cord of three strands is not quickly broken," says the writer of Ecclesiastes in the Old Testament (Ecclesiastes 4:12). There is a third strand, a third person in the relationship. This is Jesus Christ, who nourishes the marriage from its core, so that we need not lean on human willpower alone. He is the invisible strand who turns the twofold twist of human relationship into the strong threefold cord, woven together by the hands of God.

> O Lord, make me an instrument of thy peace;
> Where there is hatred, let me sow love;
> Where there is injury, pardon;
> Where there is discord, union;
> Where there is doubt, faith;
> Where there is despair, hope;
> Where there is darkness, light;
> Where there is sadness, joy.
> Grant that we may not seek so much to be consoled as
>   to console;
> To be understood, as to understand;
> To be loved, as to love.
> For it is in giving that we receive,
> It is in pardoning that we are pardoned;
> And it is in dying that we are born to eternal life.
>
> *The Prayer of St. Francis of Assisi*
> *(1182–1226)*

Appendix 1

Ready for Marriage?

How do we know that we are right for each other? What happens if we are not compatible? Is it normal to have doubts? Do we have a realistic view of married life? When you are contemplating marriage, these may well be some of the questions you are asking yourselves. Such questions must be faced honestly.

In this appendix we list *seven tests of love* which are designed to reveal whether you have the foundations upon which to build a strong marriage.[1] These tests will show not only whether you are right for each other but also whether you are ready for marriage. Marriage must be based on more than infatuation. Feelings of "in loveness" will not sustain a marriage for a lifetime. Infatuation wears off, but these following seven aspects of love can grow stronger over the years.

Test 1: Do I want to share the rest of my life with this person?

Marriage is about two individual people, who have been leading individual lives, coming together and sharing everything. Does the thought of doing so fill me with excitement or uncertainty?

Marriage does not allow you to remain as two independent people living in the same house, using the same bed, and spending a lot more time together. Marriage means being ready to share your whole life with another person.

Am I ready to share my time? I have been used to organizing my own agenda in my own way. Now we will need to work out *our* agenda together. Marriage does not mean spending every minute together, but it does mean always taking each other into account when you make your plans.

Am I ready to share my money? Could I honestly say, "Whatever is mine will become ours"? In marriage there is nothing that remains yours alone, for both of you promise that "all my worldly goods with you I share." Every possession I have, large or small, valuable or sentimental, is to be shared with the other person. Am I ready for that?

Test 2: Does our love give me energy and strength, or does it drain me?

If the relationship is healthy, you will feel more alive when you are together and more motivated to live to your full potential. The other person's love should set you free to be the person you were created to be. Marriage (contrary to many people's perception) can be liberating. The experience of a strong marriage is of living a life that is renewed by another's love.

Your closest friends or family are often the people who recognize most accurately the effect of the relationship on you. If you bring out the best in each other, other people want to be around you. Does being together make each of you more rather than less of a person?

This second test reveals whether your love motivates and inspires you. For some couples, the sheer effort involved in keeping the relationship going drains them and causes them to feel trapped. That is not a healthy basis for marriage. They may have been going out with their partner for some time and are afraid of hurting them by breaking off the relationship. But it is better to break up sooner rather than later if the relationship has no long-term future

Test 3: Do I respect this person?

There will be different aspects that attracted you to each other. Respect, however, goes deeper than mere attraction.

Do you respect this person's character? You discover someone's character by seeing the way they relate to others: how they
treat older people, younger people, their family, their peers, and
those from a different background, culture, or race. Do they
show compassion, courage, perseverance, patience, consistency,
and any other qualities you value highly? They may be stun-
ningly good-looking, have a high-powered job, be a brilliant
cook, or an outstanding athlete, but are they kind? (If in doubt,
watch the way they treat their parents, or an elderly relative.) Do
you respect their judgment? What about the decisions they make,
big or little, about career, money, or family?

"If we had a bet on
the 2.45 at Ascot —
we could double our
honeymoon budget"

Are you compatible in your core beliefs and values? It would be
unwise to marry someone with strongly opposing views on those
things you hold most dear. For example, do you agree on matters
of faith, ethical issues, education, children? To find out that your
partner does not want children can be a very painful discovery
with implications for the rest of your life.

If you are a Christian, the Bible's injunction not to "be yoked
together with unbelievers" (2 Corinthians 6:14) is important for

those considering marriage. Does this person want to follow and serve God wholeheartedly in every aspect of their life? Does he or she look to God as the one who has a plan and purpose for their life (and therefore for your life together)?

Can you say to myself, "I would be proud to be attached to this person"? A telling question to ask is, "Would I like this person to be the mother or father of my child?"

Test 4: Do I accept this person as they are?

None of us is perfect. We all have our weaknesses, quirks, and bad habits. What annoys you about this person? You need to be sure that you could live together and love each other even if none of these things were to change.

You must not get married on the installment plan, hoping to change this or that about our partner once married. You will usually be disappointed.

Addictive behavior, such as with alcohol, drugs, gambling, or pornography, will often require professional help and should be addressed prior to marriage, because getting married will not in itself solve these addictions.

Test 5: Are you able to admit your mistakes, apologize, and forgive one another?

Conflicting ideas and negative feelings are an inevitable part of any close relationship. Bestselling author, John Gray, writes "Some people fight all the time, and gradually their love dies. Others suppress their honest feelings in order to avoid conflict and argument. As a result of suppressing their true feelings they lose touch with their loving feelings as well. One couple is having a war, the other is having a cold war."[2]

Neither of these approaches works. When you hurt one another, you need to be able to bring it out into the open, let go of your pride, say I'm sorry, and forgive. This requires good communication. Have we, as a couple, settled disagreements between us in a constructive way? The point of this test is not the existence or absence of conflict but your ability to resolve it.

Test 6: Do you have interests in common as a foundation for friendship?

Do you have fun together? Friendships are built on shared experiences. Shared activities lead to shared confidences and shared memories. Have you found interests that you both enjoy? Do you derive pleasure from doing things together? Marriage does not involve sharing every interest, but it will be important to continue with those you currently share and to go on looking for other joint activities once married, to keep your friendship growing.

Test 7: Have you weathered all the seasons and a variety of situations together?

Have you seen each other through a summer and a winter—in shorts as well as in an overcoat? Or have you only seen each other with washed hair and ready to go out? Do you know the whole person? Have you known each other not only when things are going well but also when times are difficult? How do you each respond under stress or in a crisis?

Some people rush into marriage because they have been hurt by a previous relationship or a tragedy in their life. Getting married as an escape from pain is an insecure foundation for any relationship. Only sufficient time together will reveal the real person. As someone has said, "Love is what you've been through with somebody."

Some people can answer yes to all seven tests yet struggle to make the commitment to marriage because in their past someone they trusted let them down. Their parents' marriage may have been abusive; their father or mother may have left the family home when they were at an impressionable age; they may have suffered through the breakdown of a previous relationship that they had hoped would last for life.

The first step in overcoming a fear of commitment is to recognize its source. Talking about it with a trusted friend, church leader, or counselor helps. (It is generally better to discuss doubts about your relationship with someone other than your partner.)

The second step is to forgive those who have hurt us. (If this is a parent, use the prayer on page 243 as a basis.) When you choose to forgive as an ongoing decision process each time the pain, anger, or disappointment resurfaces, gradually the memories have less and less hold on us. For many, however, their fear of commitment is ultimately resolved only through knowing the faithfulness of their partner, through growing in trust, and through being part of a loving marriage first hand.

We have happily married friends who could have answered yes to all seven tests but on their wedding day were still wrestling with hesitation and doubts. It takes courage to tie the knot and to say words that will affect the rest of your lives.

We know others who have been brave enough to break off an engagement within a few weeks or even days of their wedding. Some have subsequently got married to someone else; others have remained single. They have not regretted their decision. Better by far to be single and independent, using your freedom to serve God and to reach your full potential in him, developing many friendships along the way, than to suffer the consequences of an ill-chosen husband or wife.

Appendix 2

Engagement, Sex, and the Honeymoon

Engagement

Engagement is a time of preparation, not just for the wedding, but for marriage. It is a time to develop your friendship, to understand more about one another, and, above all, to discover the expectations that each of you brings to married life. We hope that discussing the contents of this book will help. Some tension and misunderstandings are common, and the wedding plans often act as the catalyst. Learning to resolve disagreements is a valuable part of the preparation.

Sexual boundaries during engagement

Engagement can also be a time of learning to control your physical desires. God's plan is that the moment of giving ourselves to each other sexually follows the commitment you have made in your wedding vows. Mike Mason writes of the act of intercourse:

> As a gesture symbolic of perfect trust and surrender, it requires a setting or structure of perfect surrender in which to take place. It requires the security of the most perfect of reassurances and

commitments into which two people can enter, which is no other than the loving contract of marriage.[1]

Some maintain that you must discover whether you are sexually compatible before marriage. But living together on a trial basis is not a fair test.

The reason for this is that a sexual relationship makes you vulnerable. Such vulnerability requires trust, and this trust is built within the safety of the marriage vows. Within a relationship of total commitment you are truly free to give yourselves unreservedly to each other. It is not sexual experience, physical endowment, or the right chemistry that matter; rather it is committed, self-sacrificing love that produces the best sex.

The refrain in the Song of Songs, repeated three times, recognizes this need to keep physical desire in check until the right moment arrives to give yourselves to each other: "Daughters of Jerusalem, I charge you . . . do not arouse or awaken love until it so desires" (Song of Songs 2:7; 3:5; 8:4). Because of the power of sexual desire, you have a responsibility to each other not to "arouse" or "awaken" each other beyond the limits of your self-control.

We discovered a lot about the value of sexual boundaries in the four years that we were together before getting married.

Nicky
After we had known each other for sixteen months we were deeply in love, deeply committed to each other, and it seemed natural to start sleeping together.

Sila
I was eighteen, I was independent, and I loved Nicky as much as I could imagine ever loving anybody. In retrospect I recognize that

our relationship took on an intensity when we started sleeping together. In early 1974, when Nicky and I started discussing Christianity, I had no real understanding of the implications for our relationship.

Nicky

Gradually, as I started to consider and explore the Christian faith, I understood that if I were to commit my life to Jesus Christ it would mean not sleeping together again before marriage. That produced a fear that we might then start to drift apart. As a result, I kept my thoughts on this subject from Sila for as long as I could.

At the point where I knew I had to make a decision one way or the other, I remember writing down a sort of prayer: "God, I think you are there. I think I believe that Jesus Christ is the Son of God and that he rose from the dead, and therefore I need to make a commitment to you. But I don't have the strength to do so unless you convince Sila as well."

Sila

When I heard David MacInnes talk about Jesus Christ, he spoke as if he knew him personally–like I knew Nicky. This was a revelation to me. Gradually I began to see that, if I embraced the Christian faith, this would change areas of my life, including our sexual relationship. It was not that anybody had told us. It was a gradual realization that culminated in a clear conviction of the best way for us both. The evening we committed our lives to going God's way we knew that we had to wait until marriage before we made love to each other again.

Nicky

We discovered over the following weeks that the close intimacy of sleeping in the same bed without making love was too difficult for us, so I slept on the floor. Some months later we realized we would find it easier not even to sleep in the same room. We had come to see that this degree of intimacy is best kept for marriage.

Sila

It certainly wasn't easy putting in some boundaries for ourselves, but, over the next two and a half years, until we got married, we discovered our fears were unfounded. Far from drifting apart, we experienced a new freedom as other parts of our relationship had a chance to develop that had previously been overshadowed by the focus on our sexual relationship. We got to know each other in a much more well-rounded way—we found out more about each other's character, each other's opinions, and each other's interests. We started to learn to distinguish between lust and love and we also started to learn how to be more caring and thoughtful towards each other, which were all really important things to learn for when we got married, and they continue to be important in our marriage now.

Nicky

We know many couples who have decided to keep sex for marriage or (like us) to have a period of abstinence from sex prior to getting married. They've talked to us of how it helped to mark their wedding day as a new start together, as a memorable new beginning, a watershed moment in their lives—as they gave themselves to each other in their vows and then in their sexual relationship.

We also learned the need to help each other. It is easy to play a game that involves one of us arousing the other in order to get them to do something to us that arouses us that then causes us to do something to them . . . and so on. And if we go further than we had intended, "It's not *my* fault, because *you* led me on!" We came to recognize that we both needed to take responsibility to help each other.

We have put below some practical tips that we and other couples who have sought to keep sex for marriage have found helpful:

- Recognize what each of you finds particularly arousing, whether through sight, words, or touch. In general, men are quickly excited through sight, while women are stimulated through emotional intimacy. (These differences are also important to recognize *within* marriage when we deliberately seek to arouse each other.)

- Try not to put yourselves in situations where you could go to bed together with no fear of being disturbed or discovered. For example, to stay the night alone in a house or to go on a getaway with just the two of you will for many couples produce more temptation than they are able to resist. Go with other friends. Chaperones may sound old-fashioned, but they are peculiarly effective!

- We would strongly suggest not sleeping in the same bed, even if you have decided not to make love. That level of intimacy naturally leads to intercourse. Couples who have put themselves in situations that require enormous self-restraint find that this can easily lead to feelings of guilt about sex *within* marriage. One couple who regularly slept in the same bed worked so hard to restrain themselves before marriage that once married they had great difficulty letting go.
- In terms of how far to go physically before marriage, each couple will need to work out their own boundaries. Our own limits included aiming not to lie down together and avoiding being naked or partially naked together. Such disclosure should rightly be kept for the marriage night.

Practicing such restraint is hard, but you will retain the wonderful anticipation of giving yourselves to each other at the most perfect moment. A friend of ours wrote:

Before I became a Christian, I had been to a lot of weddings. Like Charles in *Four Weddings and a Funeral*, I found that hardly a Saturday passed without one. They were generally heart-warming affairs full of beautiful dresses, kind words, and good wine. However, I will never forget the first wedding I went to where I knew for certain that the wedding day marked the beginning of the couple's sexual relationship. There was something different in the air: a perceptible lightness, a feeling of awe, a sense of fragility, preciousness, and purity. The look in their eyes as they made their vows is a look I will describe to my children.

Your past sexual history

God's intention for all of us us is that both husband and wife are virgins when they marry. We have already spoken of the reasons for celibacy. But if, owing to past sexual experiences, there is pain, guilt, jealousy, or unforgiveness, these emotions need to be addressed before going into marriage.

A previous sexual relationship, whether secret or not, can tarnish your marriage. Far from providing helpful experience, it can give rise to mistrust, jealousy, and destructive memories. The Christian answer is to bring your sexual past to God and to ask for his forgiveness and cleansing for the mistakes you have made.

We would suggest revealing past sexual relationships to your fiancé(e) and asking for his or her forgiveness. Your do not need to go into details, as these will be hurtful and may cause further harm. God can then bring healing and the freedom and joy of a new start.

You may be afraid of hurting your fiancé(e), but secrets are dangerous in marriage. When secrets suddenly come to light later in the relationship, much more hurt and damage can be caused. If you are worried about how to tell each other, find a church leader or counselor who is able to help. Courage may well be required, but such confessions will ensure that your future together is firmly based on a foundation of trust, openness, and forgiveness.

It would be wise to ask advice before talking about areas such as abortion, addiction, pornography, prostitution, cross-dressing, or homosexual experiences. Find someone who understands such issues. This could start a process for dealing with the past that may take months or even years, in which case each other's support will be essential.

Some couples feel guilty about having gone farther in their physical relationship with each other than they intended before marriage. Their sexual desires have got ten out of control and one of them has led the other on to arousal against their true wishes. These regrets can be brought to God and to one another for forgiveness and restoration. As we come openly and honestly to God, his promise to us is that "if anyone is in Christ, the new creation has come: the old has gone, the new is here!" (2 Corinthians 5:17). Wonderfully, you can then enter marriage knowing a freedom from your past.

The honeymoon

Be prepared

We suggest that a month or so before your wedding you both read a good book on sex (see the "Recommended further reading" section at the back of this book) so as to be well informed. Once married, try going through such a book together. This will make it easier to start discussing your sex life openly (with each other!). It will also stand you in good stead should you encounter problems later on. Every lifelong relationship will have some periods when things don't go so well. Many men will experience a degree of impotence at some stage, most often through stress, and many women will have a lower sexual desire when children arrive.

If there are any anxieties or unanswered questions, a doctor should be able to help. Or talk to a married friend you know and trust.

Be realistic

Recognize your need to recover from the heavy demands of your wedding day. Try to organize a honeymoon that will be the most relaxing you could imagine. It is probably not the moment to go overland to Antarctica, up the Amazon in a canoe, or to climb the Himalayas. The purpose of a honeymoon is to spend time relaxing, adjusting to and enjoying each other. Too much hard traveling or sightseeing defeats the purpose. This is not the moment to plan your vacation of a lifetime. Save that for a year or so into marriage; it will probably be a lot more fun then.

Don't expect too much too soon

The honeymoon is only the beginning of a lifelong discovery. Take a long view. With regard to sex, don't expect all your Christmases to come at once. This is a time for gentleness, tenderness, and patience. Keeping a sense of humor will help you to stay relaxed. Don't panic if things don't work out as they do in the films—i.e., instant, spontaneous, multi-orgasmic sex. It may well take some time for you to experience mutual or simultaneous orgasm.

Don't be afraid to talk about what gives pleasure and what doesn't, both during and after times of making love. This will deepen your understanding of how to arouse each other. At first this may seem awkward and unnatural, but communication is essential if your physical relationship is to develop. Any embarrassment will soon disappear.

Talk about your expectations

It is easy to have unrealistic and uncommunicated expectations of each other. You should not feel under pressure to make love the second you cross the threshold of the bedroom. But feel free to. Make sure you have discussed this moment so that you do not start your marriage with uncertainty and misunderstanding. Suddenly to have crossed the boundary from "not okay" to "okay" may seem strange and you may both react in different ways.

One husband told us that his wife of nine hours was so exhausted by the wedding that she fell asleep as soon as she got into bed, while he was still in the bathroom. He stayed awake all night deeply disappointed and thinking he had made a terrible mistake getting married at all. Things improved considerably when they talked about their different expectations the next day, and they went on to have a wonderful honeymoon.

Maintain a sense of humor

Honeymoons can be unpredictable. One couple told us that they got so badly sunburned on the first day of theirs that they could not touch each other all week. Thankfully, they saw the funny side of it. Another newlywed husband described how things did not go as planned on the first night:

> When we finally got to the hotel it was eleven o'clock at night. It looked smaller than it had appeared in the brochure and I felt my heart sink. Just about the only contribution I'd made to the wedding arrangements was to choose the hotel. The day had gone well and my wife was looking radiant. I so wanted the evening to be memorable. We found our room and it was lovely, and Jane smiled when she saw the chilled bottle of wine and roses on the bed. I began to relax; everything was going to be great.
>
> And it could have been. But to my horror I noticed that there wasn't a double bed but two singles. I quickly found the manager. "This is our honeymoon, and this is meant to be your honeymoon suite," I said.
>
> The manager was very apologetic but explained that due to an oversight another couple were in the honeymoon room and were well settled.
>
> "But there are single beds in here," I pleaded. At that point I should have argued and demanded my rights. But when the manager suggested a solution I went along with it as he said it had worked before.
>
> "I'll send you up some rope," he said, "and you can tie the beds together."
>
> "Send it up fast!" I exclaimed.
>
> And so on the night I'd waited twenty-eight years for, the night I'd long dreamed of, I was giving it my best effort when the beds parted. Jane and I both crashed to the floor. I looked up at the ceiling and wanted to die, but just then Jane leant over and whispered into my ear, "Darling . . . I think I felt the earth move."[2]

Appendix 3

Working Out a Budget

According to a survey by the Marriage Guidance Service, Relate, most arguments about money come down to spending priorities. If money causes problems in your marriage, it will be beneficial to make an agreed plan of how, as a couple or family, you are going to use it. A budget is, of course, no magic formula, but the very process of working it out together has a number of benefits. The first is that your true financial position becomes clear to both of you. Second, you have to discuss how you are going to spend your money. Third, when you have allocated an amount for each area of your expenditure, you are both free to choose what you buy within a set limit.

Like any other area of potential conflict, money can either be an issue that comes between you and affects your whole relationship or a problem that you work at together, drawing you closer to each other in the process.

Working out a budget can remove the fear of feeling out of control, the guilt attached to reckless spending, and the conflict arising from mutual blame where there is a shortfall. We know of marriages that have been transformed from acrimony to harmony through discussion and decisions about finances.

If money is a source of tension, we recommend the following three steps. (They sound very obvious and straightforward, but it is amazing how few couples ever sit down and work these things out together.)

Discover your true financial position

Work out how much you own or owe
Find a time when you are not tired or distracted and are unlikely to be disturbed. Then collect bank statements, unpaid bills, savings accounts, credit card statements, and so on. Being honest with each other if you have overspent and are in debt can be hard, but it will be well worth it. Anxiety about money can easily become a dark secret. When fears are out in the open they lose much of their power over us.

Be gentle with each other–none of us gets it entirely right. If you find you are in debt, part of your discussion will need to be about how you can get out of it. Do not be afraid or embarrassed about seeking help from people with experience. The sooner the problem is faced, the more easily it can be solved.

Calculate your income
In order to plan your spending you need to know how much money is coming in and where it is going out. The simpler part is working out your joint income. You need to write down all sources and amounts of income after deduction of income tax and other deductions. This can then be worked out as an average amount for each month. Enter these figures onto a "Monthly Budget Planner," such as the one at the end of this appendix.

Work out what you spend
Many couples find themselves stretched financially but are not aware of where their money goes. As a result, they can blame the wrong items for pushing them into debt. In order to form an

accurate picture of your expenditure, it may be necessary to write down over the course of a month or two everything you spend your money on. This information, together with your bank statements and any credit card statements, should enable you to work out expenditure for an average month. (With expenses that are not incurred monthly, such as car expenses, household insurance, or vacations, work out an annual figure and divide by twelve.)

Record this information in your budget planner, creating as many other categories as necessary. Start with those areas of expenditure that are fixed, such as a mortgage payment or rent, gas and electricity, insurance and travel costs. Then put down those areas where there is room for more flexibility, such as food and housekeeping, clothes, presents, hospitality, and entertainment.

Next, you need to subtract what you spend from what you earn. (If the result does not tally with your bank records, either the bank has made a mistake or you have left something out!) You may find, of course, that you are left with a minus figure: you are spending more than your income and you need to take urgent action.

Discuss the future

The second step is to plan the use of your money, allocating specific amounts to different areas. The aim is to set a budget that is within your income and reflects your agreed priorities, putting aside enough for the unexpected.

Sacrifices may have to be made by both husband and wife, but it will always be more productive to plan the future than to argue about the past. If you cannot agree, break off discussions to allow both of you time to consider (and pray about) the other's point of view. Find another opportunity to talk again when you are at your most reasonable.

The great advantage of reaching agreement is that you can then spend money up to the agreed limit without feeling guilty or having to hide it from each other. If agreeing proves difficult, we would encourage you to seek help from a reliable source.

Decide how to keep control

Appoint a financial director
Setting a budget is one thing; sticking to it is quite another. It is helpful to decide which of you is best equipped to keep track of the finances, to pay the bills, and to initiate a regular review.

Watch the credit card
For many people, the greatest difficulty in keeping their spending under control is the credit card. There are two dangers. One is that you do not feel as if you are spending real money. The other is that there is no automatic means of keeping track of how much you have left in your budget. Some couples have therefore cut up their credit cards and reverted to cash or using a debit card that has no overdraft facility. Though less convenient, it has enabled them to control what they spend and has prevented a great deal of conflict in their marriage.

Ten suggestions for guilt-free spending
Here is one easy system. It took us around ten years to work this out.

1. Take a blank page. Keep a record of the total amount of money you have allocated for essentials (food, medicine, etc.) this month.
2. Every time you spend money on essentials, make a note of it, deducting it from your total. Both of you have to confess.

3. If you get cash out of an ATM, deduct that also. It is easy to forget ATM withdrawals, especially if you want to.

4. At the end of one week, see how you are doing. Are you going to have to cut back next week or can you relax a bit? Be honest with yourselves. Put the steak back if necessary.

5. Start a new page at the beginning of each week with your new total. Keep deducting anything you spend on essentials.

6. In the last week of the month it is not uncommon to lie, to give up, or to eat a lot of baked beans. (They are very good for you, apparently.)

7. Other expenses such as new clothes and going out can be categorized (sadly) as non-essentials.

8. Note: We don't have to buy non-essentials. We will live (albeit painfully) without the takeout curry or the football game, or the new boots. At times we will need to say no, preferably to ourselves rather than to each other.

9. Keep the same system for "non-essentials" as for "essentials." The desire to lie, forget, or omit may become more pressing.

10. When the cash is available, shopping, eating out, going away for a night, buying tickets for a festival or an away game can all be enjoyed to the full.

We have to admit that the system is only as good as its operators. There have been some periods in our marriage when money has been tight and we have had to administer it rigorously. At other times there has been more money and we have been more lax in keeping a record of what we spend. Sooner or later, however, we have had to review our finances and revert to our system to get us back on track.

Sometimes, when a couple cannot make ends meet, the problem is that they do not have enough income to support themselves. Most often the problem lies with their expenditure. Rob Parsons writes about his own upbringing:

> My father was a postman and my mother a cleaner. We lived in a rented house, and life was simple to say the least. Non-essentials like heating in the bedrooms, fitted carpets, and toilet paper (don't ask!) belonged to another world. I didn't eat in a restaurant until I was sixteen. But I had everything I needed in that home, including wise advice from a father who would take me aside regularly and recite to me the words of Mr Micawber from Dickens' *David Copperfield*: 'Annual income: twenty shillings; expenditure: nineteen shillings and sixpence–result: happiness. Annual income: twenty shillings; expenditure: twenty shillings and sixpence–result: misery.' A belief in that principle meant that my father was never in debt. You may think that he paid an unacceptable price for that. He never had a holiday away from his own home, or had his own bank account, and he never did get to taste pasta–but I have never known a man so content.[1]

Monthly Budget Planner

Work out your "Actual" (or "Estimated") income and expenditure. Then complete the "Budget" column to help you work out adjustments you want or need to make.

	Annual figures		**Monthly figures**		
Income	**Actual**		**Actual**		
Joint salaries	$	÷12	$		
Other sources of income	$	÷12	$		
		TOTAL	$	(1)	

Fixed regular expenditure	**Actual**		**Actual**		**Budget**
Rent/mortgage	$	÷12	$		$ ....
Property tax	$	÷12	$		$ ....
Utilities (gas, electricity, water, etc.)	$	÷12	$		$ ....
Insurance	$	÷12	$		$ ....
Loan repayment(s)	$	÷12	$		$ ....
Travel – tolls	$	÷12	$		$ ....
Car(s) – license, insurance	$	÷12	$		$ ....
Charitable giving	$	÷12	$		$ ....
Other	$	÷12	$		$ ....
		TOTAL	$	(2)	$ ....

Flexible "essential" expenditure	**Actual (estimated)**		**Actual (estimated)**		**Budget**
Household (food, medicine, etc.)	$	÷12	$		$ ....
Clothes / shoes	$	÷12	$		$ ....
Car fuel and repairs	$	÷12	$		$ ....
Phones	$	÷12	$		$ ....
Other	$	÷12	$		$ ....
		TOTAL	$	(3)	$ ....

Flexible non-essential expenditure	**Actual (estimated)**		**Actual (estimated)**		**Budget**
Entertainment / hospitality	$	÷12	$		$ ....
Gift-giving	$	÷12	$		$ ....
Entertainment / leisure	$	÷12	$		$ ....
Vacations and getaways	$	÷12	$		$ ....
Going Out	$	÷12	$		$ ....
Other	$	÷12	$		$ ....
		TOTAL	$	(4)	$ ....

			Actual		**Budget**
Monthly sum for savings/emergencies		**TOTAL**	$	(5)	$ ....

Add together total monthly expenditure
(2, 3, 4, 5) $ .... $ ....

Subtract from total monthly income (1) $ ....

Appendix 4

Praying Together

For some who are reading this book, the thought of praying is a strange and unknown concept. Some think that prayer is a sign of weakness or shows intellectual immaturity. They have been taught that growing up is all about learning to cope on your own. As a result, people dare not admit to themselves, let alone to their partner, that they are struggling in any area of their lives.

Others find the idea of praying aloud highly embarrassing. A woman participating in The Marriage Course told us that she would rather run down the road naked than pray with her husband. It might well make you feel exposed and vulnerable, since prayer is a highly personal and even intimate activity, but it does not need to be quite as daunting as that.

Praying together means that you are drawing upon a source of wisdom, love, and power outside yourselves. It engenders a sense of hope rather than despair. This is what some couples we know have said about the effect of joint prayer on their own marriage:

- "Prayer mainly takes the worry out of our lives. Give it to God, and we both relax a bit."
- "We try to pray briefly before we go to sleep at night. It's like a glue for us."

- "We try to pray on Sunday evening. It means we worry much less as the things we would otherwise have been anxious about have been put into God's 'in-tray'."
- "Life seems a lot more bumpy when we don't pray together, because as we come before God it brings a unity to us."

How to get started

For ourselves, praying together has played an important part in our marriage, particularly once we had overcome some initial unrealistic expectations. These were matched only by the expectations we had regarding how much we could eat.

Nicky
When we first got married, Sila would regularly cook a gourmet dinner, with enough food to feed at least six people. Several evenings a week she would do a new recipe until, after three months of bloated stomachs and a considerable quantity of wasted food, she could keep it up no longer and we switched overnight to a diet of toast and cheese or Chinese takeout.

Our praying together started much the same way. There always seemed so much to pray about and, if we managed to pray at the end of the day, it seemed to go on far longer than we could handle. It was usually late and we were often tired. After a while, neither of us would suggest praying as we couldn't face the prospect of another long session.

Then somebody recommended we tried praying together for five to ten minutes at the beginning of the day, and that made all the difference for us. We timed it so that we would only have ten minutes before one of us had to leave for work. This removed any danger of it going on for too long.

For more than forty years, our aim has been to start the day by praying together for a short time, and we have adjusted the timing according to our circumstances, the ages of our children when they were little, and the changing schedule and demands of our jobs. We do not by any means manage it every day, but having that as our goal helps us to achieve it more often than not, and the benefits make us want to do it again.

How to pray with and for each other

Praying together on a regular basis need not be strange. You need to start by praying as you can, not as you can't. For some, that might mean using a book with written prayers that they pray aloud. For others, reading a few verses from the Bible and praying silently for each other might be the place to begin. The books *30 Days*[1] or *The Bible in One Year*,[2] with verses from the Bible for each day of the year, has proved helpful for many.

Others will be familiar and comfortable with saying their own prayers out loud. Our advice would be to start where you feel comfortable and to aim for simplicity and honesty.

A few months ago we met a couple who were about to celebrate their fortieth wedding anniversary. We asked them what they had found most important in building such a strong marriage. They said a number of kind things about each other and described how they had grown together. But it was what they said next that was most revealing. They both agreed that the thing that had made the most difference to the strength and harmony of their marriage was praying together every morning.

Thinking that they had probably done this every day for the last forty years, we asked them when they had begun. They replied, "About eighteen months ago." And they added that, if someone had suggested even a few years previously that this would become important to them, they would have thought it very strange.

It is never too late to start. Equally, it is never too soon. Below we have set out some suggestions that have helped us enormously in making joint prayer achievable.

Start with thankfulness to God

Thankfulness reorientates your thinking. If you feel under pressure or overwhelmed, choosing to be thankful can dramatically change your perspective. The apostle Paul wrote several of his letters under the strain of imprisonment, yet they overflow with thankfulness and gratitude to God. "Rejoice always, pray continually, give thanks in all circumstances; for this is God's will for you in Christ Jesus" (1 Thessalonians 5:16–18). This attitude goes against the current trend of dissatisfaction and striving for more and bigger and better. Thankfulness to God, including being thankful for each other, will change your perspective.

Pray for each other

The main aim of this time is to discover each other's needs or anxieties about the day ahead and to bring them before God. Asking each other the simple question, "What can I pray for you today?" opens the way for you to be open and vulnerable with each other on a regular basis.

Sometimes the answer will be about one of your children; sometimes it will be about being short of money; at other times it is because we feel inadequate in the face of the day's challenges. If one of you is struggling to relate to a particular person, you can ask the other to pray that God would change your heart and fill you with his love for them.

Pride and stubbornness can easily get in the way of coming to God and asking for his help. But God wants you to pray about everything, especially those things for which you have no human answer.

Don't worry about needing the same prayer daily

Jesus tells us, "Ask and it will be given to you; seek and you will find; knock and the door will be opened to you" (Luke 11:9). The tense in the original text means we are to go on asking, seeking, knocking, and not to give up after one time.

> **Sila**
> When our children were small, I found myself asking Nicky to pray the same thing for me day after day. I endlessly needed more patience and more physical energy, and Nicky's prayers made an amazing difference in my relationship with our children. The fact that we need to keep on asking for the same thing does not mean that God is not answering our prayers—rather it is a recognition of our dependence upon him.

Ensure that prayers are vertical, not horizontal and manipulative

Praying is not a way to get at each other. I (Sila) should not pray, "Please, Lord, help Nicky to leave more time to get to the station!" unless of course he has asked me to pray specifically for that. Nor should we use prayer as an opportunity to communicate things to our husband or wife when they are less likely to interrupt.

Don't give up

This will be particularly relevant for those who have young children. This stage of parenting can seem to go on forever; we remember thinking that we were never going to manage to pray together again for even five minutes. We seemed to spend a lot of physical and emotional energy taking a child back to their bedroom with a toy or a book and saying, "It is not time to get up yet." Then we would rush back to our room to get in another minute's prayer before the door would open and we would repeat the whole procedure.

Was it worthwhile? Looking back, even when we only managed one prayer for each other two or three times a week, those few minutes definitely helped us. They also allowed our children to see the importance we attached to it. Children do grow up, and praying together becomes easier again.

Look to the promises of God

Becoming familiar with many of the promises of God in the Bible is a great resource for you as a couple. You grow in wisdom through reading the Bible individually and together. As you learn to apply its advice to your everyday life, it shapes and changes your attitudes and behavior.

Just as there is power in prayer, there is power in reading the Bible together. We have often found that the few verses we have read from a psalm or the Gospels before we start praying seem to apply to us very personally for that particular day.

Conclusion

Many people think that God is out to trap them or to accuse them or to restrict their lives. Nothing could be farther from the character of God revealed to us in Jesus Christ. God longs to give to us, to help us, to set us free from the past, and to enable us to look outwards to others in love. He does not force himself upon us but waits for us to respond to his overtures of love.

The biblical instruction, "Submit to one another out of reverence for Christ," is set in the context of seeking *God's* will for our lives: "find out what pleases the Lord," and, "do not be foolish, but understand what the Lord's will is" (Ephesians 5:21, 10, 17). When both husband and wife determine to seek God's will for the major decisions in their lives, they will discover a freedom from worry that will profoundly affect their marriage.

St. Paul wrote, out of his own experience, "Do not be anxious about anything, but in every situation, by prayer and petition, with thanksgiving, present your requests to God. And the peace of God, which transcends all understanding, will guard your hearts and your minds in Christ Jesus" (Philippians 4:6–7).

Praying could be the most important thing you do together.

Endnotes

Foreword

1. Rachel Schraer, "The blame game: Getting divorced in the UK," BBC News, 27 May 2018, https://www.bbc.co.uk/news/uk-44253225.

Introduction

1. For an answer to the question, "Why did Jesus die?," we recommend reading *Questions of Life* by Nicky Gumbel (Hodder & Stoughton: 2018), particularly Chapter 3.
2. From the Anglican Marriage Service, as it appears in *Common Worship: Services and Prayers for the Church of England* (Church House Publishing: 2000), copyright © The English Language Liturgical Consultation.

Chapter 1: Taking a long view

1. Mike Mason, *The Mystery of Marriage: Meditations on the Miracle, 20th Anniversary Edition* (WaterBrook Multnomah: 2005), p. 160. Copyright © 1985, 2005 by Multnomah, an imprint of Penguin Random House LLC. Used by permission of WaterBrook Multnomah. All rights reserved.
2. John Bayley, *Iris: A Memoir of Iris Murdoch* (Duckworth: 1998), p. 57.

3. Extract from Sonnet No. 116 from Stanley Wells (Ed.), *Shakespeare's Sonnets and a Lover's Complaint* (Oxford University Press, 1987), p. 130.
4. Frank Muir, *A Kentish Lad* (Random House, 2013), pp. 404–5.
5. *The Guardian*, 24 October 1998, p. 3.
6. Quoted on audio tape by Sam Thompson, "Communion in Marriage," Part 2, tape 2, Anaheim: VMI, 1984.
7. Access credit card, https://www.accesscreditcard.info/chApply 7273.aspx.
8. Quoted in Selwyn Hughes, *Marriage as God Intended* (Kingsway Publications: 1983), p. 13.
9. *The Daily Mail Weekend*, 9 January 1999 [Interview with Lynda Lee-Potter].
10. Elizabeth Grice, "Michael Parkinson prepares to get his coat," *The Telegraph*, 15 September 2007, https://www.telegraph.co.uk /news/uknews/1563196/Michael-Parkinson-prepares-to-get-his -coat.html.

Chapter 2: Planning to succeed

1. Julyssa Lopez, "Michelle Obama Shared Some Powerful Relationship Advice: 'Marry Your Equal'," *Glamour*, 7 July 2019, https://www.glamour.com/story/michelle-obama-marriage -advice-marry-your-equal.
2. Rob Parsons, *Loving Against the Odds* (Hodder & Stoughton: 2010) p. 23.
3. Hunter Davies, *Daily Mail*, 20 April 1998.
4. Gary Chapman, *The 5 Love Languages* (Northfield Publishing: 1995, 2015), pp. 29, 36.
5. Dr Henry Cloud and Dr John Townsend, *Boundaries* (Zondervan, 1992, 2017), p. 160.
6. Rob Parsons, *Loving Against the Odds*, p. 23.

Chapter 3: How to talk more effectively

1. Libby Purves, *Nature's Masterpiece: A Family Survival Book* (Hodder & Stoughton: 2000), pp. 221–2.

2. Mary Soames (Ed.), *Speaking for Themselves. The Personal Letters of Winston and Clementine Churchill* (Black Swan: 1999).

3. Cherry Norton, *The Independent on Sunday*, 3 October 1999, pp. 6–7.

4. Cited in Libby Purves, *Nature's Masterpiece*, p. 221.

5. Michael Palin in an interview about his TV documentary, "Pole to Pole," 1992.

6. Sonia Leach, "Do Men Understand Intimacy?," *Good Housekeeping*, August 1994.

7. *The Message,* a translation of the Bible in contemporary idiom by Eugene H. Peterson (Navpress, 1993).

8. Frank Muir, *A Kentish Lad* (Random House, 2013), pp. 404–5.

Chapter 4: How to listen more effectively

1. Mary Hartwell Catherwood, "Marianson," *Mackinac and Lake Stories* (Harper, 1899), p. 7.

2. Gerard Hughes, *Walk to Jerusalem* (Darton, Longman & Todd: 1991).

3. These five bad listening habits have been developed by the Acorn Christian Foundation: acornchristian.org.

4. Gary Chapman, *The 5 Love Languages* (Northfield Publishing: 1995, 2015), pp. 61–3.

5. Stephen R. Covey, *The Seven Habits of Highly Effective People* (Simon & Schuster: 1999), p. 239.

6. Bilquis Sheikh, *I Dared to Call Him Father* (Chosen Books: 2003), pp. 46–7.

7. Stephen R. Covey, *The Seven Habits of Highly Effective People*, p. 237.

8. Dale Carnegie, *How to Win Friends and Influence People* (Simon & Schuster: 1964), p. 97.

9. Diana Vaughan, *Uncoupling: Turning Points in Intimate Relationships* (Oxford University Press: 1984).

Chapter 5: The five expressions of love

1. The material in this section (chapters 5–7) is adapted from Dr. Gary Chapman's bestselling book, *The 5 Love Languages®: The*

Secret to Love That Lasts (© 1995, 2015). Published by Northfield Publishing. Used by permission. To learn more about Dr. Gary Chapman and to take the free online 5 Love Languages® Profile, visit 5LoveLanguages.com.

2. The Beatles, "I'm Happy Just To Dance With You," lyrics © Sony /ATV Music Publishing LLC.

3. The Crystals, "Then He Kissed Me" (Universal Publishing Group: 1963).

4. Louis de Bernières, *Captain Corelli's Mandolin* (Secker & Warburg: 1994), p. 281.

5 Gary Chapman, interview for The Marriage Course © Alpha International 2020. Used with permission.

6. Richard Bausch, Excerpts from "The Eyes of Love" from *The Stories of Richard Bausch*, pp. 258–9, 261–2, 264. Copyright © 2003 by Richard Bausch. Used by permission of HarperCollins Publishers.

7. Gary Chapman, interview for The Marriage Course.

Chapter 6: Words and actions

1. Ella Wheeler Wilcox, "An Unfaithful Wife to Her Husband," in *World Voices* (Hearst's International Library Company: 1916).

2. Louis de Bernières, *Captain Corelli's Mandolin* (Secker & Warburg: 1994), pp. 43–4.

Chapter 7: Time, presents, and touch

1. Jean Anouilh (1910–87), *Adela* (1949).

2. Gary Chapman, *The 5 Love Languages* (Northfield Publishing: 1995, 2015), p. 107.

Chapter 8: Appreciating our differences

1. Frank Muir, *A Kentish Lad* (Random House, 2013), p. 403.

2. Paul Tournier, *Marriage Difficulties* (SCM Press, 1971), p. 26.

3. Emma Gritt, "CLEAN FIGHT Marriage therapist reveals the

number-one thing couples argue about the most–and, no, it's not how often to have sex," *The Sun*, 10 February 2018, https://www.thesun.co.uk/fabulous/5543920/married-couples-fight-sex-cleaning/.

4. *The Times*, 12 February 2018.
5. Susan Quilliam and Relate, *Stop Arguing, Start Talking* by Relate (Vermilion: 1998), p. 47.
6. Monty Don, *My Roots* (Hodder & Stoughton: 2006), p. 116.
7. Michelle Obama, *Becoming* (Viking: 2018), p. 113.
8. ibid., p. 160.
9. ibid., p. 123.
10. John Kirkby, interview for The Marriage Course © Alpha International 2020. Used with permission.
11. John Kirkby, interview for The Marriage Course.
12. Judith S. Wallerstein and Sandra Blakeslee, *The Good Marriage* (Houghton Mifflin Company: 1995), pp. 327–8.
13. Anna Clarke, "15 of Michelle Obama's most inspiring quotes about work, marriage and motherhood," *The Telegraph*, 3 December 2018.
14. MORTAL LESSONS: NOTES ON THE ART OF SURGERY by Richard Selzer. Copyright © 1974, 1975, 1976, 1987 by Richard Selzer. Used by permission of Georges Borchardt, Inc., on behalf of the author's estate.
15. *Red*, March 2000.

Chapter 9: Focusing on the issue

1. Gabriel Garcia Márquez, *Love in the Time of Cholera* (Penguin Books: 1989), pp. 32, 34.
2. Philip Delves Broughton, *The Times*, 12 February 1998, p. 9.
3. Paul Simmonds and Mark Silversides (Eds.), *Marriage in Mind* (Church Pastoral Aid Society: 1993), p. 34.
4. Libby Purves, *Nature's Masterpiece: A Family Survival Book* (Hodder & Stoughton: 2000), p. 227.
5. Colossians 4:6; Philippians 4:5 from *The Message*.
6. Rob Parsons, *Loving Against the Odds* (Hodder & Stoughton: 2010), pp. 65–6.

Chapter 10: Centering our lives

1. Gabriel Garcia Márquez, *Love in the Time of Cholera*, p. 209.
2. *Children's Letters to God*, compiled by Stuart Hemple and Eric Marshall (Collins: 1966).
3. Alpha offers the opportunity to hear and discuss the relevance and truth of the Christian message. It is currently being offered in more than 65,000 churches worldwide. We know personally many couples whose marriages have been transformed as a result of going through this course. See www.alpha.org for more information.
4. For those who would like to know more about prayer, a good basic introduction can be found in Chapter 5 of *Questions of Life* by Nicky Gumbel (Hodder & Stoughton: 2018).

Chapter 11: How can intimacy be lost?

1. John Taylor, *Falling* (Victor Gollancz: 1999), pp. 3–4.
2. For this section, we are particularly grateful to David and Teresa Ferguson for the inspiration and insights gained through their book, *Intimate Encounters* (Nelson: 1997), and family life courses.
3. C.S. Lewis, *The Four Loves* (Fount, HarperCollins: 1998), p. 116. Copyright © C.S. Lewis Pte Ltd 1960. Used with permission.
4. Valerie Windsor, "Telling Stories," *Fresh Talent* (Sinclair-Stevenson Ltd: 1993), pp. 39–40.

Chapter 12: How can intimacy be restored?

1. Martin Luther King Jr., cited in Philip Yancey, *What's So Amazing About Grace?* (Zondervan: 2002), p. 137.
2. Cited in Walter Hooper (Ed.), *Readings for Meditation and Reflection* (Harper Collins: 1996), p. 63.
3 See "Other useful resources" on page 362 for where to seek advice and help.
4. Philip Yancey, *What's So Amazing About Grace?*, p. 97.
5. Corrie ten Boom, *He Sets the Captive Free* (Kingsway Publications: 1977), p. 38.

Chapter 13: How to get on well with our parents and in-laws

1. This quote is popularly attributed to Mark Twain, but the true origin of the quote is uncertain. The quote was first attributed to Mark Twain in 1915, five years after his death, but the actual quote has not been found in his writings. Despite the uncertainty, the quote has not been attributed to anyone else.
2. Amanda Vail, *Love Me Little* (Penguin: 1960).
3. Mary Pytches, *Yesterday's Child* (Hodder & Stoughton, 1990), pp. 147–8.
4. Victoria Glendinning, *Sons and Mothers* (Virago Press: 1997), p. 248.
5. Libby Purves, *Nature's Masterpiece: A Family Survival Book* (Hodder & Stoughton: 2000), p. 260.
6. ibid., pp. 337–8.
7. Ann McFerran, *Motherland: Interviews with Mothers and Daughters* (Virago Press: 1998), pp. 119–20.
8. Ibid., pp. 15–17.

Chapter 14: How to leave behind parental control

1. Henry Cloud and John Townsend, *Boundaries in Marriage* (Zondervan: 2002), p. 9.
2. Victoria Glendinning, *Sons and Mothers*, p. 256.
3. Ann McFerran, *Motherland: Interviews with Mothers and Daughters* (Virago Press: 1998), p. 168.
4. Dr. Xuefu Wang, interview for The Marriage Course © Alpha International 2020. Used with permission.
5. Dr. David Mace, *Getting Ready for Marriage* (HarperCollins: 1974).
6. David Brooks, "The Nuclear Family Was a Mistake," *The Atlantic*, March 2020 issue, www.theatlantic.com/magazine/toc/2020/03.

Chapter 15: How to address the effects of childhood pain

1. Alan Storkey, *The Meanings of Love* (IVP: 1994), p. 99.

2. Sue Johnson, interview for The Marriage Course © Alpha International 2020. Used with permission.

3. Ibid.

4. Viktor E. Frankl, *Man's Search for Meaning* (Hodder & Stoughton: 1992).

5. Victoria Glendinning, *Sons and Mothers* (Virago Press: 1997), p. 255.

Chapter 16: Sex–what is it all about?

1. Mike Mason, *The Mystery of Marriage* (Triangle: 1997), p. 100. Used by permission.

2. Karen Krizanovich, "Why sex just isn't sexy any more!," *Daily Mail*, 27 March 2011.

3. St. Augustine, *City of God* (Penguin Classics: 2003, first published 1467), p. 579.

4. John White, *Eros Defiled* (IVP: 1977), p. 86.

5. *The Sunday Times*, 2 November 1997, p. 14.

6. *The Guardian*, 17 October 1998, p. 3.

Chapter 17: Six qualities for great lovers

1. Alan Storkey, *The Meanings of Love* (IVP: 1994), p. 98.

2. Emma Waring, interview for The Marriage Course, Copyright © Alpha International, 2020. Used with permission.

3. UN News, 24 November 2019, https://news.un.org/en/story /2019/11/1052041.

4. Shaunti Feldhahn, *For Women Only: What You Need to Know about the Inner Lives of Men* (Multnomah: 2004), p. 100. For those with an abusive partner, please get help and find a safe place to go. Contact the National Domestic Abuse Helpline at 1-800-799-7233.

5. Emma Waring, interview for The Marriage Course © Alpha International 2020. Used with permission.

6. Henry Cloud, interview for The Marriage Course.

7. ibid.

8. Michael Castleman, *Sexual Solutions* (Simon & Schuster: 1983), p. 162.

Chapter 18: Protecting our marriage

1. Kathryn Knight, *The Times*, 17 March 1996.
2. *Good Housekeeping*, March 2000, p. 64.
3. Alan Storkey, *The Meanings of Love* (IVP: 1994), p. 83.
4. Gary Chapman, *Hope for the Separated* (Moody Press: 1982), p. 78.
5. *Good Housekeeping*, March 2000, p. 64.

Chapter 19: Keeping sex alive

1. Alan Storkey, *The Meanings of Love* (IVP: 1994), p. 164.
2. Mental Health Foundation (2019). Body Image: How we think and feel about our bodies. London: Mental Health Foundation. https://www.mentalhealth.org.uk/publications/body-image -report/exec-summary.
3. Emma Waring, *Seasons of Sex and Intimacy: For a Husband and Wife in Marriage* (Hullo Creative: 2018).
4. Various health organizations will have information and leaflets about pelvic floor exercises. You might try looking on the NHS website, for example https://www.nhs.uk/common-health -questions/womens-health/what-are-pelvic-floor-exercises/ or: Pelvic floor exercises for women: An information guide https:// www.pat.nhs.uk/downloads/patient-information-leaflets/physio /304%20Pelvic%20floor%20exercises%20for%20women.pdf.
5. Libby Purves, *Nature's Masterpiece: A Family Survival Book* (Hodder & Stoughton: 2000), p. 225.

Chapter 20: The opportunity of a lifetime

1. Ian and Ruth Coffey, *Friends, Helpers, Lovers* (IVP: 1996), p. 177.
2. Michelle Obama, *Becoming* (Viking: 2018), p. 171.
3. Martin Luther King, from a speech delivered by King on 4 April 1967 in New York City. Cited in "A time to break the silence," *The Guardian*, 18 January 2010. https://www.theguardian.com/comment isfree/cifamerica/2010/jan/18/martin-luther-king-speech.
4. *Four Weddings and a Funeral* (Working Title Films: 1994).

5. Tom Marshall, *Right Relationships* (Sovereign World, 1992), p. 24.

6. Mike Mason, *The Mystery of Marriage* (Triangle: 1997), p. 20. Used by permission.

7. Commencement address by Barbara Bush to the 1990 graduating class at Wellesley College (Wellesley College Library, Wellesley, Mass.), pp. 4–5.

8. Dietrich Bonhoeffer, *Letters and Papers from Prison* (SCM Press: 1971), p. 42.

9. Clio Turner, *Closer to God*, April–May–June 1999 (Scripture Union: 1999), p. 127.

Appendix 1: Ready for marriage?

1. These tests have been adapted from Walter Trobisch, *I Married You* (IVP: 1971), pp. 89–92.

2. John Gray, *Men are from Mars, Women are from Venus* (Harper Thorsons: 2018), p. 161.

Appendix 2: Engagement, sex, and the honeymoon

1. Mike Mason, *The Mystery of Marriage* (Triangle: 1997), p. 100. Used by permission.

2. Paul Francis, *Teenagers: The Parents' One Hour Survival Guide* (Marshall Pickering: 1998), pp. 88–99.

Appendix 3: Working out a budget

1. Rob Parsons, *Loving Against the Odds* (Hodder & Stoughton: 2010), p. 190.

Appendix 4: Praying together

1. Nicky Gumbel, *30 Days–A practical introduction to reading the Bible* (Hodder & Stoughton: 2019).

2. Nicky Gumbel, *The Bible in One Year* (Hodder & Stoughton: 2019). Also available on iOS and Android via *The Bible in One Year* app on Apple App Store and Google Play. See www.bible inoneyear.org.

Recommended Further Reading

Marriage in general

Mike Mason, *The Mystery of Marriage* (Triangle: 1997)

Rob Parsons, *The Sixty Minute Marriage* (Hodder & Stoughton: 2009)

Gary Chapman, *The 5 Love Languages* (Northfield Publishing: 1995, 2015)

Rob Parsons, *Loving Against the Odds* (Hodder & Stoughton: 2010).

Sue Johnson and Kenneth Sanderfer, *Created for Connection: The "Hold Me Tight" Guide for Christian Couples* (Little, Brown: 2016).

Building the sexual relationship

Emma Waring, *Seasons of Sex and Intimacy: For a Husband and Wife in Marriage* (Hullo Creative: 2018).

Dr, Douglas E. Rosenau, *A Celebration of Sex* (Thomas Nelson. 2002).

Michael E. Metz and Barry W. McCarthy, *Enduring Desire: Your Guide to Lifelong Intimacy* (Routledge: 2010)

Other useful resources

Restored
Offers advice and help to those who think they may be in an abusive
situation.
Website: www.restoredrelationships.org

National Domestic Abuse helpline
Tel: 1-800-799-7233

Christians Against Poverty (CAP)
Helps those struggling with debt or addictive behavior that is causing
financial hardship.
Webite: www.capamerica.org

Also Available from Alpha

The Marriage Course, developed by Nicky and Sila Lee of Alpha, has been revised and updated to provide practical tools to help couples at every stage of their relationship. This update includes talks from experts including Dr. Gray Chapman, Dr. Henry Cloud, and Dr. Sue Johnson on topics such as money, sex, love languages, healthy boundaries, and building connections. *The Marriage Course* is based on a Christian understanding of love and serves to strengthen marriages within the church while being accessible for all couples from any cultural background, with or without a background in the Christian faith.

Available wherever books are sold and at
churchsource.com and alphausa.org/marriage

Also available in Spanish

Also Available from Alpha

The Pre-Marriage Course, developed by Nicky and Sila Lee of Alpha, has been revised and updated to provide practical tools to help engaged couples build a strong foundation for a lasting marriage. This update includes talks from experts including Dr. Gray Chapman, Dr. Henry Cloud, and Dr. Sue Johnson on topics such as money, sex, love languages, healthy boundaries, and building connections. *The Pre-Marriage Course* is based on a Christian understanding of love and serves to strengthen marriages within the church while being accessible for all couples from any cultural background, with or without a background in the Christian faith.

Available wherever books are sold and at
churchsource.com and alphausa.org/marriage

Also Available from Alpha

Nicky Gumbel, Toby Flint, and Gemma Hunt, walk participants through the traditional Alpha material in an engaging way that everyone can relate to. The crew has been all around the world, filming in Canada, UK, France, Hong Kong, Israel, Kenya, and Chile. The episodes feature inspiring stories and interviews, as well as visual illustrations and motion graphics. The DVD includes fifteen episodes (30 minutes each), an introduction to the Alpha weekend (10 minutes), two required team training sessions on how to lead an Alpha small group, and how to lead prayer ministry (30 minutes each). This DVD has both English and Spanish audio with English only subtitles.

Available wherever books are sold and at
churchsource.com and alphausa.org

Also Available from Alpha

Alpha pioneer Nicky Gumbel delivers a complete set of 30-minute Alpha talks for a new generation. Filmed live at Holy Trinity Brompton Church in London, these videos provide the timeless version of Alpha talks for tens of thousands of churches of all denominations around the world. This DVD has English audio with English and Spanish subtitles.

Available wherever books are sold and at
churchsource.com and alphausa.org

Also Available from Alpha

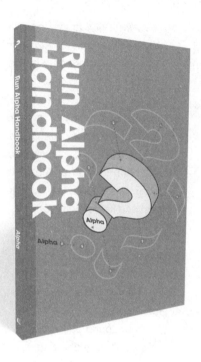

For Alpha directors and leaders, this is one of the most important tools in setting up and running an Alpha course. This essential how-to resource offers a guided tour through every stage of setting up and running the Alpha course, including reproducible resources to make it easy to recruit and train your Alpha team.

Available wherever books are sold and at
churchsource.com and alphausa.org

Also Available from Alpha

The Alpha Guide is a companion to either the *Alpha Film Series* or *Alpha with Nicky Gumbel*. This guide is divided up by session with an easy-to-read outline so that guests can follow along during each talk. With simple bullet-point organization and plenty of room for notes, the guide functions as an invaluable resource to the guest during Alpha, and as a reference tool for individual reflection long after Alpha. It is considered an essential resource for Alpha guests as well as the host and helpers on Alpha.

The Alpha Team Guide is recommended for Alpha small group hosts and helpers. It includes notes for the two required team training sessions on how to lead an Alpha small group, and how to lead prayer ministry, that can be found online or on either the Alpha Film Series DVD or Alpha with Nicky Gumbel DVD. It also provides weekly key concept summary and suggested questions to help guide the discussion time for each session of Alpha.

Available wherever books are sold and at
churchsource.com and alphausa.org

Also Available from Alpha

Why Jesus? is a concise and easy-to-read study of the very real questions surrounding Jesus that your guests might be thinking about when first attending your church or Alpha: *Who is Jesus? Why do we need him? Why did he have to die? Why is he relevant to my life today?* This booklet is an effective evangelistic tool to pass out to guests at your services or at Alpha, sharing the Gospel in a warm and relevant way.

Available wherever books are sold and at
churchsource.com and alphausa.org

Also Available from Alpha

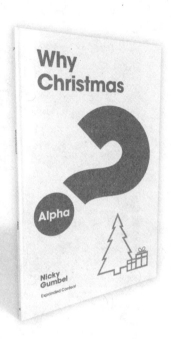

Why Christmas? is a wonderful evangelistic tool to present during the Advent and Christmas seasons. Many churches give this booklet as a gift to guests during a Christmas-themed Alpha celebration or place them inside Christmas bulletins. This booklet also makes a great addition to the church welcome packet or for your greeters to give to each guest attending Advent or Christmas services.

Available wherever books are sold and at churchsource.com and alphausa.org